BUYING INTO THE WORLD OF GOODS

Studies in Early American Economy and Society
from the Library Company of Philadelphia

Cathy Matson, *series editor*

This was the most trying hours of our lives; to take a woman raised in affluence not to say elegance and introduce her to the verriest drollery, not to say
poverty . . . To take a woman out of a painted house, not to say a fine one,
& conduct her into a log cabin. To exchange the smooth & lofty snow-
white walls of her father's hall, for the rugged and low, pipe-clayed smokey
dungeon . . . As soon as we were alone, each & both gave vent to our pent
up feelings in silent tears, words that would have expressed our mortifica-
tion, would have blazed.

In a few days we returned to her father's & in a few more we were moving to our little home. On a beautiful day in October might have been seen
a waggon loaded with a large and elegant walnut corner cupboard (glass
doors), bed, 6 chairs, ovens, plates, pitchers etc & a horse cart loaded with
poultry etc. Everything necessary for housekeeping except a table, and we
ate our first meal on a box—next day I made a cross-legged table which we
used that Fall when I took it to pieces and carried it to Franklin.

Andrew Bailey Jr., describing the early days of his September 1830 marriage

Buying into
the World of Goods

*Early Consumers
in Backcountry Virginia*

Ann Smart Martin

The Johns Hopkins University Press   *Baltimore*

This book has been brought to publication through the generous assistance of the Chipstone Foundation.

Johns Hopkins Paperback edition, 2010
2 4 6 8 9 7 5 3 1

The Johns Hopkins University Press
2715 North Charles Street
Baltimore, Maryland 21218-4363
www.press.jhu.edu

The Library of Congress has catalogued the hardcover edition of this book as follows:

Martin, Ann Smart, 1960–
    Buying into the world of goods : early consumers in backcountry Virginia / Ann Smart Martin.
        p. cm. — (Studies in early American economy and society from the Library Company of Philadelphia)
    Includes bibliographical references and index.
    ISBN-13: 978-0-8018-8727-7 (hardcover : alk. paper)
    ISBN-10: 0-8018-8727-5 (hardcover : alk. paper)
        1. Consumption (Economics)—Virginia—History—18th century. 2. Consumer behavior—United States—History—18th century. 3. Hook, John, 1745-1808. 4. Merchants—Virginia—Biography. 5. Material culture—Virginia—History—18th century. 6. Country life—Virginia—History—18th century. 7. Virginia—Social life and customs—History—18th century. I. Title. II. Title: Consumers in backcountry Virginia.
    HC107.V8C62 2008
    339.4'70975509033—dc22   2007024539

A catalog record for this book is available from the British Library.

    ISBN 13: 978-0-8018-9826-6
    ISBN 10: 0-8018-9826-9

Frontispiece: Franklin County log cabin and occupants, late nineteenth century. Quote from Andrew Bailey Jr., *Andrew Bailey, Jr. Chronicles: Life in Virginia During the 17–1800's,* ed. Eunilee Leath Bailey and Frank T. Bailey Jr. (Pfafftown, NC: privately published, 1989), 14–15. Courtesy, Photographs Collection, Library of Virginia.

Special discounts are available for bulk purchases of this book. For more information, please contact Special Sales at 410-516-6936 or specialsales@press.jhu.edu.

The Johns Hopkins University Press uses environmentally friendly book materials, including recycled text paper that is composed of at least 30 percent post-consumer waste, whenever possible. All of our book papers are acid-free, and our jackets and covers are printed on paper with recycled content.

CONTENTS

Color plates follow page 128

SERIES EDITOR'S FOREWORD

This volume in the Studies in Early American Economy and Society, a collaborative effort between the Johns Hopkins University Press and the Library Company of Philadelphia's Program in Early American Economy and Society (PEAES), offers a distinctive perspective on the economic lives of very early North Americans. One of the core objectives of PEAES has been to advance research about the early American economy which has been flourishing in recent years under the broadened umbrella of numerous disciplines, methodologies, and subjects. Alongside this book series, PEAES brings together scholars and writers working in areas such as commerce, business, banking, technology, and material culture in its fellowship program, seminars, public outreach programs, conferences, and published conference proceedings. PEAES is also engaged in the ongoing acquisition of sources that are incorporated into the collections of the Library Company of Philadelphia.

Ann Smart Martin takes an extended interdisciplinary look at the storekeeping activities of one merchant in one North American locale. She reconstructs his extensive economic engagements with myriad people throughout regional and Atlantic markets who actively shaped the production, distribution, and consumption of seemingly disconnected goods in seemingly invisible relationships. Martin's methodology is eclectic, ably blending the approaches of art historians, material culture specialists, and social and economic historians in order to reach beyond many of our typical assumptions about what a country merchant and his customers did in North America's early modern era. She recreates not only one place in time but the sweeping networks of buying and selling that shaped connections reaching outward across the Atlantic Ocean and deeply into the colonial interior. The world of exchange and consumption for her backcountry Virginia storekeeper was one of color and variety, active efforts to satisfy consumer choices, and intricate accounting for essential and exotic commodities. Each chapter takes us further into the lives of ordinary Americans on the developing frontier by highlighting a particular object and analyzing its multifaceted meanings for farmers, housekeepers, and slaves who shopped at country stores. Along the way, Martin challenges a number of our longstanding notions about how early Americans lived in a "world of goods" that carried meanings not only about credit, prices, and the quality of material objects but also about status, race, and gender in a rapidly changing frontier environment.

Cathy Matson
Professor of History
University of Delaware
Director, Program in Early American Economy and Society
The Library Company of Philadelphia

On a recent August evening in Franklin County, Virginia, vines gripped my ankles and briars scratched my face as I inched through pasture toward an abandoned house. I was in search of a fylfot, a pinwheel-like design, sighted on a decayed mantel several decades before. Such a mysterious emblem occasionally ornamented houses and furniture in the eighteenth-century backcountry, and scholars now debate its meaning. Was it an obscure Germanic blessing (symbol of ethnic pride) or a boyhood trick of the compass (display of mathematical skill)? A fylfot is a curious material expression of a complex regional culture.

My search signified just one of many efforts to reconstruct the world of the eighteenth-century merchant John Hook in backcountry Virginia. My introduction to that world came through his ledgers: scrawled words and numbers; customer names and their purchases; dates; credits and payments. Once I began viewing those transactions as triangulations between merchant, customer, and objects, it seemed important to study ever more closely the stores, plates, cabins, ribbons, corner cupboards, and fylfots outside the written ledgers Hook kept.

I first discovered the papers of the eighteenth-century Virginia merchant John Hook as a young research assistant. My job at Colonial Williamsburg in the 1980s was to search for merchants' records that listed the kinds and costs of ceramics available in Virginia. From my vantage point as a historical archaeologist, I could see that something important was unfolding in the world of goods. Even the house yards of some rank-and-file artisans living in eighteenth-century Williamsburg were littered with newfangled English creamware and exotic Chinese porcelain. This raised two fundamental questions: how could such artifacts be understood if not through an Atlantic economy and all its cultural and economic transformations? How could it not be significant that such high-style objects were part of the everyday lives of common people?

A few years later, when I began working on my doctorate in early American history and material culture, I was still carrying the memory of the records of John Hook. They were voluminous and scattered in original, copy, and microfilm formats in half a dozen archives. I had read just enough of them to know that they offered evidence that would be indispensable to solving the conundrums of eighteenth-century consumerism and local exchange.

By then, scholars were relying on computers to compile and interpret basic patterns revealed by the documents. Extraordinarily gifted quantifiers of social history like Lois Green Carr, Carole Shammas, and Lorena Walsh used probate inventories and other records to chart change across time, place, and social class in the colonial Chesapeake. Barbara and Cary Carson and a host of curators, archaeologists, and architectural historians focused on domestic spaces and furnishings. By concentrating on Hook, I was afforded the opportunity to present a particular backcountry merchant and to shed further light on various aspects of the availability, affordability, and desirability of goods.

After another decade of studying and teaching objects in interdisciplinary settings at the Winterthur Museum and the University of Wisconsin–Madison, my focus shifted toward a quite different perspective. This book continues my earlier efforts to present a nuanced history of the retail trade, including the fundamental story of credit and debt, but it also argues that retailing can only be understood if we pay attention to the desire and pleasure of consumers as well.

Our culture has many words for goods—"commodities," "objects," "artifacts," "possessions," and "things." *Desirability* is the Pandora's box in any study of goods, for within it reside devilish questions about the allure of material things. Tales of social unease about the acquisition of certain consumer goods—and about who was acquiring them—were common in eighteenth-century Anglo-America. Englishman William Blake depicted the lively debate about our grasping natures in a 1793 etching titled "I want! I want!" The lone figure shown on a ladder reaching for the moon has an uncanny modern sensibility that encapsulates my wish to understand how and why we yearn for material things beyond our reach.[1]

As scholars, we must learn to wrest evidence from individual things just as we learned how to categorize and quantify numbers of things. The dynamic energy of the duality of things as both commodities (economic systems, institutions, social exchanges) and objects (myths, cultural meanings, human stories) defines this scholarly effort. Years ago, I began the quest by examining documents on a microfilm reader, seeking to discern patterns in consumer choices. I ended my research efforts by driving on S-curve mountain roads and trekking through cow pastures in search of artifacts and stories. Those efforts and all that came between have led to *Buying into the World of Goods*.

Virginia colonists were often suspicious of Scottish merchants, thinking them to be a canny lot who cared too much about a "good penny's worth."

Merchants mistrusted Virginia colonists who were happy to take on debt but slow to pay. I am a true Virginian with a drop of Scots-Irish blood dallying long with accounts unbalanced.

Scholars who write are cited throughout the manuscript but those who study the material world too often remain anonymous. Generously offering their collections, files, and expertise were Patricia Samford, George Miller, and Terence Lockett (ceramics); Linda Baumgarten, Clare Brown, and Linda Eaton (textiles); Jon Prown, Luke Beckerdite, and Charles Hummel (furniture); John Davis, Donald Fennimore, and Fred Finster (metals); Willie Graham, Gary Stanton, and especially Carl Lounsbury (architectural history); Anne Verplanck (prints and miniatures); and Roy Clements (clocks).

Working in the Bedford and Franklin County region always gave me fresh energy and passion. Warren Moorman shared the Hook store and his lake cottage with me and Francis and Laquita Amos opened up their home and hence the world of Franklin County material culture. Folklorist Roddy Moore shared the mountaintops and music with me as well as the marvelous archives at the Blue Ridge Institute, and Margaret Gonzalez spun stories of her family at the Wade Cabin.

I spent many happy days at the Duke University library and the Museum of Early Southern Decorative Arts archives. The librarians and archivists at those special places always left me pining to head back. A Mellon research fellowship at the Virginia Historical Society helped me to dig deeper into the region, across time, and particularly pointed me to key women in Virginia's backcountry consumer society. Utilizing the extraordinarily accessible research materials at Colonial Williamsburg spoiled me for all future research. The foundation also provided much research time and support, particularly for the architectural research. The University of Wisconsin granted me several leaves of absence and the Cartography Lab prepared the maps. Tamara Mams and Emily Pfotenhauer (also a remarkable research assistant) prepared other drawings. The Chipstone Foundation is a valuable partner who constantly champions new ideas and supports me in all ways possible.

I presented portions of this work at many annual and topical history conferences covering economics, women's studies, early America, material culture, consumerism, backcountry studies, and vernacular architecture, and at each venue I received notable feedback and help. In a project that reaches back so many years, I cannot possibly thank all the colleagues, mentors, and professionals whose goodwill taught me that truly good history is often a cooperative venture.

My friends Kasey Grier, Katharine Martinez, Julie Richter, and Patricia Samford have all read pages, traveled with me to conduct research or present at conferences, and counseled my frustration with wisdom and laughter. Finally, as this book will show, family is the steely fiber of history. My parents Morgan Shelton Smart and Nancy Perkins Smart hail from Mountain North Carolina or Piedmont Virginia stock and raised me to value heritage and lore, elders and antiques. I dedicate it to Carl and Kate (along with sundry cats and a fine dog), the witty and warm household that accompanies me on all my eighteenth-century travels.

BUYING INTO THE WORLD OF GOODS

In Backcountry Time

V IRGINIA MERCHANT JOHN Hook was angry. His British suppliers had disappointed him one too many times with shoddy, unfashionable goods. He lectured Whitehaven merchant Walter Chambre in a 1773 letter, explaining that their business was absolutely dependent on "dispatch, exactness, and judgement in the choise of the goods, respecting the quality, collours, patterns, and fashions." His frustration turned to sarcasm: "for me to make money without Goods is as absurd as to suppose a Taylor to make a Coat without cloth by the needle and Shears alone."[1]

Why would a merchant on the western edge of settlement in Virginia worry about colors, patterns, and fashions? Many of his customers lived in small, simply furnished, log-built cabins. Few could even afford bound labor to clear land and grow tobacco. The majority bought primarily rum, inexpensive textiles, or agricultural tools at his New London store. But Hook evidently also needed to stock some fine things to meet his customers' tastes and desires. Mrs. George Callaway's purchases in the previous year included porcelain cups and saucers, a pinch box (for snuff), and a butter boat and stand.[2] "Free Mulatto" Benjamin Ruff bought multiple household necessities but also ribbon, embossed serge textiles, and ten strings of black beads.[3] Tarleton East purchased "one fine felt hat."[4] James Smith ("the butcher") selected simple items like rum, salt, and a small knife and paid for them with a meat credit. But Smith also chose a fine lawn handkerchief when far cheaper ones were available.[5] What did each of these shoppers hope to achieve through the ownership of such stylish goods?

In their expenditures, backcountry Virginians were "buying into the world of goods" in two senses: they were purchasing commodities and validating a set of ideas about taste, fashion, and appropriate lifestyle. This book examines how and why they acquired such goods and how country merchants brought these commodities to them between 1760 and 1810. It demonstrates that specialized distribution chains evolved to carry goods of the Atlantic world to colonists moving ever westward, spurring country merchants to compete fiercely and giving consumers multiple reasons to spend in ways that transcended traditional social fissures. Even so, class, ethnicity, religion, and race continued to shape frontier consumer patterns in compelling ways.

This study examines a particular place and time, focusing on the life and business of one country merchant, Scottish-born John Hook (1745–1809), who operated rural stores first in Bedford County, Virginia, and later in adjacent Franklin County. Further, it plumbs cultural evidence left by many individuals and the objects they chose when they shopped at Hook's store. Hook's business served as a fulcrum for social and economic relations among neighbors and family members, recording debits and credits, errands and favors. Hook may be the best-documented merchant in eighteenth-century Virginia. Besides accounts of sales and payment, his detailed records, his numerous and protracted court battles, and his lengthy correspondence with his initial partners, he left a splendid cache of business ephemera—memoranda, scrawled notes, customer lists, invoices, inventories, even detailed architectural drawings of his stores and houses. This immigrant's personal involvement with a community makes for a distinctive business story and an intensely human one.[6]

According to cultural geographers and folklorists, a *sense of place* can have deep meaning for individuals and a single place can be both extraordinary and ordinary.[7] So it was with the area in which John Hook's businesses were located. It was ordinary like all the rural places that were settled as society moved westward toward fresh farmland in the later eighteenth century. But it was extraordinary because of the interaction among groups that settled that area of the Virginia backcountry—Germans, Scots-Irish, English—and the enslaved Africans they brought with them during a time of important political, economic, and religious turmoil.

Using telling geographical nomenclature, John Hook informed his partner in Scotland in 1768 that "this and the adjacent Frontier counties is settling unaccountable fast from people below and from the Northward."[8] The people "below" came from eastern places, locales below the fall line of the James River. Those from "northward" were mostly Germans who funneled through the broad and fertile Shenandoah Valley after first landing in Philadelphia and then moving to south-central Pennsylvania. Many continued on to North Carolina, but some decided to pause in the hills of Bedford and Franklin counties. These settlers, representing different worlds in motion, enticed Scottish merchants to set up stores in this region of backcountry Virginia.

When Hook arrived in 1764, the area surrounding New London, Virginia, was by no measure a wilderness frontier. The region had received its first significant waves of European settlers in the 1740s. Population growth

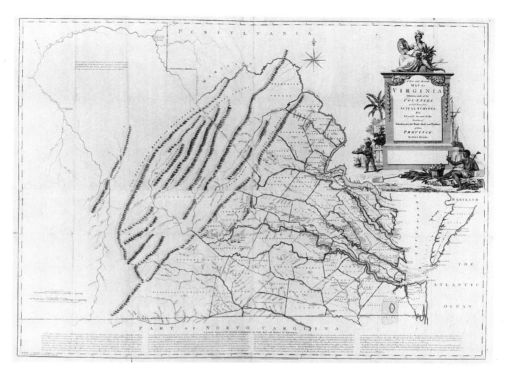

FIGURE I.1. *A New and Accurate Map of Virginia,* John Henry, 1770. Courtesy, The Colonial Williamsburg Foundation. Henry used the cartouche of the map to represent Virginia's subsidiary position as a colony within the British Empire and relegated his depictions of the slaves and tobacco to the bottom tier, well below Britannia. The map itself has some inaccuracies, which Henry's contemporaries readily pointed out. None-theless it shows a land that is well marked and understood at its east edge and fades to unknowingness in the west. *Buying into the World of Goods* is—in part—the story of this map.

slowed during the Seven Years' War, even pushing many settlers eastward, but surged anew in the mid-1760s. Carved from Lunenburg County in 1754, Bedford County lay on the sprawling western perimeter of settlement in southern Virginia. Most of it was fertile rolling agricultural land. On the far western edge rose the Peaks of Otter and the foothills of the Blue Ridge. When John Henry drew his *New and Accurate Map of Virginia* in 1770, courthouses already dotted the western Piedmont, and important geographical landmarks had names (fig. I.1).[9] New London, established as the county seat in 1761, lay at the crossroads of a major east-west road vari-ously called the Warwick Road and Salem Turnpike and a north-south road

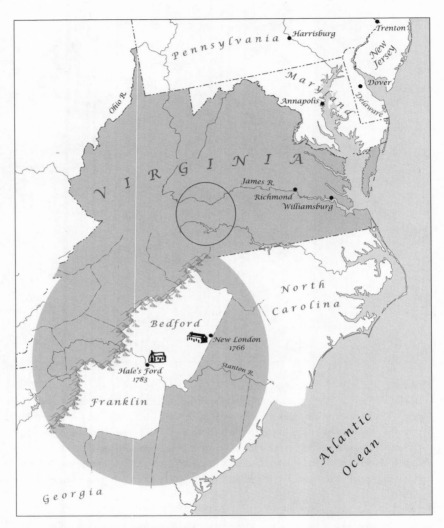

FIGURE I.2. Bedford and Franklin counties. Abstracted from *Geographical, Statistical and Historical Map of Virginia* (Philadelphia: Carey and Lea, 1822) and John Henry, *A New and Accurate Map of Virginia*, 1770. Courtesy, Cartographic Laboratory, University of Wisconsin–Madison. Hook opened a store in the early 1770s in Bedford County at New London and closed it later that decade. In 1784 he moved to Franklin County and opened a store at Hale's Ford, along the Staunton River, which remained in operation for many decades.

that carried travelers toward Carolina. John Hook's New London store drew customers from Bedford, Campbell, Botetourt, Henry, Patrick, and Franklin counties (fig. I.2).[10]

The Revolution abruptly dissolved Hook's business opportunities in New London. The loss of his Scottish suppliers as well as the locally held belief that Hook harbored Loyalist sympathies prompted him in the immediate postwar period to move his business operations to Hale's Ford, a crossing of Staunton River, twenty-eight miles south and west of New London, in what soon became northern Franklin County.[11] Furthermore, without his Scottish connections, Hook turned into a different kind of country merchant; his new store focused more on local trade, and he simultaneously ran three large plantations.

Here, in the early post-Revolutionary years, customers traveled across rivers and mountains to each store. Wagons laden with hogsheads of tobacco rolled eastward on good roads and returned with imported commodities. Distinct ethnic pockets emerged as families linked by native origin and language settled near one another on agricultural river-bottom lands or good herding hills. Mountaineers trapped animals to make hats for trade. Some slaves mined pockets of iron ore and operated ironworks at full blast, while others worked plantation lands or acreage on smaller farms.

In these decades the Virginia backcountry hovered between ordered permanent settlement and dangerous frontier. Scholars still argue about the place because it constituted the shifting edge of empire.[12] In 1760, backcountry Virginia stretched westerly from the fertile tobacco lands in the Piedmont to the lush wheat fields of the Shenandoah Valley, crossing the Blue Ridge in the process. It also stretched northerly from the south side of the James River to the Maryland border. Most settlers belonged to minority ethnic and religious groups, owned few slaves, and encountered numerous geographical barriers getting to and from market. This contrasted sharply with the culture of the Tidewater. There a settler's identity remained tightly bound to tobacco production and ownership of slave labor, and both neighbors and shops stood close at hand.[13] Another key feature of backcountry life was the one-on-one violence that surfaced even as people evinced a desire to create a stable and prosperous place. Its position as the ragged edge of empire meant that the backcountry was an unstable composition; some scholars see a "diminishment of metropolitan accomplishment," others a mediating ground between Native Americans and settlers.[14]

Merchant Hook himself viewed the backcountry in various ways. First and foremost, he considered it a location west of the river's fall line, which meant store goods had to be delivered to him by wagon. In a larger sense, he understood it in terms of a chain of purchases and sales from Glasgow to

FIGURE I.3. P. A. Alderman store, Franklin County, Virginia. Photograph, early twentieth century. Courtesy, Photographs Collection, Library of Virginia. This building is a quintessential eighteenth-century form.

several related stores in Virginia, the one farthest west being the "back store." His perception embraced the British imperial strategy that placed London at the center of a great network of exchange. Hook also looked westward from his stores, noting that the "key to the backcountry" lay still further south and west. John Hook's backcountry was paradoxical, part of the West (yet East to many settlers), rural (yet in a village), and marked by rolling fertile farmland (yet with mountains nearby).[15]

Country merchants operated as agents of commerce in far-flung places (fig. I.3). John Hook's records vividly illuminate the processes that linked Europe, Africa, and Asia with the British colonial empire in its most remote corners—places like backcountry Virginia where semi-processed agricultural goods were traded for manufactures and reexports from Scotland and England. The majority of John Hook's customers consciously participated in such market economies and made choices to buy and sell based on savvy knowledge of how to maximize benefits to themselves. But others continued to haphazardly produce petty goods that stayed in local exchange. Some people did both. Thus New London and Hale's Ford exemplified no grand revolution but a hybridized gradual shift to a market economy supported by a mix of male and female labor as well as free and slave.[16] Hook accepted hours of labor (working in his garden, raising chickens, or picking cotton), along with pounds of tobacco, cash, or bills of exchange, as payment for purchases. The local and Atlantic economies intertwine in his accounts, revealing ways that people worked and negotiated for material goods. In Hook's frontier place there were a set of constraints and freedoms, a hierarchy of ownership of land and slaves, the business of building cabins and pouring tea. A new hoe or ax made hewing a life out of the wilderness easier, and iron cooking pots helped cooks work in cramped quarters.

But do all these activities put together reveal a "backcountry" way? Was there a discernable, measurable set of strategies and options that became a lifestyle or standard? What can we tell about backcountry people's culture from examining their possessions? What do stores in the hinterlands of the British Empire reveal about the connection of consumers to each other and their identity? What role did merchants play as suppliers of goods and brokers of taste? John Hook's business provides insight into such knotty historical problems of consumerism in the early modern world. The extraordinary scholarly interest in the world of goods over the past twenty years has produced a plethora of new questions about the supply of goods, the role of fashion, and the moral practices that developed around consumption.[17] Scholars who have addressed some of these economic and cultural practices—especially those connected to fashion and refinement that announced elite men and women's new preferences—have identified the geographical dispersion of people who would have had the opportunity to reinvent themselves through possessions. They have also examined the role that rising competition for social position and a growing awareness that knowledge of the latest fashion carried power played in consumerism.[18]

Bedford and Franklin counties provide a test ground for the theory of invented identities and social competition. Both counties had plenty of newcomers who could have dressed and strutted in ways the locals deemed fashionable, but few did so. Admittedly, the choices of some residents were constrained by enduring poverty. Others in the county had money to buy fineries, but instead they invested in land and slaves, embraced religious beliefs that privileged simplicity, or adhered to ethnic custom. Furthermore, the substantial distances separating neighbors limited families' opportunities for sociability, thus leaving some new objects unnoticed or unneeded. But an array of backcountry men and women—rich, poor, and enslaved—did purchase from John Hook, who liberally extended credit to those who wanted to buy. And in accepting crops, cash, and services as payment for debts, he drew all of his customers into larger economic and cultural processes. In backcountry Virginia, consumer goods did not have to be expensive to be powerful. Small items fulfilled many consumer desires and obliged all layers of backcountry communities to repay debts. Even Hook's poorest customers purchased ribbons, hats, and rum or whiskey. Many of these buyers do not reappear in any public record during the decade after they entered Hook's store. They moved through the Virginia backcountry yet remained outside institutional systems that categorized the population and taxed property, or they were transient and mobile in ways previously underestimated— they stayed poor or moved on.

John Hook's records pull many other people out from the historical shadows. Because the store trade relied on a credit system that had a legal foundation, most accounts are in white men's names, which in the past led historians to presume that Virginia stores operated as white male bastions. But an accounting system is a language of commerce with a set of conventions and codes. Since most females were not liable for debt under Virginia law, what many women were up to remains tucked behind recorded male names or disappears into lists of cash sales. John Hook's extra-careful record keeping permits a nuanced reading of his stores' accounts and demonstrates how at both stores, women actively participated in choosing and paying for goods, and on a daily basis. At the same time, rural women occasionally traveled long distances to trade the products of their own labor for consumer goods, hence bypassing the debt system of trade.

Hook also welcomed slaves as customers. The number of slaves who made purchases had grown so large and their activity so regular that by the turn of the century, Hook's storekeeper at Hale's Ford began keeping a separate account book for their purchases. The goods that slaves bought, the frequency with which they traveled to purchase them, and their method of payment demonstrate the flexible relationships of slaves with owners, merchants, markets, and consumer goods.[19]

Buying into the World of Goods heavily depends, first of all, on material culture analysis. Its theoretical component opens by describing the protean role of consumer goods as desirable *objects with values*—values that can be defined through production skills, craft mastery, cost, pleasure, or utility. Second, it also argues that the increasing local availability of inexpensive manufactured goods proved to be a powerful agent in whetting consumer demand. Third, it assesses how residents of the rapidly growing settlements in backcountry Virginia understood and employed urbane ideals of respectable consumption.

Of course, there was some trepidation about these expenditures and what they meant. Benjamin Franklin had already warned his fellow colonists against the "common man's petty vanity of tricking out himself and his family in the flimsy manufactures of Britain" with an "Ambition to become gentlefolk."[20] Similarly British author Thomas Alcock bemoaned the "unnecessary expense of the poor," deploring their predilection for "smoking and chewing tobacco, taking snuff, tea-drinking, . . . and 'dram-drinking'" and their desire to wear "ribbons, ruffles, silks and other slight foreign things."[21] When William Eddis visited the mid-Atlantic colonies in 1771, he observed how quickly merchants had moved to supply "the real and imaginary necessities" of those who lived in the backcountry.[22]

But others were already leaning toward the view of Adam Smith, who proposed that man, as a social animal, defined his "necessaries" by that of his neighbor; "whatever the custom of the country renders it indecent for creditable people, even of the lowest order, to be without."[23] He continued, "when we say that a man is worth fifty or a hundred pounds a-year . . . we mean commonly to ascertain what is or ought to be his way of living, or the quantity and quality of the necessaries and conveniences of life in which he can with propriety indulge himself."[24] We might not be able to say just what backcountry Virginians were worth, but we do know that they navigated within these community ideals of value, lifestyle, decency, and consumer indulgence.

John Adams, one of the few eighteenth-century writers on either side of the Atlantic to reflect on the cause and effect of fashion and necessity, understood why consumption was powerful. He explained that when a man sees another whom he considers his equal with a "better coat or hat, a better house or horse, than himself, and sees his neighbors are struck with it, talk of it, and respect him for it . . . he cannot bear it; he must and will be upon a level with him." It was not the hat that caused the desire. It was the attention that the hat drew and the respect it bestowed on its wearer. This behavior was in evidence in "every neighborhood, in every family; among artisans, husbandmen, [and] laborers" and had a ratchet effect: "those who claim or aspire to the highest ranks of life, will eternally go to a certain degree above those below."[25]

Two basic material culture principles inform this study: the first holds that objects do not merely reflect culture but also are the means by which it is created. They symbolize and communicate intangible ideas, build relationships, and proffer pleasure. They are, as I have argued elsewhere, "complex bundles of individual, social, and cultural meanings grafted onto something that can be seen, touched, and owned."[26] These meanings are derived from processes and structures of production, design, and marketing and are unstable. In ferreting out meanings, we must assess the roles of the manufacturers in England, the partners in Glasgow, and merchant Hook in New London in the consumption process. We must also remain open to the possibility that customers likely brought to bear their own meaning or perhaps a meaning appropriated from a visit to a local wealthy planter's home. In sum, we must be open to the notion that consumer goods from the heart of the British Empire came packed with associations, values, and meanings that subsequently could change through ownership.[27]

The second major precept is that value is determined in multiple ways, by using techniques that, for example, assign prices and by probing more subjective and personal perceptions of worth. In backcountry Virginia, some people valued an object most when it remained just beyond reach, a state in which ownership could be imagined. That acquiring an object might decrease its value in the consumer's eye accounts in part for the self-extending pattern of consumer desire.[28] Others were drawn to objects because of their novelty. Many goods offered by John Hook were new, different, better, cheaper, and more exotic. Assessing purchases in these terms permits us to address how the people in Hook's world used material goods to navigate change. Moreover, race and ethnicity introduced particular ways for people to interpret objects that were in other ways similar on a store shelf. A material culture approach to history allows objects such as a cupboard in a cabin to become a powerful starting point for evaluating how a preference for newness or an interest in fashion on the rough edges of empire became entangled with rural people's larger perspectives on class, governance, and the American Revolution.

ONE

The Business of Revolutions

John Hook and the Atlantic World

T HE BUSY PUBLIC library in Rocky Mount, Virginia, is of interest to
historians of colonial Virginia for two reasons. The first is that it is
home to the Gertrude Mann Public History Room, which holds an array of
local documents, including photocopies of scrawled accounts related to the
business of several Franklin County merchants. The other is that it contains
a glass case of local memorabilia, including a leather pocketbook embossed
in gold with "John Hook / Virginia / 1758" (fig. 1.1).[1]

Whether the pocketbook was presented to him by family members as he
left for his new life in Virginia in 1758, purchased by Hook in Williamsburg
shortly after his arrival, or ordered later to commemorate that important
date in his life likely never will be known. However, we can surmise that it
mattered a great deal to someone, probably Hook himself, and that it is significant that the date coincides with the year that he sailed from Glasgow,
Scotland, to Virginia hoping to make his fortune.

John Hook traveled to Virginia as a 13-year-old apprentice clerk and
shopkeeper. His father, Henry, was likely a small-scale manufacturer—he
later would open a soap manufactory—and had some wealthy distant relations and good friends in the Scottish mercantile world. Of his seven children, his five sons scattered to make their fortune; three went to Jamaica,
one to the East India Company, and John, his fourth, to Virginia.[2] In the
phrase of historian Alan Karras, the Hook sons were classic "sojourners":
young, educated eighteenth-century Scotsmen who saw little possibility for
financial success in Scotland. Their hope was to make enough for a comfortable, respectable existence—back in Scotland.[3]

Although unable to help his sons become established financially, Henry
Hook could provide connections. For his son John, that business link was
with the Donalds, one of the largest families operating in the Chesapeake
tobacco trade. John Hook was to go to Virginia to work and learn the tobacco business. Like so many other young Scotsmen who spread throughout the British Empire seeking their fortune, he was youthfully optimistic
that he could earn quick riches yet faced the realities of a chaotic Virginia

FIGURE 1.1. Pocketbook, c. 1758. Leather with gilt embossing. Gertrude Castor Mann Room, Franklin County Public Library, Rocky Mount, Virginia; photograph, Ann Smart Martin. The wear on this accordion-folded pouch indicates its owner, John Hook, carried it for many years. Although few everyday accessories from the eighteenth century survive, this one did, and family members included it among the many papers and books of John Hook's business that they deposited in the library.

economy, intense competition among a community's merchants, and the extraordinary social and economic dislocation of the American Revolution.

When war came nearly two decades later, most of his Scottish competitors fled home, but Hook remained a settled member of the local society. He had married Elizabeth Smith, a wealthy planter's daughter, in 1770 and through business and marriage had accumulated large landholdings. He had in many ways achieved the merchant's ultimate success; he had moved from commerce to landholding. Yet by most Scotsmen's measures, true success—returning home a wealthy man—remained an unfulfilled dream.

The life of John Hook illuminates how the retail business functioned in early Virginia. As one of the best-documented merchants in Virginia he demonstrates how consumerism works. He squabbled with rivals, complained to the firm's partners in Scotland, and grew discouraged that he had not achieved the dream of great wealth. Yet in only a quarter-century, Hook went from doing menial tasks in an established Tidewater store, to managing a store in the Piedmont, to imagining expanding business as the line of European settlement roared westward.

Just as important, his vantage point from Virginia looking back to Glasgow throws the Atlantic world into sharp contrast. By the end of his nearly twenty-five years as a Scottish merchant in the Virginia backcountry, his complaints might have seemed shrill, but he desperately needed shipments of the right goods at the right price in order to succeed. The consumer goods drove his business, not the purchase of the tobacco crop. Hook offers a bird's-eye view of consumerism—the world of goods with all its attendant meanings. He is also the first actor on our stage.(?)

The Retail Trade in Early Virginia

Early settlement patterns in Virginia profoundly affected the evolution of the retail trade there. Traditional patterns of exchange in England might have predicted that in the New World there would be markets, towns, and centers of higher and lower order and of larger and smaller size as well as more or less complex institutions. Virginia, however, did not evolve in such a fashion. Seventeenth-century planters quickly spread out along the colony's many rivers in dispersed patterns, and ships, which could travel far inland, were able to deliver goods more cheaply than overland transport. Hugh Jones, a visitor in the 1720s, opined that this access to water made it easier for "any thing to be delivered to a gentleman there from London, Bristol, etc. than to one living five miles in the country in England."[4]

Other factors discouraged town growth in Virginia. Because British policy mandated using the colonies to produce agricultural commodities and to supply other desirable raw goods while simultaneously discouraging manufacturing there, the need for points of manufacture and distribution in Virginia remained low. The first retail trade thus constituted a kind of waterborne peddling in which merchants traveled to countless private landings to buy tobacco and sell goods.[5]

Settlement patterns along the rivers represented only part of the problem. Tobacco, the major crop, constituted another part. It was a difficult commodity. It was bulky and difficult to transport, and only a seasoned eye could judge its quality. These factors quickly discouraged the untrained who might undertake a small trade venture, made collection of debts difficult, and, perhaps most important, kept ships in Virginia for months on end, waiting while their captains scurried about the colony trying to acquire a full return load.

Incipient forms of other distribution systems developed in the first hundred years after Virginia's settlement. Prominent planters ordered goods from Britain and sold them from their plantations to neighbors until the assortment ran out. Some entrepreneurs roamed the countryside like peddlers, purchasing tobacco and selling goods. Some stores opened and closed, depending on the goods available.[6] The cost of transporting tobacco, however, remained a key problem; in 1730, for example, Governor William Gooch estimated it cost a merchant 3 to 6 shillings a hogshead to bring tobacco to shipping points.[7]

The establishment of permanent stores at specified locations nonetheless heralded the beginning of a real solution to the problem of supplying

Virginians with manufactured goods. Four factors made this possible. First, the Tobacco Inspection Act of 1730 in Virginia enabled the issuance of tobacco notes, entitling the bearer to a certain amount of tobacco in a warehouse, and created a system of inspection, placing the onus of judgment of the quality of tobacco on the inspector rather than the merchant. This solved many of the problems confronted by earlier merchants. Second, settlement density increased. A larger population base permitted merchants to stock a wider variety of goods and to do so on a year-round basis. Without the fear of a dearth of goods, consumers could purchase regularly and even impulsively. Third, as the tobacco trade itself became more organized, permanent merchants began to operate in the colony, which led to greater efficiencies. Ships thus spent less time sitting idle and goods were sent abroad more frequently. By midcentury, that greater efficiency meant two annual shipments—spring and summer goods shipped in February and March and autumn and winter goods shipped in late summer and early fall—instead of only one. Fourth, British firms reorganized the trade by establishing regular mercantile houses in Virginia, and each sent an employee to manage their business in the colony.

Hence, by the time John Hook arrived in Virginia in 1758, the retail trade had become institutionalized. There were two major forms of distribution. The consignment system, which persisted from earlier days, shipped tobacco at a planter's own risk and cost to an agent in Europe, who sold the crop to the owner's best advantage, served as a banker the planter could draw on for bills of exchange, and purchased goods as requested, all in return for a commission.[8] This remained the most common form of sale for more wealthy planters who could afford the costs and risks of transportation as well make do without a return profit for at least a year. The consignment trade centered in southern England, mostly London and Bristol, and generally took in the best quality tobacco for domestic use. On occasion, some merchants also involved themselves in the cargo trade, in which case they supplied a quantity of goods on credit to the planters.[9]

Local sales, the second important system of distribution, involved direct purchases or factor trades, in which a group, most often of British partners and investors, combined capital to purchase stock, open a retail store or chain of stores with an employee (factor) in charge, and return tobacco in payment. This trade centered in northern Britain—Glasgow, Whitehaven, and Liverpool—and purchased the lesser quality tobacco, often for reexport to the French monopoly for cash. While a small retail shop in the Chesapeake was a relatively minor investment, the capital required to stock a year-round store and to take tobacco in trade was quite substantial. A minimum of nearly £3,000 was necessary for a true store, although a Glasgow firm more commonly had a capital stock of £10,000 to £20,000.[10] This was the famed Scottish system of trade.

Successful, well-funded, and well-supplied stores in the Chesapeake to-bacco trade often worked in a network. A partner in Britain, most often in Scotland, handled the European end of the transactions. A partner or em-ployee operated a store in the Tidewater, where he could supervise loading and unloading of goods and crops. A third might open a store at the fall line of one of the rivers, the transfer point from land to water transshipment. A fourth might open a store in the rural west where fresh lands promised good crops and attracted droves of settlers.

While Virginians and English-born merchants traded tobacco for goods in the Chesapeake, Scottish merchants captured the lion's share of the mar-ket. By 1769 more tobacco went to Scotland than all the English ports com-bined. The Scottish merchants had several advantages: a faster (and shorter) route by two or three weeks, greater available credit, fewer expenses because of cheaper Scottish labor, and the consolidation of purchasing in the hands of a few large firms. One English merchant wrote in exasperation that year that the Scottish "Ships are perpetually coming—They never stop buying," and had overpaid planters for tobacco several times that year. Their large shipments had "thinn[ed] the Warehouses."[11]

The firm of James and Robert Donald owned five ships that joined those Scottish argosies. Connections to various Donald firms proved important to John Hook for nearly two decades. The number of Donalds—often with the same first name—engaged in the tobacco trade to Virginia often leads to confusion. One historian calls them the "endless Donald connections," noting that James and Robert Donald and Company were known simply as "the Company" among the Donald clan.[12] The firm's large number of retail stores—possibly as many as nine—meant that each ship could be filled with consumer goods on the outbound voyage to the New World and with tobacco on the inbound crossing to Scotland, avoiding any outside shipping costs.[13]

John Hook began his career working for the James and Robert Donald firm in Blandford (near Petersburg), where he performed various jobs to learn the mercantile business. As an apprentice he initially swept out the store every morning and put goods in their proper places. During the day he and all other assistants waited on customers. The firm assigned a more senior as-sistant to bookkeeping, which needed to be "Posted up every Night."[14] By age 18 John Hook had risen from apprentice to storekeeper and worked at Warwick, near Richmond, on the James River.[15] The terms of his employ-ment were generous. He received £40 per annum and free room and board, and most significantly, as he informed his father, he had "liberty of trade as much as I pleased so as I did not interfere with their trade." He could import £250 of goods a year, shipped free in the firm's ships, to sell for himself, separately from those he sold for the company.[16]

In January 1764, Robert Donald allowed his distant relation William Donald to hire 19-year-old Hook to keep books for William's store at Pages on the York River.[17] Although William Donald did not increase Hook's salary, he did promise the young man a post as storekeeper in an upcountry store after one year with a £10 raise and permitted Hook to import several hundred pounds sterling of goods to sell for his own profit on the side.[18] Although elated with his promised future position, Hook grumbled to his father that "a young man without a fortune or good friends will be all his lifetime at it before he can make more money than he could just live on." He reported that he only wanted to make enough money in Virginia to carry him "Gentily out of it" but was afraid achieving such a goal might take two to three years.[19]

By the end of that summer, Hook's optimism returned. He was "blessed with a good constitution to undergo any fatigue and withstand hot weather." No "business can be carryed on to Advantage" in the mercantile way without "application and industry," and he had much of both.[20] John Hook remained committed to the goal of other Scottish "sojourners": to return home and be able to take up a genteel—that is, comfortable and respectable—lifestyle. He also began to think about ways he could increase his profits. He yearned to be "far from the Noice and confusion of the Troublesome Planters" and wished to establish trading relations and information channels with other Scotsmen.[21] Cognizant of the success of other Scottish family networks, he began with his own family, turning to his brothers Thomas and Duncan, living in Jamaica. He suggested they send him consignments of rum and sugar, for which he would send "pork, corn, beef, flower, [and] peese" in return.[22] Nothing came of that plan.

Indeed, few of Hook's business schemes at this time reached fruition; too often he had to put aside his own personal business ventures to spend time chasing debtors, going from courthouse to courthouse in an attempt to force planters to pay their old debts or issue mortgages.[23] Nor had he received his promotion. Because Alexander Donald, William's brother, had not returned home to Scotland as planned, the promised position of storekeeper had not opened up for Hook. Concerned that he had wasted several years, Hook once again planned to return home to find a new backer or partner.[24]

Mercantile migrants such as John Hook had high expectations of quick and ample success. Some who had gone to the Chesapeake years earlier—dubbed the tobacco lords—had returned to Glasgow extremely wealthy men. That was the myth and ideal, but John Hook, like most who went to Virginia, was disappointed. It took eight long years for Hook to achieve the status of factor, becoming a partner in his own store. In 1766 he formed a joint partnership with William Donald (who then returned to Scotland) and his brother James Donald. Under the terms of their agreement, William would receive the normal commissions for managing the business at home in Scotland, James would set up a new store at Warwick on the James River, and Hook would open a store on the "frontier" in Bedford County with the £500 he convinced his partners to lend him at simple interest.[25] Hook knew he needed to find a good location, one where he could buy good crops with minimal competition from other merchants, and the backcountry beckoned. Even more importantly, he recognized that his success would depend on a well-chosen stock that fit the needs and desires of his customers and that he would have to buy goods cheaply so that he could offer low prices.

Getting the Right Goods

Operating as true emporiums, Virginia stores would sell everything from nails to novels. John Mair's popular English manual *Book-keeping Method-iz'd* urged a varied and complete stock for a Virginia or Maryland store; "the greater variety . . . the better; for wherever planters find they can be best suited and served, thither they commonly resort."[26] Mair himself suggested fifteen different broad categories for Virginia merchants, if only to help organize the thousands of items they stocked.

Furthermore, a properly stocked Virginia store offered two levels of quality. For example, merchants had to have basic textiles such as coarse linens for the less wealthy and for slaves as well as provide a wide variety of more luxurious, colorful, and fashionable items that appealed to the more affluent, albeit limited, market. Thus Falmouth, Virginia, merchant William Allason stocked silver and gold lace even though he only managed to sell a tenth of it in two years. Despite such small demand, Allason pointed out that he needed "a good assortment in order to keep my customers to myself without going to my neighbors for trifles."[27]

Problems arose at both ends of the market for clothing. Chesapeake merchants complained bitterly about the poor quality of goods shipped by English suppliers. Merchant Francis Jerdone fussed to his partner Neil Buchanan that the English tradesmen—"some of them overcharging in the prices, others Sending very mean and unsaleable goods"—had "grossly abused" them. The color of one piece of fabric, he complained, was so out of style that he planned to return it, and he accused the sellers of packing up goods "that have been shopkeeped for some years."[28] In Falmouth, shopkeeper Arthur Morson became livid when he unpacked his October 1773 shipment: "never [have I] seen such a parcell of Motheaten, rat eaten, Mouse eaten, damag'd trumpery in the whole course of my life." To add insult to injury, he could have purchased the same osnaburg—coarse linen—locally at a price less than the wholesale cost he had paid for the shipment![29]

Such complaints form a common refrain: English tradesmen routinely passed off poor quality, damaged, and old-fashioned goods for shipment to Virginia. Writing his partners, Henry Fleming noted that he had a long list of problems with particular fabrics that had been sent including a "quantity of very high-priced printed Cottons, very bad patterns, very much darn'd," and most remarkably, he had received half a piece last year and had just been sent the other half at a higher price. Fleming blustered that the "people of Whthavn who have not been in Virginia. . . . hold the doctrine 'that since such an article is going to Virginia & tho it will not sell here it certainly will there.'" He reminded his partners "the people in Virginia are to be full as nice & curious as in England," and the firm's success entirely depended "upon having neat & fresh goods to suit such."[30]

The notion of eliminating a middleman and buying directly from a man-ufacturer clearly appealed to Hook and other Virginia shopkeepers; how-ever, many supply problems did not originate with the British commission agents. Unsupervised manufacturers and shopkeepers also took advantage of shipments destined for distant markets. When Maryland merchant John Semple suggested that his Glasgow partner James Lawson send to London for more fashionable goods, the partner argued against it. Lawson had the first choice of a selection made by a fellow Glasgow merchant who traveled to London twice annually to personally select British silks for the home trade, and so he obtained the "very Newest and Best fashions" from Lon-don. If the tobacco firm ordered from a London export merchant like James Russell, there would be no supervision over the selection of the goods, as Mr. Russell "gives in his orders to a shop that makes them up without his seeing of them."[31]

The availability of goods also varied. German osnaburgs often seemed to be in short supply. Prices for textiles might fluctuate wildly, as in 1759 when the raw material for a kind of woolen cloth went up 20 percent.[32] Af-ter traveling to manufacturing towns, the most "capital" being "Gloucester, Tewkesbury, Bromsgrove, Birmingham, Coventry and Woodstock," Joshua Johnson reported with disgust that the current arrangements among the firms stymied his efforts to gain better quality goods at a cheaper price. These manufacturers' agents, who were well aware of changes in prices and who were part of an established network, had little incentive to deal with inde-pendent small buyers like Johnson.[33]

Surviving letters often reveal how storekeepers obtained goods, but only a rare few name the suppliers and allow a view of the complex chain of distribution linking English goods and Virginia consumers. Most Scottish firms treated the partner in Scotland as the source of their shipped goods and offer no further details. The firm of John Lawson of Glasgow and John Semple of Port Tobacco, Maryland, however, stands as an important exception for it lists the names of specific suppliers or manufacturers next to the list of goods shipped to the Chesapeake.[34] John Lawson turned to Staffordshire potter John Baddeley at Shelton near Newcastle-under-Lyne for white salt-glazed stoneware "neat and genteel" that he wanted as cheap as possible to "encourage future dealings." Baddeley's account books in turn reveal the place Semple and Lawson's orders occupied in his business. Between 1753 and 1767 this successful potter not only shipped more than one hundred crates every few months to Amsterdam but also maintained a sizeable local trade in surrounding towns and, occasionally, with local nobility in Staffordshire. He also sold crates of pottery to middlemen in Glasgow, Edinburgh, and Liverpool, some of which likely ended up in the American colonies. By 1771 even rival Josiah Wedgwood acknowledged Baddeley's products as "the best ware perhaps of any of the potters." Wedgwood marveled that the Shelton potter had made an "ovenfull of it Per Diem" and had led the way in lowering prices. Perhaps this reputation had spread to Glasgow, prompting Lawson to specifically order these cheap and well-made tea- and tablewares for his Virginia and Maryland customers.[35]

Lawson also mentions the names of other suppliers. Lawson purchased rugs and white cottons from Mary Wakefield and Sons in Kendall, light gowns from Manchester warehousemen Robert and Nathaniel Hyde, and cotton gowns from Kennedy and Bell of Glasgow. Scottish manufacturing firms benefited greatly from this export trade—Lawson mentions, for example, the "Port Glasgow ropeworks," the "Delftfield House of Glasgow," the "King Street Sugar House," the "Kilmarnock Wooling Manufactory," and the "Smithfield Factory." Lawson visited dozens of Scottish craftsmen to fill his orders, including at least three shoemakers (who supplied different kinds of shoes and pumps), cloth calenderers, stay-makers, and silversmiths. From London he acquired glass, china, looking glasses, spices, silks, guns, furred hats, and other fine goods. For a single December 1757 shipment of goods totaling £1,808, Lawson dealt with forty different manufacturers, craftsmen, and merchants. The assortment included everything from ropes and house brooms to "one dozen dressed babies," fiddle strings, and "silk sun capes laced at 6/6 each."[36]

The "Art, Caution, or Judgement" of Pricing

Of course, colonial shopkeepers needed to sell their stock at competitive prices. Virginia merchants were always on the lookout for a good "pennyworth"—a bundle of goods that could be bought cheaply. Pricing of goods remained a complicated and intricate process that was set in motion by the producer and concluded by the consumer. For one thing, goods came in at invoice price with an "advance" at the bottom that represented both profit and conversion to sterling in a single calculation. Fluctuations in the exchange rate could occasionally wipe out much of a merchant's gross profit, as happened in 1770–71. For another, the prices charged on the invoice by suppliers varied by the method of payment (cash or credit). The long distance and uncertainty of business meant that few Virginia merchants could pay cash or make returns quickly enough to secure the lowest wholesale price.[37]

Even if every item came at the identical price to the Virginia shopkeeper, the advance that he charged varied by buyer, method of payment, length of credit, and particular kinds of goods. For example, the advance might drop as goods became more plentiful and competition for business grew. The advance might also vary by the purchaser. James Robinson reminded his new storekeeper to base his prices on the nature of payment (cash or credit) and the trustworthiness of the buyer. He further warned him to undertake such actions with a "great deal of art, caution, or judgement." Robinson suggested his storekeeper remember three points when coming up with price: the quality of the article, the ability of the purchaser to pay, and the prices set by neighboring merchants. Some storekeepers showed the planters their invoices so that they would know exactly what the wholesale cost was and offered a set price above what was listed.[38] Henry Fleming, for example, sold his hardware at "15 percent Sterling and advance upon goods and packages to very particular customers." Others he charged 17½ percent markup. Fleming was, he said, "allowing as other people do." Moreover he also maintained special relationships with other merchants: to fellow Whitehaven merchants, partners Eilbeck and Ross he traded his goods at a 10 percent markup and they did the same. Simultaneously, he and Hector McAlistair traded goods at no advance, in essence a straight exchange.[39]

Varying their prices according to circumstances as opposed to offering a set price almost always stood to the merchants' advantage. Controlling the paperwork, they could manipulate a conversion from local currency to British sterling cost. They could also offer a higher price for the tobacco they bought from planters by inflating costs 25 percent for the merchandise they sold the planters. Finally, they could add false charges such as insurance on the foot of an invoice.[40]

Finding the "Right Birth": A Backcountry Location

In 1759 new partners Walker and Company advised William Allason to set up a store where "there are not too many already settled, where ye people are not much in debt & pretty free birth, near some Warehouse of good Character." His partners reiterated for good measure—lest Allason miss the point—that his success depended on "falling on a right birth to open store at."[41] Allason chose Falmouth. Ironically, the remarkable growth rate of Bedford County and nearby New London had attracted the attention of several other mercantile firms. Allason's partners should have been more precise: too much of a good thing brought a number of merchants running to compete. The right berth should not be too crowded.

In 1766 John Hook headed up the James River to open his own store. Located 120 miles above the fall line, Bedford County lay in the western edge of the Piedmont, a region poised to become the prime market in Virginia for tobacco growth and sales. The exceptionally fine quality of the leaf grown there could command both an English and a French market.[42]

The volume of shipping makes clear the level of economic development that had been achieved in the upper Piedmont and the western lands south of the James River. In 1766, the year of Hook's arrival, nearly half of the colony's tobacco, one-third of its iron, and two-thirds of its wheat exports cleared from that district. By 1773 one-fourth of *all* tobacco imported into Great Britain came from the Upper James River naval district.[43]

John Hook's journey belonged to a steady line of new settlers. To succeed he had to break into a new location and attract business. Opening a new store often required wooing customers away from other merchants by offering them additional credit or lower prices, an especially difficult task in the fiercely competitive and rapidly expanding backcountry. Another goliath of Scottish stores, Cuninghame and Company, had begun to expand aggressively on the James River.

In 1770, when the Cuninghame firm appointed Thomas Gordon director for their new store in Halifax County, the head factor for Virginia, James Robinson, wrote a lengthy letter giving instructions and advice. His words help us to understand John Hook's future successes and failures and some rather specific requirements of doing business in the backcountry. Robinson urged his new employee to pursue actively the planters at the warehouses. Offer to pay all cash, if necessary, to increase his "importance and interest amongst them," Robinson advised, rather than expend credit. Always buy from the planters rather than other merchants, for "by the one you engage an excellent customer for goods in future, by the other according to the old adage you lend a staff to break your head." He promised his storekeeper as much cash as he might need, for if the price of tobacco was agreeable, "you must not on any account be stinted in money." The company had high hopes for the new area. "You have a large field before you, on which to raise your name high in the mercantile world," Robinson glowed. "Advance boldly, but let prudence be your guide."[44]

Robinson wrote a similar letter to John Turner, the new manager of the Cuninghame store in Rocky Ridge in October 1771. Even though Turner had worked at another store, the importance of his new position engendered an extraordinarily long and detailed missive of advice. Robinson urged Turner to "use the utmost . . . vigilance and attention to promote their [the firm's] end by every prudent, legal, and justifiable method in his power." Setting profit level depended on local custom. Robinson noted that the custom on the James River was to "advance" the price of goods (i.e., raise the cost from wholesale) some 65 to 75 percent but advised Turner to conform to his competitors' practice if they offered a cheaper price. Robinson required that before Turner made any new agreements with planters to supply goods at a particular special price he obtain a written agreement stipulating a method of payment.[45]

The second important topic covered stocking goods. As manager, Turner must keep the store regularly supplied and closely supervised, for he alone held the responsibility for its success or failure. Robinson urged particular care in the ordering of goods, down to the "minutest articles." But do not overbuy, he cautioned, especially those goods that could "decay by lying." If Turner should have an overstock, which might be expected in the first year or two, he was to get clear of it on good terms to another merchant, even if at less profit than through a retail sale to a customer. He also could exchange them for items at other Cuninghame stores.

Having addressed the issue of the proper quantity and quality of goods, Turner could turn his attention to extending cash and credit. To achieve the all-important goal of getting on "solid footing," Robinson advised him to consider taking a short-term loss, for "there is no acquiring an extensive influence without sinking a considerable sum in debts." If merchants pay for tobacco in part in goods and in part in cash, Turner should follow the custom of the place. Cash would be the grease of the first year's operation, and Robinson urged him to set an absolute fixed price with no wrangling. When an anticipated ship filled with earthenware and salt from Liverpool reached his location on the James River, Turner must have at least a hundred hogsheads of tobacco ready to fill its hold, even that very first year. Tobacco constituted the firm's main business, and other commodities, such as corn, hemp, and wheat, should be secondary.

Robinson reminded Turner that the final key to extending influence lay in securing customers farther west in the backcountry, those who traveled greater distances to the stores. In this, store location played a vital role. Like the Donalds and Callaway before him and "per the custom of James River," Turner must "fix one or more stores in the Back Country." The factor at Richmond, probably Andrew Chalmer, had already recommended Falling

River in Bedford County, but Turner should check around. Robinson provided detailed instructions for choosing an appropriate place for a back-country store. Turner must carefully judge the local soil and the financial abilities of people within a radius of twelve to fourteen miles, the maximum reach of such a store. Those planters should be able to sell him at least three hundred hogsheads annually, and they should not already be too much in debt to other merchants nor too rich (with their own source of goods) nor too poor (with no ability to buy).[46] Yet judging the creditworthiness of customers proved harder than it looked; one fledgling merchant, for instance, advised his cousin that in their future store endeavor "there is little doubt that you may sell whatever you please, the difficulty however is getting paid."[47] Selling was easy in a generous credit economy. Collecting was the problem.

Finally, Robinson offered personal advice about the kind of relationship Turner should establish with his customers: "live on good terms with his neighbors in town" but at all costs avoid "too great an intimacy with any of them." Turner must keep secret all manners of business but should regularly consult with the firm's storekeeper in Richmond so that they could jointly adopt such measures as might be "for the best" for the firm.[48]

The vying for the proper location that went on reflects the increasing number of merchants, the overall population growth, and the heightened competition for planters' tobacco. James Robinson reported to the Cuninghame firm that one rival had chosen a store site merely to prevent the Cuninghames from establishing one there.[49] Discouraged at the decline in his business as competitors set up shop, a merchant at Charlotte Court House blustered, "Now . . . if you do not exactly Suit them in every article they may want they go immediately to some of our Neighbors and there lay out their tobacco." Because the other merchants gave credit to high-risk customers, he decided to trust only those known to be "Punctual forehanded men" who would pay off what they owed.[50]

Meanwhile, John Hook's disappointments continued. He had advised William Donald to send £4,000 in goods annually, £1,000 to each store in autumn and again in spring, and his first autumn's shipment of £967 of goods arrived in October 1766, too late for much of the season's business. He informed Donald that had the goods arrived by the first of September "he could have stopped upwards of half the Bedford people from going down to Warwick or Rocky Ridge for their fall Goods." He urged Donald to ensure that the next shipment of goods arrived by mid-June for "its hardly creditable to think what a Manifest Advantage a back Store (especially so far back as this)" would have "over those Below" (i.e., located at the river's fall line) if the goods were to show up in a timely fashion.[51]

Hook faced other daunting challenges. New London was already home to one store, run by William Callaway and his son James, some of the wealthiest planters in the region.[52] Furthermore, the attractive position of Bedford County had enticed Hook's old employers, Robert and James Donald, to plan to open a store there in the next spring that would be run by Robert Cowan. Hook initially regarded the Donalds's entrance into the local trade as being to his own advantage, anticipating that the strong Scottish presence would drive out or at least weaken the Callaways, leaving plenty of local trade for both Scottish Donald firms. Hook would gain some of Callaway's customers, even if the new Donald firm would regain most of their "loland Customers" who traded below the fall line and who used to "daile" [dally] with Hook for convenience.[53]

Hook's business had a disastrous first year. The tobacco crop—as well as the hemp and ginseng crops that he also relied on—failed miserably. Attempts to raise hemp were hampered because Bedford County planters had little skill in its production and little market for its sale. He still hoped in December to send off £1,000 from collection of retail debts, but he encountered difficulties in this realm because the planters with their failed crops expected to be indulged until the next season. They refused to sell their land in order to pay Hook, and he hesitated to sue them for fear of damaging business. To add to his woes, Robert and James Donald had followed through on their plans—Robert Cowan had opened a "well assorted Store . . . back'd by an able company."

The two Scottish companies did not, in the end, band together in an effort to break up James Callaway's business. Indeed, James and Robert Donald continued to supply Callaway with goods even as they competed with him, prompting Hook to grumble that it seemed as if they wanted to drive Hook out of business. He hastened to assure his own Donald partners that, if needed, he could either move his store to a spot where they would not have such powerful rivals or break up the trade. He remained optimistic that the extraordinary population growth would render the latter option unnecessary.[54]

The three competing mercantile firms jostled for position during the next several years. The two Donald firms pursued the same strategy for tapping backcountry trade. Each positioned one store at the fall line of the James River (James Donald, the brother of William Donald, on one side, and Robert Donald and Alexander Stewart on the other) and another in the "backcountry" at New London with John Hook and Robert Cowan respectively managing their businesses. Each had a large amount of capital centered in Scotland and a coterie of bookkeepers, assistants, and slaves in the colony.

The third competitor, James Callaway, followed an alternative, older business model of the Virginia mercantile trade: that of a planter who purchased a few goods and sold them on the side. More serious about the mercantile business than many, Callaway had opened a retail store to gain patronage in the infant town of New London in 1761 and sited the store on lot no. 1. At first Robert Donald and Company supplied him with goods, but by February 1770 he had adopted a partner named Peterfield Trents at Rocky Ridge and entered a correspondence with Dobson, Daltera, and Walker in Scotland. Callaway and Trents also may have expanded their operations in the backcountry, perhaps in Pittsylvania County, for their correspondence to their new suppliers mentions fixing a store in "a large extant of Country, the lands fresh and good for Tobo, the planters clear of Debt and no Store to interfere with us." They confidently predicted that, in exchange for goods, they could ship one hundred hogsheads of tobacco and five thousand pounds of deerskins for payment annually, pointing out that Callaway had been able to collect that much tobacco and that many deerskins the preceding year while working with goods that were "not well sorted or good in quality." Dobson, Daltera, and Walker sent goods with a wholesale value of more than £1,000 in the autumn of 1770 to stock the Callaway and Trents stores at Rocky Ridge, New London, and another unspecified backcountry location.[55]

The handful of Bedford County merchants maintained ambivalent relationships. They cooperated in supplying each other with goods when necessary, although not at the most favorable terms. Hook and Robert Donald both received numerous goods from one another and supplied them to one another. Different merchants carried each other's letters to partners. They knew each other's prices and suppliers and occasionally shared wagons. Often Alexander Stewart (of the firm of Robert and James Donald) left goods for wealthy planter John Smith of Pocket Plantation to pick up at James Callaway's store. Yet these same merchants competed head to head for the purchase of tobacco. Hook would later often complain to David Ross, who had become his partner in 1771, that he was at a disadvantage because Ross firmly set the price he was willing to pay for tobacco, and Hook was outbid. Hook had to buy all his first year's tobacco for cash, knowing that if he had not promised to pay the planters in cash (rather than in store goods), his competitors would have prevented him from gaining customers.[56]

Those relationships were also determined by the differing personalities involved. Robert Cowan may have cajoled and flattered shoppers to make sales; at least John Hook thought he did. By June 1768, he reported to his parent firm with relief that the "leading men of the County" and those smart planters "who have any penetration" thought merchant Robert Cowan "insincere and guilty of flattery," an opinion that was hurting Cowan's business.

He even predicted that Cowan would soon "play the Girls a Trick by marrying a Widdow with four or five children" and quit the business.[57]

Nonetheless, Hook continued to look over his shoulder, and with good reason. Once again, family connections would trump long-term service. His parent firm, William Donald and Company, decided to close the Warwick store in 1769, and sent James Donald to join Hook in New London. Soon after, another Robert Donald, the youngest of the Donald brothers, arrived in New London for training. John Hook, who had been an independent storekeeper and decision-maker, became an adjunct employee in the very business he founded. His dissatisfaction increased daily and by March 1771 he complained that "two manniagers won't do" and that he had too much "spirrit to be an underling."[58]

With the copartnership about to expire and his frustration at a fever pitch, Hook desperately cast around for another partner "with a heavier purse" than his own. Writing to a number of established merchants, he inquired if they might be interested in opening a backcountry store and stated his terms.[59] Hook's inability to contribute capital earlier in his career had been a stumbling block, but now he was able to supply, or at least promised to supply, £1,200 between the autumn of 1771 and October 1773.[60]

Hook had reached several tentative agreements in the spring of 1771. One involved a business with Petersburg merchant James Lyle. Hook would open his own store in New London, and a second store under the operation of Gross Scruggs would be opened in Falling River. Hook enthusiastically praised Scruggs as a future employee and offered a telling explanation of the characteristics of a good storekeeper: a man who had experience in the business and one who had selected a good helpmate. By choosing a "a plain planters daughter" who was a "good oconomist" and received "no visitors," Scruggs had acquired immunity from those female weaknesses that might diminish his value as an employee.[61]

Hook knew the area around Falling River, having already purchased three hundred acres of land there, and considered it "the key of the back Country."[62] Further, Hook hoped to expand westward by opening a store on the New River. The New London and Falling River stores would each need £2,500 to acquire the assorted necessary goods for sale and the western store at New River only £800. Hook's salary would be but £50, and he would require another £15 to £25 for managing the whole backcountry setup. Hook believed he no longer stood on the edges of the retail trade—a store to the west of him was already possible.

Hook's ideas reveal a sweeping vision. He believed that he had established good connections and relations with local planters. He had identified several potential experienced employees and had convinced them to stay clear of other engagements pending the success of his own plans. He had scouted the area, found what he thought to be the best places for stores, and calculated the capital and servants that would be needed for success. Looking around him, he saw an area experiencing immense growth and noted that planters to the north and west, "the Augusta and Botetourt men," preferred the roads on his side of the river.[63] With the addition of a store on the New River, he would create a network through which he might tap much of the expanding southwestern backcountry.

Hook moved aggressively to squash future competition. In the spring of 1771, merchant Alexander Banks was constructing a store and outbuildings at a local plantation and toying with the ideal of a trial run in New London. If successful in town, Banks planned to sell the rural buildings. So Hook made a preemptive strike to prevent Banks from setting up a trial store in New London: he rented the only unused store building, confident that this, combined with the £500 Banks was sinking in new buildings elsewhere, would discourage Banks from moving to New London.[64] Even the smallest fish represented competition, and about six months later, Hook strove to disadvantage another opponent, urging David Ross not to allow one of their suppliers to continue selling to a local Bedford man who wanted a small quantity of goods to retail locally.[65]

Unfortunately for Hook, reaching an agreement with potential backers proved elusive. Gross Scruggs could no longer wait without commitment and accepted an offer from Callaway and Trents. Hook found another store-keeper candidate for Falling River in John White Holt, former sheriff in the lower district, a man of "good character . . . good education and good sense," and best of all an individual with many connections in the lower part of Bedford County and the upper part of Charlotte, where he grew up.[66] Disappointed at the loss of Scruggs and impatient to begin, Hook urged his intended partner in June to at least make a pretense of building on Falling River to discourage a competitor from coming in.[67] But Lyle demurred and by the end of the summer of 1771, he had bailed out. A demoralized Hook once again contemplated returning home and placed an advertisement to run in the *Virginia Gazette* of August 19, stating his plan to sail for Scotland unless he found a suitable position to keep him in the colony.[68]

The day before the advertisement appeared he wrote to merchant David Ross about another business matter. In the course of the letter, he explained his current employment situation and offered to travel to Petersburg for an interview. Soon thereafter, he met with Ross and gained a new job.

Hook had worked with various Donald firms for two decades. He began in 1751 sweeping floors and tidying stock, then moved on to keep accounts, collect debts, and open a store in a booming economy. He had located employees and proposed a grand network to potential new partners that could take advantage of the rapid expansion of the backcountry. But working for the Donald clan always had left him at risk. Not a family member, he could be, and was, supplanted by Donald relatives. Not a partner, he had only limited opportunity to make his fortune. The harder he worked for Donalds, the less time he had to come up with his own projects—the deals that his arrangements with the Donalds had promised, at least on paper, he could pursue.

The firm had enjoyed extraordinary expansion and wealth during the decades of Hook's employment. Even in the face of fierce competition, these were halcyon days for large mercantile firms. The letters of Hook and other merchants show an economic climate that liberally extended credit, generously stocked consumer goods, and ran up the price of the staple product to pay for it all. As settlers pushed farther out, Hook and other employees of the mercantile firms arrived fast on their heels to supply the backcountry trade.

Hook's business venture with David Ross began just before these good times came to an end. The overall ruinously competitive business conditions, most especially the bidding wars for tobacco, had brought disastrous results for Virginia merchants. By the 1770s, prices paid for Virginia tobacco often almost equaled European prices, which meant tobacco arrived in Britain at a bookkeeping loss. Increasingly any merchant's profits had to come from the goods he stocked and that, in turn, required a significant outlay of capital. By 1775 a London commission firm needed about £8 of stock for every hogshead of tobacco imported.[69]

Ross and Hook, 1771–1774: A Beginning and an End

John Hook and David Ross signed their articles of partnership in September 1771, agreeing that Hook would run two stores in the backcountry: one in New London and a smaller one at Falling River in the southeastern part of the county. Of the total capital investment of £4,500, Hook contributed £1,000 and received 25 percent ownership of the company. Hook had finally located a senior partner with immense capital. Ross operated a Petersburg warehouse and had an extensive network of stores in the backcountry, landholdings in Bedford, and an interest in local ironworks. By the late 1780s Ross would be the richest planter in the state, owning more than one hundred thousand acres throughout the Piedmont and the Shenandoah Valley, four hundred slaves housed in seven different counties, and eight hundred cows and operating a burgeoning urban provisioning trade.[70]

By October an optimistic Hook had personally selected store goods from David Ross's warehouse and had ordered others, spending almost £800. He purchased a double lot for a store and a new house for his bride, Elizabeth,

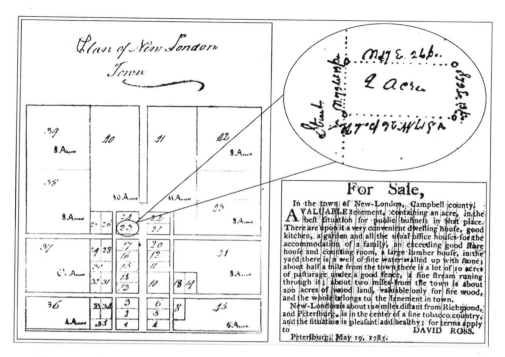

FIGURE 1.2. John Hook in business in New London. Left: plan of New London, 1754, Bedford County Deed Book A, p. 434. Top right: detail of deed for purchase of John Hook's lot in New London from William Callaway on May 16, 1772, Bedford County Deed Book 4, 1711–73. Lower right: advertisement in *Virginia Gazette* of May 19, 1785, for the sale of the real property of the Hook and Ross firm. Courtesy, The Colonial Williamsburg Foundation.

that would allow them to live near the courthouse and his new father-in-law, the planter John Smith (fig. 1.2). The new business required one more important thing: construction. Early in 1772 his two acres, a large lot even by colony-wide standards, sported a forty-two- by twenty-foot store building, the long side of which faced the street (fig. 1.3). The ground floor housed a store room (that is, the store itself), a counting room, and a storage room, possibly what Hook termed the "lumber room." This structure does not still stand, but its appearance was comparable to Farish Print Shop on King Street in Port Royal, Caroline County, which has a quite similar plan and size.[71]

Even as he was setting up his new business, his competitors faltered. In February 1772, James and Robert Donald decided to close their New London store.[72] Ross was ecstatic for he believed that under them the New London trade had become ruinously competitive. He derided "the folly and extravagance" of traders who sold their goods for no profit, paid too much for

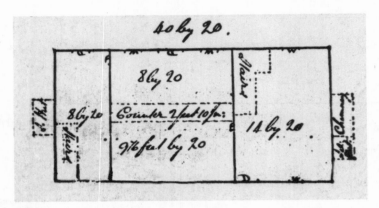

FIGURE 1.3. Plan, John Hook store, New London, 1771. Hook Papers, Duke University. This is a typical commercial floor plan, but Hook gave the store a larger footprint than most others in the region.

commodities, advanced cash to the planters, and took their debts on them. He also blamed their "extravagance in their manner of living and carrying on their business."[73]

Notwithstanding his fortuitous new partnership and the Donald firm's retreat from New London, Hook endured his own share of worries in the early 1770s. Robert Cowan had begun employing what modern economists call "price leaders" as a marketing strategy when he sold one of the most common items below cost; namely Norfolk rum at the Norfolk price, thus foregoing a profit and having to cover shipping costs to boot. Although incensed, Ross urged Hook to stay out of the bidding wars and "by no means advance a shilling for those long-winded chaps. . . . Let every one have the full swing that way," he wrote, "they can't carry off the Land." He further predicted that Cowan's mercantile firm would soon be tired of him and "have no great cause to like the Bedford trade."[74]

Intense competition wracked the mercantile community in Bedford County. Robert Cowan (who had by now become an employee of Alexander Spiers, Bowman, and Company) gave up his store at Walkers Place and moved to town.[75] Robert Donald and Company continued to retrench by closing their Rocky Ridge store.[76] In May, Ross again addressed the "present situation of the dry Goods Trade in general and in your part of the Country in particular." He pleaded with Hook to exercise caution in extending credit to "doubtful people" who will "be very apt to lurch you at the last." He wrote with scorn of "your Gentlemen that have hitherto made so much noise in the Country with their lending the planters money." They "now cut a Shabby appearance . . . one day swaggering about looking for opportunity to be security for planters and to lend them money and perhaps the next day not able to discharge the demands against themselves."[77]

Ross's disdain grew out of his awareness that merchants at the landings on the Upper James River had become so intent on gaining customers and filling the holds of ships that they had bid up the price of tobacco to unreasonable levels. Such indulgences had spoiled the local planters. Certain that highly inflated prices would prove impossible to sustain, Ross forecast that the merchants would be "cured of their madness" that very autumn. Ever the shrewd businessman, Ross predicted that when the fall-line merchants rebuffed planters' demands, the planters would turn to the new Ross-Hook store at Falling River.[78]

But it was not just the overextension of cash and credit, the result of merchants jockeying for position, that led to the financial ruin that occurred in 1772. Distant and far more serious economic problems intruded on Bedford County. Following the breakdown of nonimportation agreements, the colonies had enjoyed two years of general prosperity. The trade boycott had allowed planters to reduce their debts, and in 1770 planters resumed spending on British goods with all due force. Over the ensuing two years, a business boom in Great Britain led to a rapid expansion of credit and ultimately risky speculation. The bubble burst when a Scottish bank failed; the resulting financial panic throughout England forced a number of banks to suspend payments.

The credit crisis of 1772 hit Virginia hard, as English and Scottish banks tottered and no longer honored bills of credit.[79] In August, David Ross wrote at length to Hook about the "Melancholy accounts from home."

> A great many of the principal Merchants in London are become Bankrupt it is said that every capital house in Edinburgh but three are stopt payment two houses in Whitehaven are also broke, the Carion Company has also stopt, thare are as yet no very particular accounts from Glasgow but the most sensible people here expect dismall news from there. The Nobility of England & Scotland have many of them entered into asociations & some of them even mortgaged their Estates to procure Money to support the tottering Banks—When the Ship left London that bro[ught] in our Goods the Capt. could hardly procure Specie Suff[icient] to clear out his Ship—the Banks were shut, no Mercht to be seen in the Exchange everything was in confusion.[80]

Ross pessimistically warned Hook, "Credit will be vastly curtailed," which surely would have an immediate effect on the prices of Virginia commodities. The merchants in Petersburg shared his "great consternation as we have not heard the Worst of it." Ross held out little hope of escaping unscathed: "I know not how it will end, every body largely engaged in Trade stands on a ticklish footing. They are so linkt together."[81] The Atlantic and local economy could not be separated; the loss of stable credit could be everyone's downfall.

Within a month, Ross received new information that enabled him to better assess the situation. He decided that the price of tobacco would "from very plain & natural causes" be sunk by the failures of the banks. In Scotland alone, £2 million in paper currency would be pulled out of circulation. Tight linkages between all involved in the tobacco trade would produce a ripple effect, for if the French monopoly and the "Rich manufacturers" in England waited for a low price, "men in a tottering situation" would not be able to "hold out and must accept of any price." Since most of the tobacco currently in Britain lay in the hands of those stricken, he feared the whole importation was doomed even if not all were incapacitated. His apprehension of financial ruin was now clear: "I tremble for the Tobo the Co[mpany] now has got at Market."[82]

Dire news arrived a month later. Ross reported that Alexander and Robert Donald, who had earlier retired to Scotland, had both hastened back to Virginia to collect their debts. "If old standing Houses such as those are on the brink of Bankruptcy what prospect do you think is there for beginers," he moaned. He grew increasingly frantic and implored Hook to "immediately lop off any unnecessary expense (if any)" and move quickly to make the best collections possible.[83]

Reporting that the Virginia merchants in Petersburg and Blandford had decided to meet to discuss the situation, Ross predicted that these worried men would unanimously agree to raise the advance on goods to 75 percent, which meant that some additional profit could be eked out of the goods for sale to counteract the expected losses on low-priced tobacco. He also expected that the merchants operating stores at the fall line of the James and the backcountry would soon follow suit.[84]

The stage was thus set for four merchants of New London—John Hook, Robert Cowan, James Callaway, and Robert Donald—to meet in October 1772.[85] Following the lead of the merchants at the river landings, the four "Bedford men" agreed to cooperate to control prices and per their instructions from partners set a profit of 75 percent for their retail goods. Furthermore, they contracted to sell some of their most important articles, including sack salt, bar iron, molasses, pot iron, West Indies and Continental rum and peach brandy, at the same prices and on the same terms. Certain large planters with whom they had special arrangements were exempted from the new pricing structure until the following September. Still distrustful of one another, each man made a promise: "Whereas doubts are likely to arise of some taking advantage of others by eluding there Engagements hereto in some evasive manner, we pledge our Honour and Credit to each other that we will by no means attempt to Inveight or Draw off the Custom of others by promises of selling Goods under the prefixed prices."[86]

Bedford County planters howled in protest. Although Ross had derided the Scots for being too generous with them when trying to woo their business, many farmers were of the opinion that the Scottish merchants had taken advantage of them. True, the merchants had extended liberal credit, but they also encouraged consumer desires and overcharged for goods. Planters contended that the merchants made immense fortunes. Resentment against Scottish merchants had simmered for years. The previous October, for example, "Junius Americanus" used his letter to the *Virginia Gazette* to heap scorn on the "junto of North Britains, whom the favor of the Virginians had raised from beggary to affluence."[87]

Bedford planters met in 1773 to protest the "destruction and total combination of the merchants against the people and inhabitants of this colony."[88] They agreed not to sell their tobacco under a set price and suggested a cooperative arrangement controlled by local planter Richard Stith to market their own tobacco, thus bypassing the Scottish merchants. Their complaints and their reaction cast a light on the whole trading system. A blistering letter in the *Virginia Gazette* recounted the doleful history.

> The Scotch nation about fifty years ago, being informed of this valuable Country, and of the weak and blind side of its inhabitants, chose some of them to quit their packs, and leave their poor fare, and baren country, and make an experiment in the tobacco trade which by a little industry, and the mechanik turn of mind and the artful craftiness and cunning natural to that nation, they soon not only raised great estates for themselves, but found a plan to enrich their country and raise Glasgow from being a small petty port, to one of the richest towns and trading points in his majesty's Dominions, and all by Fawning and Flattery and outwitting the indolent and thoughtless planters.[89]

"Let us Bedfordsmen lead the way to liberty and renown" the anonymous author continued, "and turn the channel from centering in Glasgow (richly overflowing all Scotland, and aggrandizing all Scotchmen) to center in Virginia." They proposed that all Virginians join them by boycotting any merchant who did not reside in the colonies and spend his riches there. They wanted commercial liberty from the "craft and cunning" of Scottish merchants.[90]

The threat of imminent commercial disaster should have caused the merchants to band together. It did not, and personal animus continued to divide them. Hook's letterbooks are oddly silent on the details, but apparently he did something that produced a firestorm of angry recrimination among the merchants. Hook scoffed that the whole complaint or suit stemmed from an accusation that he had reportedly claimed to one of Cowan's customers that his goods were better bought than those of his rivals. Written but marked out, however, in Hook's scratch letterbook is information that Hook stood accused of breaking the association's price agreement.

The action and reaction demonstrate the vehement animosity within the merchant community. Alexander Banks (factor for James and Robert Donald at Manchester) had written Hook a letter, which Hook answered in fury. (Neither is extant.) Outraged about the whole affair, Hook wrote a letter to have the suit quashed, and in his copybook draft of the letter, he alternates between threatening to "depreciate the goods, credit and trade" of his rivals and proffering soothing platitudes about giving in for the "sake of living in friendship and good society with a number of respectable gentlemen." Any merchant, especially one setting out, he opined, could not notice every "Ill-natured thing . . . said of them." But, he sniffed, "there is no man [who] meddles less with his neighbors affairs then I do or is at more pains to do every thing in his power to set our Trade on a more respectable footing." If the other merchants were similarly disposed, they would "all be better friends and our connections gainers thereby."[91]

Despite his protestations of generous good will, Hook's correspondence and actions reveal a pessimistic man, driven to succeed, sensitive to perceived slights, and quick to complain. This mindset also affected his relationship with his trading partner. Even though the price of tobacco stabilized in 1773, and the two men had weathered the financial storm, Hook took little pleasure in this. Instead, he believed that Ross, the senior and more experienced partner, had slighted, ignored, and badly dealt with him. Certainly, Hook stood at a disadvantage because he had to follow Ross's directions about prices and could not freely negotiate with customers on a case-by-case basis. That he had to rely on Ross to send needed goods from Petersburg incensed him. Furthermore, he thought that Ross injured their trade by not obliging his requests. Hook thereupon demanded to meet with Ross four times a year personally to address their problems and, getting to the heart of the matter, urged a reconsideration of and amendments to their agreement.

Fifteen years after his arrival in Virginia, John Hook had managed to climb the chain in the store business only to find himself mired in squabbles with his Scottish and English competitors and his own business partner. As important, he increasingly felt derided by the local planters. He had married into a well-established local family, built his own store and house, and opened book credit to many locals. But all was not well; his Atlantic world and his local one began to separate in earnest.

Bedford County planters and Scottish and English merchants clashed over the very core of their relationship. When crops and profits were good, merchants multiplied in a single region and overextended credit, which prompted customers to snap up more consumer goods than their future crops might pay for. Credit did much more than allow the purchase of necessities or enable an ambitious planter to acquire more slaves and land. Credit increasingly encouraged the purchase of many niceties—"articles of fashion"—that made life more comfortable and pleasant and could mark a man or woman as a person of substance or notoriety. One colonist alleged that overweening pride and luxury compelled Virginians "to seek after and desire many articles which we do not really stand in Need of, and which we cannot afford."[92] As Benjamin Franklin put it, England was like a "Mad Shopkeeper, who should attempt, by beating those who pass his Door, to make them come in and be his Customers."[93]

John Hook helped bring that world of goods to the backcountry. He likely cajoled and flattered customers so that they would buy things and then harangued them to pay. His store offered enticing sensory pleasures—exotic smells of other lands, visual delights of color in a drab winter landscape, smooth porcelains and silks in a rough world of wood and stone, books that led the mind to God or to distant places. The relationship between Virginian and Scotsman rested atop a delicately balanced fulcrum of consumer desire for objects and a merchant's desire for crops. The fulcrum could handle economic ups and downs but not political change. As Franklin had warned members of the House of Commons seven years earlier, consumer goods in the colonies were "mere articles of fashion, purchased and consumed because [they were] the fashion in a respected country." When that country lost the respect of the colonies, fashions were easily rejected and shackles thrown off.[94]

In June 1777, a jeering crowd of fourteen headed by Col. William Mead surrounded John Hook's house. They threatened to burn the structure unless the merchant came out, and they even considered tarring and feathering him. When Hook appeared, they took him by force to John Page's house where Mead produced two papers for Hook to sign. One was an agreement signed by about twenty of the county's principal men to suppress the "Tory" party; the other, in Mead's own hand, accused Hook of treason.

Hook reported that he was "charged by Mead on behalf of the Mob at my Perell not to carry on any kind of Trade in this County till after Court." In his complaint's closing, Hook claimed that William Mead said, "Law or no Law, we (meaning the Mob Associators) are determined to proceed against Hook and they did."[95]

The members of the mob joining William Mead that June day included Mead's 15-year-old son Nicholas, wealthy planters Zach Callaway and Jacob Early, and nine other less affluent yet important men. Ten of the twelve adults were Hook's customers; most of them owed him money. Perhaps something more than Toryism or treason was also at stake.

WILLIAM MEAD'S SCOTTISH CLOCK

When William Mead stood at the head of the mob outside John Hook's house, he was a magistrate and one of the most wealthy and powerful men in the county. Like many others, he and his bride had made their way down to the Shenandoah Valley from Pennsylvania. By 1751, this carpenter had purchased land in sparsely settled Bedford County, Virginia. Mead quickly rose in power and fortune. After his wife Ann died in childbirth in 1769, he married widow Martha Cowles Stith, the daughter of a wealthy planter from Charles City County. He helped incorporate the town of New London in 1761. At various times, he occupied the offices of sheriff, deputy-surveyor, justice of the peace, lieutenant in the militia, and vestryman of the Anglican parish. Using skills perfected as deputy-surveyor, he accumulated more than forty thousand acres of land before 1769.[96]

Mead was the kind of man that historians recognize as a county leader. He must have been well respected or at least politically adroit to serve at local, colony, and church office levels. The records of John Hook illuminate another facet of his life: William Mead as a leader in gentility, style, and fashion. As he grew in wealth and power, Mead aligned himself with an Anglo-American ideal of consumption that most residents of Bedford County did not—or could not—share. He was "buying into the world of goods."

Col. William Mead first ordered a few special items from John Hook in 1772. He sent for a carpet measuring twelve by sixteen feet, two dozen black leather or horsehair chair bottoms, a dozen silver tablespoons monogrammed with his initials, and a clock with "Moon Age to Shew the Days of the Month with Mahogany Case." He directed Hook to specially order the clock from John Barr at Port Glasgow, Scotland, at a cost of £8. Fearing that the clock face might fall off, he stipulated special care in its packing, noting that clocks recently ordered from other Virginia-based merchants had received considerable damage in transit.[97]

When he ordered his clock, Mead was following the consumption patterns of the clergy, a small group of learned men in this backcountry region. Living by clock time constituted a way of being more modern, more commercial, and more punctual—a remeasuring of time that continues today. Moreover, any clock that charted the moons, sang the hours, and counted the minutes exemplified the magic of technology. A clock that regulated and ordered the cosmos surely also legitimized its owner as a man to elect and follow. Serving as the head of a mob, however, was something altogether different, for that linked Mead with the twelve angry men before him. Perhaps he even goaded them. Hook certainly thought so.

The other men in the mob could have, like Mead, ordered such a clock from abroad if cash had lined their pockets, but none of the householders recorded in probate in Bedford County between 1768 and 1777 owned a clock, not even those who had the financial wherewithal. Indeed, none of the inventories of any of Hook's customers who died locally in the next quarter-century lists a clock of that magnificence, nor did Hook himself own one.

William Mead's order is puzzling. Why did this man living in the backcountry want a clock, and why did he order it from Scotland when, like furniture, it could have been made in Virginia or one of the nearby colonies?[98] These are two basic questions about supply and demand or makers and users; these are the concepts that quite often lie at the heart of historical analysis.

So why did William Mead order from Scotland? One reason might have been that clockmakers working in Virginia before the American Revolution were often assemblers of parts, not fine metalsmiths who made their own works. Further, Scottish merchants in the backcountry had greater connections across the Atlantic than to a small town like Alexandria, home to the sole working clockmaker documented in Virginia before the American Revolution.

If well-to-do Virginians had any desire for the better things in life, they could special order them from the merchants who sold their tobacco and supplied their goods. It was thus perhaps natural that Mead ordered (or tried to order) fine things, such as the leather chair bottoms that he wanted from Norfolk, using Hook's business connections. As for the clock, British clockmakers had a fine reputation; Scottish-bred Lord Dunmore, for example, who arrived as the new Virginia governor in 1772, had transported his Scottish tall case clock among his household goods.

We don't know why Mead named a specific clockmaker in his request, but John Barr was established—several of his marked clocks may date to the middle of the century—and he supplied other Virginians. At least one other member of the Virginia elite (either in Mead's locale or that in which his second wife had moved before marrying Mead) owned a John Barr clock, and it represented a commodity that could be packed and delivered across an ocean. Barr worked in Port Glasgow from at least 1761 onward and still listed himself as a "watch and clock maker" in the 1783–84 Glasgow directory. Barr made sophisticated, fine quality mechanical works and housed them in the latest style cases (fig. 1.4).[99] John Barr was one of a legion of clock makers in Britain, but he was a good one and in the competition between nations for market, British watch and clock makers ruled.

The larger question remains: what motivated Mead to buy an expensive tall case clock? Historian David Landes's observation that by the end of the eighteenth century, England had become a nation of timekeepers suggests one answer. England was urbanized and its middle ranks were large. Timekeeping soon spread into the countryside. While industrial factory-type production had been going on for a century, the putting-out system—working at home with materials supplied by others—did not demand precise time. The idea of working in a factory, on the other hand, went hand in hand with the notion that work began and ended at set times, and if a labor force had no clocks, the employer had to send around people to serve as "wakers."[100] Therefore, it is not surprising that by the turn of the century, watches and clocks were extremely common. Inexpensive wooden clocks could even be found in the homes of the laboring poor.

Rural Americans may have lagged behind their British counterparts in the need for clock time. In the Hudson River Valley, a consciousness of time in terms of hours or minutes did not become prevalent until the 1820s but then quickly became common practice. The ownership of clocks there preceded notions of labor and time ownership—clocks were rather measures of class distinction.[101]

So why would a Virginia planter want a clock in the late eighteenth century? Tobacco growers worked to a rhythm of light or dark, not by hours and minutes, and lived by routine, not clock time. Traveler Adam Hodgson found that backcountry residents still kept their time by the sun a half-century later. "If you ask them what time it is," he averred, "it either wants so many hours of noon, or it is so much before, or so much after sun-down" and "meals are regulated by the sun, even in families where there is a clock, or a time-piece as they call it."[102] Nonetheless, a clock that showed the face of the moon did have special advantage: moon regulation enabled its owner to predict safer night travel and the rising and falling of tides.

Did this signal a rising tide of consumerism, when luxuries became amenities, making a new set of equipment socially acceptable as appropriate for a certain lifestyle? One study that asked that question found that timeliness did grow in importance by the end of the eighteenth century as theater,

FIGURE 1.4. John Barr, tall case clock, Port Glasgow, Scotland, 1780. Mahogany, brass face. Courtesy, Roy Clements and Pendulum of Mayfair, London. During the colonial period only one clockmaker actively advertised in Virginia, and many planters found it more expeditious to order clocks from abroad. Generally, they worked through local merchants like John Hook who had close connections with partners in Britain and thus could handle special orders that specified the striking mechanism and clock face as well as the woods and embellishments for the case.

mail, and travel became scheduled in Virginia's towns. Yet clocks remained at fourth or fifth place in the category of objects consumed by wealthy households (after silver, ceramics, mahogany furniture, and the like) right up through the second quarter of the nineteenth century.[103] These individuals purchased clocks only after they had bought other luxury items.

This pattern contrasts markedly with households of German extraction located in the counties arcing across southwestern Pennsylvania at around the same time. Material culture specialist Benno Forman considered clocks a veritable icon of that culture's successful yeomen. Of course, those well-to-do men chose clocks for many of the same reasons as their British neighbors, such as that they expressed success and cosmopolitan values. But in many Pennsylvania German households these hugely expensive clocks sat amidst relatively modest furnishings, provoking Forman to ask, "What modern American would invest 6 percent of his net worth in a timepiece?"[104]

William Mead's desire for a tall case clock thus continues to intrigue. Few people except the clergy had clocks in William Mead's backcountry world. What did it mean to buy an expensive clock when so few people owned one? The clock belonged to a cosmopolitan culture quite different from the world around him. Was he "buying into a world of goods" that satisfied a desire to be considered learned (like the two local ministers), successful (conspicuously spending on luxuries), or enlightened (admiring of new mechanic marvels)? As new rich and poor residents poured into the backcountry, Mead might have felt the need to mark his power in multiple, increasingly material ways. Owning a clock would have allowed him to do that. Like what he had to do to establish and sustain his leadership, it too began with a serious capital expenditure outlay (for the mahogany case and precision assembly of gears) and, if given appropriate attention and care, would function smoothly week in and week out. Perhaps Mead's ability to lead in a changing, even volatile, world was based on a careful display of power and material things.

Maybe the secret resides in William Mead's second marriage. A life-cycle shift often provoked increased consumption by colonists.[105] The second Mrs. Mead was a beautiful and wealthy widow who loved to entertain. She may have expected to live like the elites of Amelia County, where she and her late husband had lived—amidst fine things and sociability. To woo her into the backcountry, William Mead may have needed an appropriately furnished home in which she could live in a manner she was accustomed to. The tall case clock he purchased around the time of their marriage was a fine amenity.

William Mead's clock alerts us to the complex relations of the British imperial world of goods. John Barr made fine Scottish clocks. He plied his craft in busy Port Glasgow, no doubt to take advantage of trade patterns. Into such ports flowed goods from places local and exotic. Perhaps Barr used precisely fashioned metal parts from Birmingham to make the machine work and carefully chosen mahoganies from the West Indies to make it lovely.

What did the clock mean to William Mead? We shall never know, of course. But several hypotheses have emerged. As an expensive luxury, the tall case clock signaled Mead's wealth and social rank. A timepiece was a particular kind of luxury, for it also functioned as an index of modernity. If considered as a high-end household good, it was a present for a new wife in a new household. It could have represented a shared investment in group identity, given that Germans and German-Americans were familiar with clocks and created a market that promoted mechanics that could assemble them. Finally, if the clock was actually ever delivered, William Mead would have become an owner of time, like few others in his world. But the longing for the clock, the meaning of the clock to the local Bedford folk—mob or no mob—was a fine amalgam of changing European skill and trade and colonial wealth and desire.

After the Revolution, scores of watch and clock artisans set up shops in the small towns up and down the Shenandoah Valley. Most of their clocks had imported works housed in locally made cases. To fulfill desire in the world of goods, Virginians first depended on British production. They then took the old and mixed it in with the local. Ultimately, America would not need the British; Eli Terry's clocks—often cited as an early nineteenth-century harbinger of American industrial prowess—would lead the world. Clocks then began crossing the Atlantic in the opposite direction.

TWO

Getting the Goods

Local Acquisition in a Tobacco Economy

IT IS RELATIVELY easy to see how goods like expensive tall case clocks marked wealth, power, or, in the case of the clergy, perhaps culture or learning. Although the number of clocks owned by those in the middling ranks would rise as the end of the century approached, there were still few people who had them. If we limited our view to just such elite objects, we would uncover little evidence of a rise in consumerism in eighteenth-century Western Europe or America. It is the increase in small, less expensive man-ufactured and processed goods that tells the story. A bit of tea, a printed handkerchief, a looking glass, or a creamware plate, each of these are the kinds of new objects that entered into people's lives in the backcountry.

William Mead purchased such items of everyday life in 1771: textiles, thread, handkerchiefs, shoes, hats, nails, even a teakettle. Each represented a common item, but his hats were "fine," his handkerchiefs "printed," his rug "silk," his textiles "Irish" linen, and his teakettle copper. Not only were many of his purchases of better quality; they were also often on a larger scale—a thousand nails or thirty ells of osnaburg. Sometimes he personally traveled to the store. Occasionally he sent his son Mahlon or another of the men from the plantation. On November 16, 1771, slave Daniel bought two pair yarn hose on his account. Further, although Mead purchased many things at Hook's store, using family, servants, and unrelated men to conduct his business, he did not make any payments on these purchases that autumn.

Like those of many customers, William Mead's account with John Hook reveals consumer choices. It reveals prices and qualities of goods. It reveals patterns of behavior, such as Mead's predilection to shop for large quantities when court was in session, intimating that he was then in New London attending to business, playing the traditional masculine role of a tobacco planter. Finally, the store account reveals relationships—John Hook, William Mead, and clocks, representing the triangulation of merchant, customer, and consumer goods. Those relations, rippling out and multiplying, explain much about the large economic and social changes of the eighteenth cen-tury. They offer up the drama in the world of goods.

Buying from John Hook was one way to get household goods in the backcountry. There were also numerous outlets, a range of specialists, and a set of suppliers that complicate our efforts to assess customer choice, supply, and access. Any schemata that tackled this system would be a complex matrix that used distance traveled, degree of choice, and kind of establishment as variables of supply and wealth and gender, elements of customer freedom.[1] A sizeable body of evidence suggests the existence of a hierarchical demand system in which wealthy families who had more to spend and who had extensive and powerful business and family networks were given greater latitude by merchants on the issue of debts. On the other end of the spectrum, merchants allowed the poorer sorts to arrange for the extension of small amounts of credit and to make payments through numerous petty forms of exchange, from labor to home-produced goods. There were also systems that had no exchange component, such as inheritance.

Most Sovereign Consumers: Elite People's Web of Goods

The wealthiest people in Virginia had a range of options in acquiring goods. A consignment system allowed planters to order almost anything desired. For example, in 1770 Henry Fitzhugh of Stafford County ordered from England a man's "Neat, Fashionable Gold Watch to run upon a diamond, the works to be cased and Enameled," a "neat light post Chariot," and a "Woman's suite of Rich Brocade ready made up," including with his order the young woman's measurements and a color sample that he wished the new gown to "be agreeable with." In addition, he ordered Brussels lace, a "Paste Necklace and Ear Rings set in Gold Suitable to Above Brocade" and a matching pair of women's fashionable silk shoes, a stomacher, and sleeve knots.[2] In all, he needed a London shopper with taste and knowledge to serve as consumer proxy in creating the desired matching ensemble. The consignment system gave the purchaser almost unmediated access to all the shops in England, constrained only by the diligence of one's merchant factor or friend. John Mercer sent a lengthy shopping list to his son George in London, even naming specific shops and street locations, such as the Bible and Sun in St. Paul's churchyard, advising that it was the best and cheapest place for books for the instruction and amusement of children "from two to six feet high." He also asked his son to arrange annual shipments of articles from London merchants, ranging from slave clothing to the *Gentleman's Magazine*.[3]

Wealthy planters went to some remarkable lengths in their personal trade with England; Richard Morriss of Hanover County shipped to England old hard metal plates to be cast into new ones, a service almost certainly locally available. Perhaps getting the latest mode or design outweighed any inconvenience. Or perhaps it cost him less to ship the plates to England

and have the work done there. Dealing directly with merchants or friends abroad allowed one to avoid the profit markup that local merchants took as middlemen. Even the wealthy were looking for a bargain, particularly for bulk goods: Morriss wrote in glee to James Maury about the secondhand clothes that his friend Thomas Lewis had shown him: even with the cost of transportation from London to Liverpool, this would allow his rapidly growing family (i.e., labor force) to be clothed "much better as well as much cheaper than heretofore."[4]

The letters of countless planters who consigned their tobacco on commission to London houses such as John Norton and Sons are also filled with orders for household and personal goods "for when they [Virginians] send to London it is to get the best of Goods in their kind not so much regarding price as quality."[5] Yet the London agent for Norton seldom supervised the goods being sent, provoking a constant chorus of complaints that the goods were of poor quality and out of date. The concern of these wealthy consumers for correctly selected goods was shrewdly acknowledged by merchant William Lee of London: nearly every solicitation by him for a new patron was coupled with the soothing promise that "Mrs. Lee will be attentive in the choice of anything."[6] Such merchants and their wives essentially carried out long-distance shopping functions.[7]

Options for the acquisition of goods exploded for the wealthy. They could tap into vast formal and informal local systems used by ordinary Virginians. Furthermore, they were far more likely to be linked with business relations in eastern Virginia or travel to higher-order towns in which a greater selection of goods existed. Planter William Preston left Botetourt County for Williamsburg in July 1771 with a lengthy memorandum, the details of which are significant. He needed to take care of his own business ("see Treasurer for overpayment," stop by the securities office, get some papers signed, check his bill at Mr. Prentice's to see if a balance was due, and "remember Hargrave's affair") and to take care of business for others (searched the auditor's office to see if Tom Moor's thousand-acre tract had been paid for and if necessary pay any balance).

But he also had shopping to do. This included buying a blank book, two ivory books, and six pencils, asking the masters of the College of William and Mary for several education books, picking up three silver thimbles for "Betsy and her Mammy," and getting Betsy, someone he presumably took with him on the trip, "to buy Gauze and make some caps for Betsy Preston." Yet most of the errands involved making purchases for other people: a saddle for T. Smith; a set of "genteel Buckles for Mrs. Buchanan"; a London lancet ("not too spear-pointed") for Capt. Fleming; an ounce cochiniell for Mrs. Armstrong; a slave for Col. Breckinridge; and if Fleming should pass by Rocky Ridge on the way home, he needed to pick up a good saddle for Capt. Smith and a piece of good linen and two pair shoes for Mrs. Smith. Finally, he was to pick up two full "compleat Setts of Queen's China" for his own use. The earliest reference to Queen's ware—also known as cream-colored ware—in Virginia dates from 1768; by the summer of 1771, a wealthy Tidewater planter had reported that Queen's ware had attained popularity among his peers. That Preston also purchased "Queen's ware" on his 1771 trip simultaneously illustrates his awareness of fashion and the absence of large sets in his own local market.[8]

Another way to broaden your available consumer options involved having goods sent to you by a merchant elsewhere in the colony. A backcountry planter with good crops would likely be very well looked after by his merchant at the fall line. The John Smiths of Pocket Plantation received a near constant stream of items from the family merchant partner at Rocky Ridge.[9] Although the plantation lay only twelve miles from New London, Smith preferred to deal with Alexander Stewart of the Donald chain, who had a store at the fall line in Rocky Mount. Smith might "dally with" John Hook for minor everyday items, but he turned to Stewart for most business transactions.

John Hook, too, shipped goods to some planters. His memorandum book in March 1773 notes a varied list of promised goods: a brass kettle to Robert McAfee and a dutch oven to George McAfee, both in care of T. Boye; *Johnson's Dictionary* to John Taylor in Fincastle (care of Majr. Ingle), a best men's saddle, with cloth and bags, to Nathaniel Evans, textiles (pink and blue "wosted" binding, brown Holland), chamber pots, and sugar to Col. Preston, and "26 yards red and white thread fringed furniture Bed Curtains and weeding hoes" to Col. Thomas Maddison.[10]

Thus few barriers confronted wealthy Virginians who wanted to acquire particular goods, even luxury ones. They could use the web of relatives and friends and business associates and mercantile partners locally and abroad. As long as their credit was sound, they could promise a future crop as payment. Their one disadvantage was perhaps time, for if a good proved to be of poor quality, badly sized, or simply unsuitable, even the richest buyer had to wait months for its replacement.

Peddlers

Rotating into this local system of the distribution of household goods was the peddler—"one of the Honourable Fraternity of Moving Merchants."[11] The early nineteenth-century diary of one peddler traveling the backcountry of Virginia gives invaluable evidence of the trade and travel of these elusive entrepreneurs who carried trunks or packs throughout the backcountry, stopping at courthouses, inns, and private residences. Many peddlers tried to time their visits to coincide with court days that attracted many surrounding planters and their families to town. As a contemporary put it, "In Hopes of doing a very good Business," peddlers occasionally "put the Best foot foremost" and hung "their Rags to the Public Eye, in order to induce a Sale."[12] In some locales, particular peddlers had built stands, which the first peddlers to reach the scene quickly appropriated. Others considered porches at the courthouse fair game, lest bad weather otherwise force them to pack up all their goods—ranging from textiles and used clothing (their "rags," if English precedent is an accurate guide) to guns, hats, and saddles.[13] But we would be remiss to categorize peddlers' customers as the poor or the peddlers' stock as marginal items. Priscilla Fleming, daughter of Col. William Fleming spent more than £10 in 1798, buying textiles, clothing items, and accessories—even "morocco slippers" from one peddler. Her sister Anne made a more modest purchase the following year: "gloves, needles, and pins."[14]

Peddlers swarmed across the landscape in Franklin County in the late eighteenth century. Perhaps they capitalized on the burgeoning consumer interest in goods; perhaps stores remained too few and far apart for many families to get to. In any case, the numbers of licenses issued to peddlers seeking to supply goods to backcountry residents rose steadily; in 1803 the county licensed nineteen peddlers, hawkers, and retailers of "goods of foreign manufacture." In 1806, it licensed nineteen peddlers alone. Their number declined in the 1820s, but only after more stores had opened throughout the county.[15]

Auctions

An obscure part of the local economy involved the auctioning of goods to satisfy sanctions of wills or pay off debts, to sell off overstock or the estates of stores. In 1775, an auction in Campbell County dispersed the estate of Edward Goldman. The twelve slaves, livestock, barrels of pork, and corn and an impressive list of household furnishings fetched £418. The purchasers included some of the wealthiest men of the region. James Buford took home two desks—one cost him £3, the other only 5 shillings—and a chest. Richard Melear bought tin pans, pewter plates, a few pails, some wheat, and chairs. William Howard carried home a churn; Thomas Fuqua bought a tub. Elias Hammond left with butter pots and a teapot. The brief listings do not permit an analysis of whether "secondhand" purchase remained significantly cheaper than new items at a local store, but obviously such sales provided an alternative, if only occasional, venue for the purchase of goods. That this sale took place at a time when local merchants were desperately trying to collect debts and, in many cases, had stopped importing goods should not be overlooked.[16]

The Goldman sale attracted a large cross-section of Bedford residents and within a matter of hours transferred the household goods of one man into the homes of some three dozen others. Such a scene raises numerous questions. Was the bidding frantic or laconic? Were there unspoken rules that allowed Thomas and Richard Goldman, perhaps Edward's sons, to purchase all but one of the slaves?

Other auctions, called vendues in the eighteenth century, played an important role in the social world and provided a way to move goods through society. On December 6, 1786, Col. Francis Taylor of the Northern Neck attended the "sale of Chews attachment on J. P. Adams effects." Although the day was cold and cloudy, the sale attracted many people. Taylor bought a half-barrel of ochre for a relative and seven pair of leather breeches for himself, on the relatively ungenerous terms of two months credit with interest. The next day he returned to the sale, buying two dozen pewter plates and some thread and scissors. Then the wheeling and dealing began, as the purchasers broke down what seemed to be larger lots and sold them among themselves and to others. Taylor bought a bridle and three tin basters from James Gaines, sold thread and a pair of scissors to several others, and exchanged one pair scissors with Johnathan Waugh for a pair of thread stockings. The formal sale continued the next day although little was left. Taylor left security for £5.4.0, "36/ for Breeches & 45/ for plates etc bot by me & 23/ for Oker bought for G. T. F. Madison paid me £6.0.0." Straightaway the next morning he went to Lee's store and traded six pairs of the leather breeches (which Lee valued at £2) for three stamped and one silk handkerchief, 2 yards of green plains, 5½ yards of linen, one hat, and two pounds of sugar. The next day Taylor sold a relative a final pair of leather breeches and came out with a small profit.[17]

Merchants sponsored such vendues, especially if a particular market location was glutted with goods. Matthew Read and Hugh Johnson's ledger in Staunton in Botetourt County, for example, is filled with customer charges for goods bought at vendue in the late 1760s.[18] Another reason for a vendue was to close a business. In 1809 John Hook's personal and store goods went on the auction block. Page after page of his 1809 accounts list the customers who came to the court sale and took home bargains.

Inheritance

Wills of Bedford County residents seldom listed specific household goods; more often they specify bequests of land, slaves, and livestock. On occasion,

widows and children received specific legacies. Jacob Hickman left extraordinarily detailed directions for building a house for his widow and supplying her with foodstuffs—fruit, wheat, and beef—as well as hemp, flax, tow,
and wool for clothing and household use and a good pair of shoes a year.
Even if she remarried and left the farm, she received two cows, her chest and
her "spinned wheel," a bed and bedstead, and "housin fresh such as Basons"
equally divided among her and the children. He went on to stipulate that the
rest of the farm animals—horses, cows, sheep, and dogs—and household
furnishings be sold and divided equally among the widow and an unnamed
number of children.[19] Wealthy planter and owner of Washington Iron
Works Jeremiah Early also provided for his widow during her natural life-
time, granting use of the plantation, eight slaves, numerous livestock, the
riding chair and two horses, all the plate, pewter, and "every other kind of
household and kitchen furniture necessary for her maintenance."[20]

Fathers also left household goods to their daughters. Robert Ewing's be-
quest to his daughter Patty included the best family bed and full half of his
"Table Furniture" along with her own chest, saddle and horse, her apprentice Sukey, and four hundred acres of land in Kentucky.[21] A bed (most often
the most expensive piece of furniture in the house) constituted a common
household good specifically designated for a daughter, although more frequently daughters received bequests of slaves, livestock, cash, and even land.
Bequests for sons tended to include land, although special household items
that may have been considered male possessions also were passed down
through the male line, such as the writing desk that Guy Smith specified go
to his son Bird B. Smith. The elder Smith also designated that all his books
be divided between his two sons, carefully noting that they not break a set.
His seven daughters received hunting saddles, part of his slaveholdings,
and, when each married, a horse. Moreover, after the death of his wife,
his extensive household estate valued at more than £1,000 (and including
prints, teawares, armchairs, and silver spoons) was to be divided among their
nine children.[22]

Other people, perhaps unrelated, received bequests of household furniture and consumer goods. To Elizabeth Hunt "for diverse good causes" John
Adams left a feather bedstead, bolster, and two blankets; a chest, small
trunk, and cotton wheel; a pewter dish, basin, quart pot, and two plates; a
half dozen spoons and a candlestick; two chairs, a pot, and a coffee pot. This
constellation of goods was enough to maintain a basic household.[23]

Most specific bequests vastly overrepresent the wealthy and date from
after the Revolution. The majority of wills left by Bedford Countians merely
stipulated dividing an estate equally among the children or passing most of
it to an older son after the death of the widow. Daughters often received small

sums of cash; men generally received livestock or land. Peter Funk's whole estate was valued at £52 in 1792. His only furniture was two beds, three chairs, a chest and a small table, yet he carefully designated their disposition; they were to go first to his wife and then to be divided equally among his children.[24]

Artisans

Surprisingly few specialized artisans settled in Bedford and Franklin counties, perhaps owing in part to the vagaries of town development. The population of New London, one early center, shrank after court proceedings were moved to the town of Liberty in the post-Revolutionary period. When Franklin County laid out its new county seat on the lands of James Callaway at his iron foundry, no town grew around that courthouse because Callaway refused to sell lots.

The absence of trade centers prompted residents to urge the new state government to establish new towns. The petitioners for establishing a new town at Wisenburgh argued that it would promote business: when numerous artisans are centered in one place in a town there is a "lawdable spirit of emulation in each to excel." Such a clustering would also "reduce the Price of manufactured Necessities" to—as they rather testily phrased it—"something of their real value."[25]

Local artisans provided another structured means of acquiring goods. John Hook's records, although replete with details of other merchants, stand remarkably silent about artisans. Hook kept no personal household accounts of expenses that show the work of artisans providing household services to humor his family, and the few bits of evidence he provides about local craftsmen come from various forms of barter accounting, that is, using store accounts of debt to exchange or pay off others. Merchants like Hook supplied the vast majority of imported goods; artisans supplied the many bulky, simply produced, or processed needs of local people.

William Mead's order of clocks and fine chairs aside, merchants seldom imported bulky items of locally available materials like furniture; the backcountry was filled with men who had woodworking skills. In some ways, the search for these artisans in the backcountry should not be difficult. Diligent local historians and material culture scholars have located multiple pieces of domestically and locally made furniture that descended in area families. At least two signed pieces survive. Clusters of furniture types have identified yet another artisan's patterned work, but no scholar has successfully tied those to a specific individual's name.

Although furniture could be roughly hewn and made with simple tools, the more refined pieces required specialized tools and the hand of a trained skilled artisan. One of the early lawsuits lodged in Bedford County involved a dispute over making a desk.[26] A furniture maker needed tools, skills, and customers. While more research may uncover other specialist artisans, it is likely that multipurpose woodworkers produced the majority of locally made early furniture of Bedford and Franklin counties.

By the early 1820s, just two or so generations later, the booming towns of Salem and Lynchburg had attracted cabinetmakers capable of making specialized goods and with a large enough clientele to perhaps make only furniture rather than general woodworking. Three had settled in Lynchburg by 1805. Still, as late as 1828, John Wibert, for one, continued in the general tradition of being "a cabinet maker and house carpenter" near Salem. In a modishly constructed walnut chest of drawers he penned an advertisement on a handwritten label. He offered pieces for "holesale and retale" and a warranty of one year's satisfaction. If "good care was taken" but it was "disapproved of, the chest of drawers could be returned to him at Jane Mason's creek, one mile out of town."[27]

Benjamin Lenier likely set up shop further south, in the mountains of Henry, then part of Patrick County. Like Wibert, the only record of him survives in the wares he marked. He made furniture that was ebulliently and enthusiastically constructed and ornamented. He knew the vocabulary of classical motifs that gained popularity in the first quarter of the nineteenth century and used them with abundance. Lenier inserted a paper behind a glass on one of his bookcase desks, dating from 1805 to 1815. On the upper left of the four panels was his name, to the right was "Cabinet maker," and on the lower left and right, was the name Joseph Scales (figs. 2.1, 2.2).[28] John Wibert's work was in style but quite restrained when compared to Lenier's. In terms of the way furniture "looked," Lenier's work was like those exuberant Shenandoah Valley pieces that celebrated the skill of veneering and inlaying with multiple wood types and made a visual statement of religion and ethnicity.

Other backcountry craftsmen produced assorted versions of utilitarian household goods, some of which competed with imported items stocked in profusion at John Hook's store. Samuel Darst, for example, moved from Shenandoah County, which had multiple active potters, to Franklin County where he acquired 220 acres of land that had good potter's clay. When he died some years later his estate included potter's tools and earthen plates and dishes.[29]

A single household might pay multiple individuals for specialized goods and services, as the records of William Jones's estate settlement demonstrate. The estate paid Elizabeth Cook for weaving; Josiah Hundley and Peter Daniel for shoes (with Peter Daniel being given repeated business); Sarah Wood for making five suits of clothes and for "waiting on one negro

FIGURE 2.1. Benjamin Lenier desk and bookcase, Patrick County, 1805–15. Walnut with lightwood and cherry inlays, glass and paper insets. 98" x 41⅝" x 19¾". Private collection; photograph courtesy Old Salem, Inc. Unlike artisans who scratched a pattern that referred to geometric stringing (see pl. 6), he used inlay abundantly and positioned it in unusual places.

woman" (probably as a midwife); James Stepp for making a powder tub and other coopering services; and W. (perhaps Williston) Talbot for smith's work. In addition the executor paid an unnamed craftsman 7½ shillings for casting pewter and paid a local slave 2 shillings to provide cotton.[30]

Household Economy

The slave's sale of cotton illustrates how families might obtain household goods through an exchange that lay outside traditional craft definitions. Despite the important work of multiple scholars on household production

FIGURE 2.2. Detail of the Lenier desk and bookcase. Courtesy, Old Salem, Inc. The placement of the maker's name on paper in a glass inset is an unusual form of advertising. The significance of the other name remains unknown.

and the market, the household as a locus of consumption and shopping remains, quite simply, an economic black box about which we know little. Agency (who controlled access to resources and initiated purchase choice), action (who physically moved about the landscape to acquire goods), and authority (who was the final arbiter in consumption decisions) remain enigmatic realms.[31]

However, the household perhaps in part remains a black box because historians have been inclined to the view that the male head of household dictated how family labor was maximized and consumer choices made. Such a view overlooks the extent to which buried within the notion of relationships are ideas about the successful functioning of the family in promoting wealth and social standing and passing property to heirs. Therefore it misses women's contributions to the household economy and the massive purchase of women's commodities in the eighteenth century.[32]

A dramatic tension existed in eighteenth- and nineteenth-century households over authority, ownership, choice, and decision. One contemporary noted that the husband was "still the master upon whatever the monied concerns depend." That power lay at the crux of the marital relation and "however much the wife is adored or valued she feels the dependence in this which regulates her conduct." and "the husband thinks he must be kind and he endeavors to render her life happy."[33]

Still, women could step in as needed in many ways. For example, because Landon Carter of Richmond County had no wife in 1770, his daughter Lucy actively attended to her father's business and went to stores to lay out tobacco and arrange the delivery of cotton and osnaburg for slave clothing.[34] John Hook's partner David Ross relied on his wife to take care of his business when he was ill. He reported to a business colleague that he "gave Mrs. Ross what little money I had to pay out occasional claims and to put in a little ticket [a bill notation] of the amounts paid and to whom."[35] This allowed his wife to serve as his deputy accountant, and it vested her with financial authority.

For the less well-to-do, being a helpmate often meant actively working to bring home income or resources. Overseers' wives commonly spun and wove, made butter, or sold eggs.[36] John Harrower urged a neighboring overseer to marry the woman he had already spent several nights with because if the two joined households, she would be able to save him money through her own efforts. "One in his Business," opined Harrower, "cou'd afford to live better married, than a man in any Other Bussiness whatever." A wife could make at small expense a great many articles in the house, articles that "run away with a deale of money from him when he went to the store."[37]

These exemplify the myriad and flexible ways in which women had connections to and experience with the workings of cash economies and consumer goods. The patriarchy of earning power—women's complete dependence on their husbands—similarly could be mitigated by control of some portion of resources. An early eighteenth-century chapbook scene presents the proverbial honest John and his fiancée Kate. John looks ahead to their marriage by imagining a booming poultry yard that would send her to market. She asks him squarely who would control the money made "with those odd things?" The young man replies amiably that she already understood the "way of the farmer's wife . . . for they had rather have a little purse to themselves, than the knowledge of five hundred pounds of their husbands."[38]

Women were hardly the only players in these petty economies. The ledgers reveal numerous men trading services and small crops with John Hook for store goods. About the same time, a youthful Daniel Drake in Kentucky spent his spare time "weaving shot-pouch straps, belts, and garters" and then exchanged those items for "a day's work, or making a hundred nails." With pride, Drake pointed out that even as a boy, he could exchange his labor with a full-grown man for an equal length of time.[39]

Other systems of economic exchange, for multiple products, also developed in the backcountry. The advertisement David Ross sent to planter John Smith at Pocket Plantation in July 1780 announced that tobacco, bacon, beef, coarse linen, allum, salt, brown sugar, and coffee as well as bar iron and castings were for sale at Oxford Iron Works.[40] Although he stipulated cash payment, Ross simultaneously offered to buy for Smith, and presumably other planters to whom he had sent the announcement, all of the above provisions for resale. Implicit in that offer lay the potential for trading one kind of commodity for another, even though the transaction itself would be recorded in cash terms. The kinds of things for sale at the ironworks may have been related to wartime shortages, but the point remains that a market for coarse linen, perhaps even that made in the home, existed.

Producing surplus items in the domestic economy offered a way to pay taxes, tithes, and rent and to buy salt and tools—indeed, to cover all the everyday costs of the most mythical of "self sufficient" farms. But beyond this lies a more dramatic point. Petty cash earned by women in the neighborhood economy constituted a purposeful form of production. For many, producing goods provided a means of consuming. Such products of sale became a set of resources that a woman could specifically control, and control of those resources gave her a set of choices for buying consumer goods. That motivation is highlighted in the records of some agricultural women themselves.

Jane Frances Walker Page lived a little eastward in the Virginia Piedmont, but her detailed account book demonstrates the depth and breadth of such exchange relations. Page methodically paid her slaves for fowl and eggs. Paying slaves for produce was not unusual in eighteenth-century Virginia; however, this housewife also used small quantities of retail goods like thread to barter for products made in other households. This woman thus stood at the center of a large web of domestic economy. She traded with and bought from slaves, overseers' wives, and other women in the community, and she traded with and bought in the larger world of British goods from Britain.[41] This system was not part of a bucolic world of rural sharing. The participants all accorded the items a cash value.

Such household accounts as Page's knitted into store accounts in multiple ways. A few examples from John Hook's accounts illustrate how petty goods afforded entry into the new consumer world for groups traditionally viewed as standing outside the cash economy of eighteenth-century Virginia. Lucy Bailey's four grown hens and dozen chickens bought her a pewter dish in August 1772. Sarah Tisdale chose ribbon, a wax necklace, and expensive fabrics—muslin, silk gauze, and chintz, that totaled more than £4—and she paid most of her balance with 30½ yards of Virginia cotton cloth valued at 2 shillings a yard. Ruth Mosse took home 6 yards of red-

striped Holland at the end of one month and returned with a dozen bags
that she probably made of coarse cloth or hemp.[42]

John Hook: An Atlantic Man in a Local World

It is this kind of local system that intertwines with the Atlantic economy in
John Hook's business ventures. His experience in the backcountry trade
provided him with many insights as the endeavor with David Ross proceeded. Recognizing that his two former employers and a third merchant
might offer substantial competition, he stressed to Ross, right from the very
beginning of their partnership, the importance of having quality goods at attractive prices at the proper time of the year. He pointed out that the other
merchants' stores were already well stocked. Hook found "difficulties enough
to get my best friends" to frequent his business and wished that he could ex-
ceed his rivals in "the Qualities of my goods," asking always to be sent the
best of their kinds. Soon after receiving £800 of goods that first autumn, he
reminded Ross to remember him if he saw any "pice of goods in your Cargo
that is Nice and Saleable even if it is not put down" on his orders.[43]

Hook's shelves remained incompletely stocked, and he included a long
list of necessary goods when he wrote Ross in November. He suffered "in
the purse" for want of feathers, for which great demand existed. He also
needed pepper, allspice, sixty pounds bohea tea and one hundred pounds of
Gloucester cheese. He needed a good assortment of ribbons, books, playing
cards, cotton cards, more white and brown sheeting (this was "material," he
insisted, as was duffel and leather and calamanco shoes), two pieces of clear
lawn, and yellow and pale blue shalloons and stuff for women's winter
gowns. Additionally, he requested more bed blankets, worsted stockings,
women's cloaks, colored and spotted rugs, a good assortment of ribbons,
and snuff.

The quality, variety, and fashionability of the items he stocked belie the
pervasive currently held notions of rugged, self-sufficient, backcountry life
(pl. 1); his customers could thumb through the *Spectator* or *Johnson's Dictionary* and handle backgammon boards, china teacups, or feather plumes. But
the ledgers indicate that most commonly Hook sold his customers the necessities of everyday life. Hook stocked assorted nails, crosscut saws, gim-
lets, socket chisels, gouches, mortise firmers, tenon saws, best Newcastle
adzes, hinges, and locks, all items used to carve a home out of the wilderness and keep it in repair. Paint—white, spanish brown, prussian blue, and
yellow—transformed the natural hues in this built environment. Hook also
sold garden spades, bramble scythes, and hoes for clearing, weeding, and
grubbing, allowing the settlers to turn fertile earth into tobacco, corn,
hemp, wheat, and vegetable fields. He offered guns for protection and food

procurement; ones four feet long with half-inch bores or break-off guns, along with flint, powder, shot, and pistol locks. His stock addressed the vast equipage for transportation—riding horses and hitching wagons—and ranged from curry combs to two superfine lady's hunting saddles, with polished arched mouth bits and green saddle cloths embroidered with gold sprigging costing almost £2 each.

The household items for sale at Hook's store included brass candlesticks, hair brooms, scrubbing brushes, pepper boxes, and iron pots, the last of which weighed from 1½ to 40 pounds. He offered pewter dishes—the sturdy tablewares of country living—and white salt-glazed plates, and he sold tin pints, hard metal (high-quality pewter) "bellied" drinking pots, and creamware mugs, any of which could serve the ever-popular rum that Hook sold daily. Customers also could buy pewter spoons, molds for spoons, silver teaspoons, in addition to a wide array of knives and forks. That Hook also offered large printed teapots, enamel-painted creamware sauceboats, and tablecloths suggests that his customers had a heightened interest in entertaining. For those who wanted to further display their wealth, hospitality, and good manners, Hook's store had fine painted teapots, Chinese porcelain cups and saucers, English-made cut-glass Madeira decanters (engraved), enameled wine glasses, and cut-glass cruets (fig. 2.3).

The vast range of textiles, sewing notions, and clothing constituted the most significant items available to John Hook's customers: buttons of glass, ivory, and brass or beads; fine silver thimbles; twenty-five grades of linen, ranging from coarse to fine; and vast quantities of undyed sacking and sheeting, along with more colorful linen and cotton checks (pl. 2).

Hook complained to Ross about many of the goods he received; the copper pans were charged to him at 3 shillings 6 pence although they were marked 3 shillings 2 pence. Hook also believed the pewter too expensive, and he asked Ross to check with his rival Peterfield Trents to see at what price that pewter came in. Although Hook liked the printed handkerchiefs "blue ground and white" and asked for more, he believed the silk handkerchiefs at 27 shillings no better than those for which he had paid 24 shillings. The powder he received was so much glazed that it would not ignite, and he returned half a barrel in exchange for the "ragged" kind. He could not find the buttons necessary to match the fabrics sent and sent swatches back with the buttons, explaining he could not sell the cloth without the right ones.[44]

A month later his complaints continued. He strenuously objected to the sugar, as its poor quality "prejudices and disgraces the Retailer," and he directed Ross to supply good quality sugar or none at all. Most other complaints in this long letter focused on prices charged him, and he stipulated those items that could be bought cheaper in London or Glasgow than

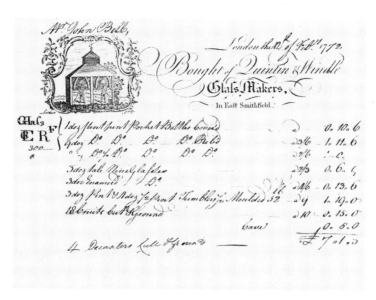

FIGURE 2.3. John Bell shop note, London, 1772. Hook Papers, Duke University. Shop notes are rarely found in Virginia merchants' records because middlemen generally combined multiple orders into a few shipments. This note indicates that East Smithfield glassmakers Quinton and Windle had filled an extensive order: dozens of glasses and tumblers, a few cruets, and four cut and engraved decanters. Hook, who at the time sold more pocket bottles than other glass items, frequently complained about the size and shape of those he received.

Whitehaven, but he also groused about quality and packing. Half of the poorly packed, expensive pewter had arrived in damaged condition. Moreover, the firm's new supplier Walter Chambre had neglected to even send "such a material item" as pewter plates. The large crate used to ship the crockery weighed so much that breakage was possible. The blue and white counterpanes were terrible—the blue ones were no "better than stained with something as [torn] as fig blue," a common bleaching dye. The first time they were wet, he reported, the stain could hardly be seen. He reserved his lengthiest comments for the agricultural implements in the shipment. The crosscut saws could only cut one way. The mill saws were thinner at one end than the other; they needed to be of heavier substance and equivalent thickness from top to bottom. The sickles were of such bad quality he doubted he would sell a single one. The scythes were too slender in the blade and back, and "Our Farmers oppinion" was that they were meant for work in meadows rather than for cradling grain. The hoes had not enough of a square shoulder for Virginians' taste and were poorly shaped, which made them

thus unsaleable. In short they were too broad, too straight, and too small.
Ross needed to find ones with more weight behind the eye so that they would
better cut in the ground, and they should be 3½ to 4 inches wide.

Despite these complaints, many of the merchant's goods had sold. He
was already out of handkerchiefs and women's bonnets and hats (the black
satin bonnets having found the readiest market). He needed a hogshead of
jugs (in two- and three-gallon sizes), butter pots (two to five gallons each),
chamber pots, a few pair of firedogs, assorted bottles, and a barrel of vinegar.[45]

The stress of trying to hold the business together during tough financial
times increasingly wore on the merchant, and Ross's placating responses no
longer quelled Hook's anger over the availability, quality, and price of the
goods shipped to him. In April 1773 Hook coldly informed Ross: "I cannot
refrain from complaining of my orders for Goods, both European and West
Indian being too much neglected when ever I rite you I am answered with
Complaints, with Appologies and With Instructions." That their Whitehaven supplier did not send osnaburgs to him or his Falling River storekeeper last year "was such capital blunders that there can be no excuse for it."
Why should he have to pay 5 percent commission for shipping his goods or
tobacco, he asked with annoyance, pointing out that the level of the service
was so poor and that Callaway and Trent received goods freight-free so long
as they used their partners' ship to send their tobacco and only paid 2½ percent commission on top of that.[46]

In June he resumed his harangue: "So much of our business in trade depends on Mr. Chambre or whoever buys up our goods in Britain adhering
strictly to the orders sent for them." Surely the company "had more unsal-
able and fewer salable well chose Goods within these 28 mo. past than any
Mercht in the Colony that has imported to the same extent." He demanded
to meet with Ross four times a year to adopt a method of solving their problems and wanted their copartnery reconsidered with necessary clauses an-
nexed to their agreement.

Hook's final complaint in June concerned goods that he had special ordered for wealthy local planters: prints for Thomas Maddison and hides of
black grain leather for chair bottoms for William Mead. Neither had come
to hand and the neglect of these commissions made him look ridiculous.[47]

A displeased Ross replied with sarcasm: "I am at present (as I observe
any other Merchant) struggling hard to make Remittances in order to avoid
the general ship wreck of Credit [so] what must my apology [be] for not
attending so minutely to prints, chair bottoms, and ruffles as you would
wish?" But the harried partner did promise to formulate a plan to keep
Hook's store supplied "whereby the goods do not pass through my hands,"

essentially agreeing to let Hook arrange for his own goods with Chambre in Whitehaven.[48]

Hook took to his task with relish, advising Chambre that the success of their business in New London was absolutely dependent on the "dispatch, exactness, and judgement in the choise of the goods, respecting the quallity, collours, patterns and fashions": sales and collections "depend on the goods." Lest Chambre miss his point, he continued, "cargoes well assorted of good quallity well bought and to have in good season will command the Custom of the best and ablest paymasters." His own trade had suffered greatly because his competition was much better supplied; he chided that "for me to make money without Goods is as absurd as to suppose a Taylor to make a Coat without cloth by the needle and Shears alone."[49]

Hook claimed his store shelves lay absolutely bare of goods and directed Chambre to act quickly. He especially needed "the Material Articles, the Linens Shoes Duroys and Sagathys with the trimmings," although he then reiterated that "every article is material as we are extremely bare." He also scolded Chambre for not shipping his commission goods, explaining that disappointments on orders of this kind were very prejudicial to the company's interest. Wealthy local planters were the kinds of customers to take pains with for they stood ready to make payment when the goods arrived. Delays in filling their orders made the company look bad, and left Hook in the uncomfortable position of personally bearing their displeasure. Finally, he also directed Chambre henceforth to let him know where and from whom each object was purchased so the two businessmen could monitor the choices and act accordingly.[50]

During 1772 and 1773 Hook's complaints grew increasingly bitter. Stocking his store with well-bought and appropriately assorted goods remained a problem in his dealings with David Ross and the Whitehaven partners and suppliers. Customers shared Hook's disappointment and faced three choices: await the next shipment, take their business to another store, or try to buy a locally made version of the commodity.

In summary, all of these entrepreneurial activities worked to a certain degree, and they all supply us with a certain amount of information. The disposal of estates, for example, offer an outline of domestic goods and the precise value placed on even the most basic household furnishings that heads of household attempted to provide, usually in some equitable or conventionally unequal fashion, for their widows and children. The value placed on items traded and services provided illuminates the growing variety of goods available emanating in ever-widening circles from a locality, a region, a colony, and England. Overall, however, these data provide little detail about clothing for the majority of residents, and they do not give a clear picture of consumer behavior. The unsystematic nature of such documentation means that it is difficult to precisely reconstruct the material lives of Bedford County residents.

By teasing and tugging at a number of different sources we can create a sense of what the consumer's world was like. What has emerged is a series of images—a rich daughter buying fancy slippers from a peddler's pack, planters hauling complete sets of dishes over rocky roads or wheeling and dealing with leather breeches or scissors and thread. Amidst this John Hook operated his business, which offered customers a world of fashion and style and comfort as well as ideas for improvising when either the desired goods or the money with which to buy them remained in scarce supply.

THE IRON PLATE

Almost two centuries ago, someone in Franklin County poured iron into a mold to make a table plate in a stylish Staffordshire form. That plate—along with a small number of other plates, bowls, and mugs found nearby and in other backcountry counties—stands as remarkable evidence of how local people amalgamated the raw resources of the new nation with the industry and power of England.

The working of iron—its heat and power—conjures up the mythic and heroic status of a blacksmith and the echoing and pounding refrain of steel-driving folk heroes like John Henry. While it has not similarly crossed into historical memory, a furnace in blast stage was a marvel. Benjamin Franklin included a drawing of the Principio ironworks in Maryland in his very first *Poor Richard's Almanack* in 1733.[51] In the Shenandoah Valley of Virginia, the furnace and foundry that lit the sky was aptly called Vesuvius.

Paradoxically, even as it celebrates labor and brawn, iron making represents a prescient form of industrialism. And in the colonies, the scale of capital, labor, skill, and organization in ironworks led to the evolution of a special Anglo-American version of "industrial bondage," a reliance on an enslaved labor force. Backcountry Virginia possessed numerous rich ore veins, and by the mid-eighteenth-century entrepreneurs were producing basic iron for the colonial market. The Oxford and Washington ironworks in Bedford and Franklin counties produced ammunition and weapons for the American Revolution and protecting the two ironworks became an important mission of the Virginia war effort. These and other local ironworks played important roles in the evolution of American ironworking. Toward the end of the war Thomas Jefferson claimed that James Callaway's Washington Iron Works forge supplied almost a quarter of the bar iron and the furnace about 14 percent of the pig iron manufactured in Virginia.[52]

The American colonists used two distinct methods to produce iron. The simpler and more direct form relied on a bloomery, a large square hearth with a chimney atop akin to a barbecue pit. The chimney had an outside funnel (tuyere) through which a water- or air-operated bellows propelled air, and the heat source was wood charcoal that had smoldered for several days under the watchful eye of the collier.[53]

When all was ready, the bloomery fireplace was fired and charcoal and iron ore were placed atop it in layers and air-blasted. During the burn, the furnace men added limestone as a flux to lower the temperature and to remove impurities. The melted ore puddled at the bottom, where workers stirred it until impurities were burned out, leaving a dense mass called a bloom, measuring about five inches around and weighing one hundred pounds. Yet other workers hammered the "bloom" into bar iron. (Ultimately, foundry owners turned to a water-powered mechanism that alternately raised and dropped the hammers in the final refining step.)[54]

An ironworks, or furnace, differed from a bloomery in both size and scale. An ironworks needed a huge stone tower—sometimes thirty feet tall. The tower was canted inward to decrease its diameter toward the top and leaned toward a hillside, to which it was connected by a bridge, so that charcoal and iron ore could be added at the very top. The molten ore rolled to the bottom of the tower, where a worker used a vent and a plug to direct it into long slurries (called sows) and small side vents off the streams (called pigs). (The whole operation resembled sows nursing their young.)[55]

Bedford County had one of the earliest ironworks in the region. Pennsylvania investors began the Oxford Iron Works as early as 1768. It had commenced operations by 1773 and three years later was sold to David Ross, John Hook's mercantile partner, who was quickly becoming one of the wealthiest men in the colonies. A second ironworks, initially established as a bloomery, belonged to John Donelson. Local magnates James Callaway and Jeremiah Early bought the business from Donelson, and by the middle of 1779 had a blast furnace in full operation.

Washington Iron Works (renamed to honor the leader of the American forces) proudly announced that it produced a variety of products: "to wit, POTS, KETTLES, CAMP-KETTLES, OVENS, SKELLETS, FLATIRONS, SPICE MORTARS, FIRE DOGS, SMITHS ANVILS, FORGE ANVILS, FORGE HAMERS, WAGGON BOXES, STOVES, or any other kind of castings that may be wanted."[56]

The rapidity with which the owners promised to deliver such a wide array of everyday wares is striking. Many fall into the category of castings—

FIGURE 2.4. Stove plate fragment, Franklin County. Cast iron. 20" x 12". Private collection. Recovered during excavation within Washington Iron Works, Franklin County.

wares created from molten iron that was poured into molds suspended in a stratum such as sand. Because at least one wood carver incorporated the name of the ironworks into the mold he made, researchers have been able to identify several stove- and firebacks and fragments made at Washington Iron Works.

The advent of the iron industry changed the area around Bedford and Franklin counties in at least three profound ways. The need to guard it during the American Revolution heightened the local awareness of the value of the industry. Simultaneously the appetite of each furnace (an acre of woodland for each day during a six-month run) depleted the supply of wood in the immediate vicinity. Third, the furnaces represented a massive investment. In 1820, the output of Washington Iron Works depended on eighty-nine slave workers (fifty-four were involved with the ironworks, and the remaining thirty-five worked as loggers and haulers, both transporting required wood and delivering the finished iron to retailers) and grew the needed agricultural crops to feed those who worked there. Its capital investment, estimated at $100,000, yielded an annual profit of $7,000.[57] It was an iron plantation.

Historians can imagine skillets, Dutch ovens, and pots bubbling on hearths because cast-iron pots are still made and used for camp cooking.[58] Decorative iron stoves to radiate heat or stove plates to reflect heat from the back of fireplaces are other items that make sense given the properties of iron and possible uses for wares made of iron (fig. 2.4). Merchant John Hook offered imported iron pots from Scotland, ranging in weight from 1½ to 40 pounds. But understanding the iron plates for eating or punch bowls or

FIGURE 2.5. Plate with molded edge, Franklin County, c. 1800? Cast iron. Diameter 9".
Private collection; photograph, Gavin Ashworth. This Virginia-made cast-iron plate
has the same rim, depth of well, and width of marley as Josiah Wedgwood's Royal shape
Queen's ware and a very similar footring on the back.

mugs for drinking, all of which likely originated in Franklin County and
surrounding backcountry Virginia, is more difficult (figs 2.5, 2.6; pl. 3).

Food plates made of iron remain all but unmentioned in the literature on
ironwares of colonial America.[59] The disincentives for making and using
iron dinnerwares are both practical and real; iron conducts heat quite effi-
ciently, which would make iron dinner plates difficult to handle. Iron products rust easily. Iron surfaces are difficult to decorate, except through molding. Iron is also heavy; these particular iron plates weighed around 2½
pounds each, and the footed bowl weighed 7½ pounds.

Functional equivalents to iron dinnerwares were widely available. Ceramic dinnerwares were both locally made and imported. Wooden plates
could be made locally and with relatively simple tools. Most pewter versions
were imported but could be easily cast and repaired locally.[60] Thus a *functional* reason for making a cast-iron dinner plate did not exist. Furthermore,
this particular one emulates a Queen's ware plate with a molded, smoothly
undulating rim, a pattern that Josiah Wedgwood, official potter to the English king, marketed as "royal" and that dining plates, whether of silver,
pewter, or ceramic, often featured in the late eighteenth century. The bril-

FIGURE 2.6. Mug, Franklin County. Cast iron. 5" x 4½" x 2", excluding handle. Private collection.

liance of creamware, a lead-glazed refined white body, reflected its ability to attach a certain cachet to a shape made of common earthenware. The ware was a phenomenon unmatched in the history of English pottery, perhaps unmatched in the history of household goods. Soon the Russian queen—Catherine the Great—commissioned a lavish set of individually hand-enameled pieces. Wedgwood conquered markets around the world and consumers clamored for his wares even in undecorated forms. By the early 1770s similar creamware was available in the colonies and at an affordable price. Its popularity had prompted backcountry planter William Preston to travel to Williamsburg to acquire two whole dining sets of Queen's ware in 1771, and Hook sold such plates in his own store for 1 shilling 6 pence per dozen. He also imported British pewter ones for 7 shillings per dozen.

Evidence of mold lines and snapped-off sprues (the lines for pouring iron) on the bottom of many of the iron plates indicated that they were cast in a mold, probably one placed in sand. Most such castings relied on a two-part mold made of some other material (such as wood, clay, or pewter), which clamps held together during the pouring and as the molten iron cooled.

Other evidence may shed light on the plate. The first iron plate found, the one with the molded edge, turned up in a field about two miles from Carron Forge, which James Callaway owned. The 1814 inventory of that

Franklin County forge lists a dwelling house and kitchen, thirteen slaves, and some household effects, including two iron dishes, four tins, five plates, two dishes, and a basin.

After the Franklin County plate popped up in a field, ten other individual iron plates, all documented to the southern Virginia backcountry, surfaced.[61] These discoveries in turn prompted a hunt for other common food and drink wares made of iron. This search turned up three bowls, and they too originated in the southern backcountry. The shallowest of the three may have served as a washbasin. The middle one may have had multiple functions. The large footed one may have been molded from a porcelain punch bowl. (Plate 3 compares the profiles of porcelain and iron punch bowls.) John Hook's inventory of his store when he died in 1809 included fifty-six iron bowls. In addition to the bowls, two iron mugs have surfaced from this region—the larger measures a fine liquid pint. Both mugs have the same profile and exaggerated and thickened handle. Finally, a set of six handleless iron teacups molded on a multisided ironstone ceramic form popular in the mid-nineteenth century proffer the somewhat astonishing idea that iron was used to hold hot liquids. Like the other iron dinnerwares, they too can be traced back to within a few miles of Washington Iron Works.

Questions remain. For example, how much of the allure of Queen's ware could be captured in an iron version? And why make teacups out of iron and tolerate the hazard that must have been posed by drinking hot tea from them? The idea of making iron versions of ceramic wares used for social pastimes like dining, tea drinking, and punch drinking puzzles twenty-first-century sensibilities. We must think like a man or woman of the backcountry or perhaps even like an ironworker. John Hook's store offered fashionable ceramics that customers could see, admire, and purchase. But these same forms could also be *created*, perhaps for free. Slaves manned the forges and ironworks of the colonial backcountry, and perhaps these workers made ironware plates, cups, mugs, and bowls for themselves, perhaps as end-of-day wares once the production work had been cast.

In a culture of iron, many things are possible. One child remembered touring Vesuvius foundry with the local grade school of Rockingham County. Her brother pressed his hand in the sand, and a workman brought a pot of molten iron and poured it in the imprint, making "such a perfect replica that the lines of his hand showed plainly."[62] A cast-iron mask of a man's face even exists, purchased in a neighboring ironworking county, perhaps made to celebrate a life of work in the death of an owner. When iron was so available, it is perhaps not strange that those who worked with it might also have explored other uses.

Material culture analysis begins with an object and moves to makers and users. An object made in a different ironworking district suggests ways to consider iron objects in particular contexts. In 1795 Bates How, a joiner living in northwestern Connecticut made a bureau and signed his name to it. In its construction How used bits and scraps of wood and an unusually large number of screws, some of them decorative, and added rope detailing that resembles the twisting of the screws. These elements might suggest the artisan was both creative and idiosyncratic but to stop any analysis would be to miss important elements. Other factors played a role in determining the appearance of and techniques used on this bureau. Nearly every head of household in the region was allied with ironmaking in some way. As important, the region produced nail rods out of which screws were locally made in profusion.[63] For Bates How, the use of a readily available material that seems anachronistic to us now was a viable option.

In southwestern Virginia someone molded an iron plate in the fashionable royal shape, sometime in the late eighteenth or early nineteenth century. Perhaps backcountry people took their knowledge of fashion and made their own version. Perhaps an enslaved worker made it for his personal use. Whatever the reason, it is the object that raises questions about making do or making better, about how an iron plate mattered. Does the plate signify "buying into the world of goods" in backcountry terms? Is it the hybridizing of African skills and European goods? In either case, clearly something different is going on in the larger Virginia backcountry.

THREE

Accounting for Life

Objects, Names, and Numbers

I N LATE JULY 1801, John F. Price spotted a man crossing the river between Bedford and Franklin counties carrying a "Sack Bag filled with something on his horse." Although he could not swear positively, witness Price some years later averred "from the shape of the article in the Bag, I have no hesitation in saying I believe they were the Books."[1] The books in question held the early 1770s accounts from the Virginia store of John Hook; the horseman was Hook's son-in-law Bowker Preston. For six years, these documents had been the subject of litigation between Hook and his former partner David Ross, who claimed that Hook had not fully paid him when the Revolutionary War terminated their partnership.

Hook had steadfastly refused to appear and produce the books for circuit court commissioners to examine and had been found in contempt. The court finally ordered a sequestration against Hook; his property would be seized until he produced the books. The stage had been set. One morning in June 1801, a group of four men gathered in the yard of John Hook's large house in Franklin County. Three of them were court commissioners, who brought hammers and nails to board up the doors after turning Hook and his family out of the house. When they arrived with their order to inventory Hook's property, they found wagons loaded with goods being removed from the premises, a bold act in defiance of the court's order. Hook had also hidden the keys to the store and cellar.

Hook still alleged that it was his understanding that the court order did not cover the books. Price fumed at Hook's arrogance, but the commissioners thought it too cruel to order Hook's innocent family from the premises. Hook invited all to dinner and the commissioners ultimately left with the standoff unresolved. When they returned the next day, the merchant at first acknowledged that he had arranged to have the books removed but then claimed that they had been stolen. According to the testimony of Price, the clerk of commissioners, the tears in his eyes "were those of a Crocodile merely shed to deceive." Hook finally accused the commissioners of having, themselves, stolen the books after interrogating his "mulatto servant man Dennis" or a neighbor's slave who was Dennis's "confident and associate" and discovering where the servant had hidden them outside the locked store.[2]

The saga of the books continued. After Price claimed he saw Hook's son-in-law with the books in his saddlebags in late July, the commissioners testified in September that they had found Hook's personal ledger on the bed in the counting room and had taken it into their possession. Somehow Hook "or some of his young men" had secretly ferreted the ledger away without their noticing and hid it with all his other books. Somehow all the missing books fell into the hands of Charles Simmons—a local "drinking man"—who promised to return them for the $30 reward Hook offered. When pressed for information about where he had obtained them, Simmons said only that he found them by a "magic rod or divine stick." The books then appear to have been lost again. Just as the judge prepared to issue a ruling, without access to the crucial documents, Hook's lawyer, Edmund Randolph, claimed that the books had been in *his* office for some time, but he needed more time to examine them. The case remained in litigation for another forty years.[3]

These episodes provide an entertaining and rare combination of intrigue and comedy—books whisked from behind the backs of officials, drunks with divining rods, conspiring slaves, mysterious gunnysacks, and a sprinkling of crocodile tears. But Hook's books record far more than trouble with a former business partner. The contents of these volumes bring to life the world of goods of eighteenth-century Anglo-America—tools that built, textiles that warmed—and the process of their acquisition. They evince actions, desires, and relationships.

Perhaps John Hook's account books were charmed. They could vanish, be mysteriously whisked away by an unknown hand, hidden by slaves and their compatriots, found by a conjurer, and lost again before reappearing in the office of a jurist. They possessed great powers of truth; containing a formulaic code of words and numbers that a court of law stood ready to accept as verity. Without even being opened, their contents were recognized, for when Bowker Preston forded the river "the shape of the article in the Bag" alone convinced John Price that the horseman carried John Hook's missing account books.[4]

"Book-keeping is called an Art," declared John Mair in his often-reprinted *Book-keeping Methodiz'd*, "an art that through precise recording enabled a man of business to know the true state of his business, in whole and in every part."[5] The double-entry, or Italian, system of accounting required keeping multiple books to post business by date and cross-reference by name. Cashbooks, stock books, books for inventories and invoices—all played a role in the complex eighteenth-century business world. Every act of commerce engaged in by a human being must be recorded, ordered, accounted for; all awaited a reckoning. As John Hook demonstrated in his many court cases, the books provided the essence of business.

Hook's books show consumer goods moving into the hands of a broad cross-section of backcountry residents. Rich and poor, male and female, black and white—when these individuals crossed the threshold to Hook's store, they entered into a relationship with the merchant. The entries, listing goods purchased and payments made, demonstrate complicated patterns of commerce and lifestyle. Operating within a society economically and politically structured around white men and their property, the faces of some customers remain blurry or missing. Yet the need and desire for consumer goods washed over economic and political boundaries; women, renters, transients, and the enslaved did join those white landowning men at the merchant's counter. Through the scrawled entries, images of people on the move emerge—crossing streams, riding down mountain passes, walking down the streets and roads, alone or in groups. Their actions punctuate the rhythms of the agricultural calendar—court business or shopping trips, a broken hoe or a cold snap, a treat for bringing in the harvest.

The words and numbers in account books are a type of code, but one that does not tell all. To operate a successful credit mechanism, both merchants and customers had to deal in faith using a legally recognized system of book credit that could be upheld in a court of law. The merchant generally listed a name, a date, a brief notation about goods or services received or sold and whether a debt or credit ensued. He recorded debts on the left hand page; credits on the right. Each line of writing constituted a "transaction," whether in the form of a "debt" (usually a purchase or a cash loan) or a "credit" (paid with cash, a service, or goods). While the name on the account belonged to a particular (white, male) individual, other people associated with him might conduct a transaction on that account, including a wife, child, sibling, a slave, or even a person whose relationship to the account holder is today unknown. Hook assiduously listed who actually made each transaction, whether the account holder or another party, denoting the latter by the word "per" and the third party's name. That very practice illuminates the ambiguities of consumerism and the difficulties of keeping his economic system within prescribed channels that located a head of household as the single point of decision-making power. The eighteenth-century store trade was as much about relationships as it was about commerce (fig. 3.1).

Perhaps because of his own litigious nature, Hook remained remarkably punctilious in his record keeping throughout his career. After reviewing the accounts in connection with the suit brought by David Ross, the commissioner pronounced that "the great attention paid to the debts is uncommon,

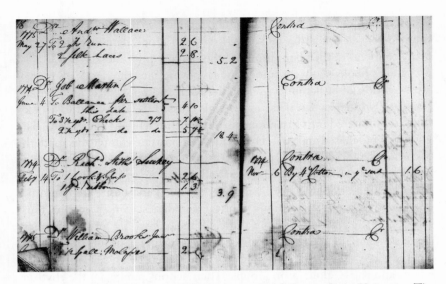

FIGURE 3.1. John Hook Mercantile Ledger, p. 12. Hook Papers, Duke University. The left-hand page lists purchases, the right credits.

indeed 'tis extraordinary for a Retail Business." He marveled that Hook conscientiously reviewed every open debt account and after about six months time charged interest "with great exactness even to the sum of 5½ d or 6d."[6] What an accountant admired was anathema to the local customer who was accustomed to greater leniency.

Reaching a modern-day understanding of the depth and breadth of Hook's business dealings requires studying the multiple books he kept and doing so in ways that produces an analysis that ranges over both time and kind of account. Among the 103 surviving volumes is a daybook detailing the beginning of his partnership with David Ross in the autumn of 1771, which led to the establishment of his store in New London. It lists both named credit and anonymous cash business. A second daybook details purchases at Hook's second, more rural store located at Falling River in 1773–74. These two books were the kind of traditional ledgers kept on premises, one recording events as they occurred, the other posting up a day's work. Two additional small books—a petty ledger and a mercantile ledger—list small accounts during 1773–75. These record less structured accounts and contain lists of small purchases and barter payments. In the former, Hook recorded small debts, actions he subsequently posted to a larger ledger, no longer extant. The mercantile ledger itemizes purchases made through exchange for a vast range of goods, services, and foodstuffs. These two small account books record 674 purchases by 127 customers between 1773 and 1775. Hook also kept a memorandum book where he jotted down daily orders, promises, and obligations. Hook used these smaller pocket-size books while on the road, and they formed part of the intricate system of memory and notes that allowed the accounting to function.[7] They also contain the names of poor whites and African Americans, customers from the more marginalized groups in society.

The Revolution ended Hook's participation in the Scottish tobacco trade, but he did continue to operate a small plantation store in the ensuing decades, for which several account books as well as the records of the estate sale in 1809 survive. Of particular interest is a small book from 1803 to 1805, labeled and catalogued as a blacksmith's book, in which Hook listed purchases by slaves. In combination, all these records kept by John Hook open a window into the retail trade in the backcountry as settlers transformed the region from colonial outpost to early national "frontcountry."[8]

Analysis of Store Account Books, 1771: The Tobacco Business

Between September and December of 1771, John Hook recorded almost four thousand individual transactions in the store's daybook. Although recovering from the downturn of 1770 and soon to experience a massive dislocation, known today as the credit crisis of 1772, the economy in the waning months of 1771 appeared relatively stable.[9]

Autumn constituted a merchant's busiest season. Farmers needed supplies and tools to process the harvest and feed and clothe the workers. They later brought in their harvest or payment; the merchant credited the value against purchases previously made. They were in essence creating a "buy now, pay later" consumer culture. Indeed, of all the customers recorded in Hook's daybook from September to the following April, 246 made at least one purchase in the fall between September and December.[10] Moreover, in Virginia economic activity was high, particularly in places like Bedford County in which rival merchants jostled for new business. New London had three other established merchants. To take advantage of the busy season, Hook had opened his store before all his stock arrived, and he remained short of goods until the end of October. Still, 371 named customers patronized his store.

Their names are rare and important, but they also raise a problem: how to move from reading names to reconstructing lives. Who was Guy Smith? Simmons Everitt? In Virginia, as in many colonies, the documentary evidence about store customers is slim because most documents before the American Revolution deal with court business and land management. Only after the establishment of new state codes in 1782 did Virginia government systematically assess taxes on land and personal property at the county level. Local tax lists, court records, marriage records, and deed books do, however, help flesh out biographies and wealth holdings for some of Hook's 1771 customers. So does a search through public records in several counties, letters of local gentry and businessmen, and varied other small accounts.

Yet one out of every eight men remains unmentioned in the surviving official records of Bedford County and surrounding counties. Part of this omission may be explained by the nature of the personal property and land tax lists themselves. The lure of fresh opportunities in lands to the west and south may be another factor; any number of transient settlers no doubt just passed through. Death and the dislocations of war may account for the absence of yet other names from the records. Still, John Hook's strategy of extending credit to gain customers did sweep some of those previously unknown and marginal white men onto the historical stage, demonstrating that women and slaves are not the only common people missing from government records.

Eighty percent of Hook's customers at the New London store were from the large pre-Revolutionary Bedford County, with another 11 percent residing in Botetourt and Fincastle, located to the north and west (fig. 3.2).[11] Only about 40 percent owned slaves (table 3.1), mirroring overall slave ownership in the county as a whole (table 3.2). Half owned land, but only about a quarter owned both land and slaves. Two-thirds of his landowning customers owned tracts of less than two hundred acres. John Hook drew his customer base from the middling and poorer sorts of society (table 3.3).

Debit and Credit

The practice of accounting frames the life of any community by sorting debts and credits, obligations and promises. John Hook's accounts, as his autumn 1771 records show, served as a fulcrum, balancing the debts of the local and global economy, both in the store and among the community. More than 70 percent of his transactions involved a named customer making purchases on credit. Another 4 percent of the debt that Hook carried on his books owed to his customers' borrowing of small amounts of cash, often to pay taxes or third parties. Hook actually loaned out more cash than he received in payment in the same time period. They were as frequent as the popular sales of sugar or powder; moreover, they were large, an average of £3 each during in the autumn of 1771. He also more commonly took payment in goods and services rather than in main cash crops. Equally important, customers used Hook's books to pay each other; that is, they paid for another's accounts through goods and services.

Hook's business operated as part of the Chesapeake tobacco trade, a

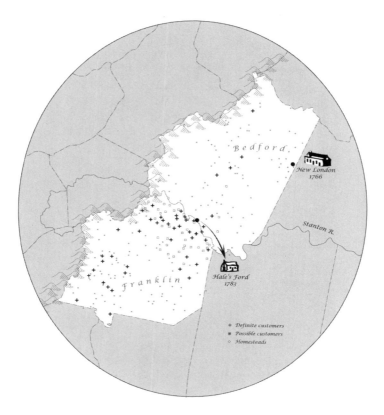

FIGURE 3.2. Bedford and Franklin counties. Drawn by James Carrot based on Bicentennial Maps. Completed by Cartographic Laboratory, University of Wisconsin–Madison.
This map is based on place names appended to twentieth-century historical maps created from deeds for Franklin and Bedford counties. Two caveats are necessary. (1) Because those maps stop at the current county lines, they do not encompass those customers
who traveled from further distances. (2) Some of the names on the Bicentennial-era
maps belong to a family rather than the individual mentioned in Hook's account. The
map indicates how the river and mountain passes combined to direct customers to
Hook's stores. In the postwar years some customers tramped past James Callaway's store
in Rocky Mount and went the further distance to shop at Hook's Hale's Ford store.

trade essentially defined by the extension of long-term credit for goods in
exchange for crops. Yet closer analysis measures the surprising mutability of
that system. Nearly a fifth of his transactions involved goods sold for cash,
which meant he had no need to list the buyer. He entered these transactions
on separate cash pages several times a month. Such entries helped Hook
control and account for inventory and liquidity—all part of the language of

TABLE 3.1. Slave Ownership among Hook's Customers, 1771

Number of slaves owned	Percentage of customers	Percentage of store sales
0	59.3	62.2
1–5	22.1	22.4
6–10	10.1	10.6
11+	10.2	4.8

Sources: John Hook Daybook, 1771, and Bedford County Will Book 1, 1763–87, Library of Virginia.

TABLE 3.2. Slave Ownership in Bedford County, 1768–77, 1787

Number of slaves owned	Percentage of probated estates, 1768–77 (n = 80)	Percentage of tithable households, 1787 (n = 1,214)
0	62.7	67.1
1–5	28.0	21.8
6–10	6.0	7.0
11+	2.7	4.1

Sources: Bedford County Will Book 1, 1763–87, and Personal Property Tax List, 1787, Library of Virginia.

TABLE 3.3. Land Ownership Patterns in Bedford and York Counties, 1782

Property size	Bedford County	York County
1–99 acres	7.7%	27.8%
100–199	29.1	22.4
200–299	26.7	15.1
300–399	11.9	7.3
400–499	7.6	9.3
500–999	11.6	11.7
1,000–1,999	4.6	5.4
2,000 or more	1.2	1.0

Source: Bedford County and York County Land Tax List, 1782, Library of Virginia.

Table 3.4. Most Common Items Sold at Hook's
Store, 1771

Item	Percentage of all goods sold	Average price per sale (shillings/pence)
Rum	6.5	2/8
Osnaburg	4.7	7/2
Hats	3.8	5/7
Handkerchiefs	3.8	3/2
Buttons	3.5	1/3
Powder	3.3	1/5
Sugar	3.2	3/1
Thread	3.0	0/1
Linen	2.6	12/1
Hose	2.5	3/5
Cotton	2.3	13/0

Source: John Hook Daybook, 1771, Library of Virginia.

double-entry bookkeeping. These small cash transactions added up to a significant £82 in just a five-month period and provided a needed inflow of capital into the business. The kinds and scales of cash transactions varied, ranging from 1 pence for a bit of thread to £24 for a hogshead of rum.

Buying Patterns

Store records provide detailed testimony about the nearly 250 different kinds of items Hook sold in late 1771. These included a few fashionable items of dress (green women's riding hats) and a few specialized tools (joiners' rules). Many simple improvements to daily life were made by single-sale items: a medicinal elixir, a reading primer, a glass pane to repair a window, expensive tools such as an ax, a flatiron, a scales and weights, and a watch key.

The dozen most frequently purchased items constitute the very ones Virginia merchants constantly fretted about with their suppliers: inexpensive goods (table 3.4). Hook had constantly reiterated to his suppliers the importance of "material items" such as rum and coarse textiles, and these items were indeed the most popular. The majority of these items were ones that customers had to replace or replenish often. Rum topped the list, outselling the second-ranking item, buttons, by two to one. Next came everyday linens, hats, handkerchiefs, thread, and hose followed by sugar and gunpowder. Thus textiles and clothing items provided the mainstay of his common business. Items for personal decoration and hygiene such as combs

Table 3.5. Purchases at Hook's Store, 1771

	Percentage of gross sales	Percentage of transactions		Percentage of gross sales	Percentage of transactions
Textiles	35.3	21.8	Sewing items	3.5	14.8
Clothing	10.7	14.4	Craft items	1.4	1.5
Alcohol	11.1	7.1	Building materials	1.3	1.8
Bedding	7.3	2.5	Misc. household items	1.3	1.0
Groceries	6.7	9.1	Tools	1.0	1.5
Saddlery	5.8	3.2	Books	0.2	1.6
Foodways objects	4.1	5.2	Miscellaneous	6.8	8.0
Hunt/fishing equipment	3.5	6.5			

Source: John Hook Daybook, 1771, Library of Virginia.

and ribbons stood in the top twenty-five as did only three nondomestic items: nails, shot, and cuttoe knives (multipurpose short-blade knives).[12]

Any analysis attuned to intense variety often misses a larger structure. Thus the top three categories of goods—alcohol, textiles/clothing, and cooking/dining must be examined in more depth (table 3.5). Some of these goods were expressive of lifestyle. Others were visually communicative. Still others gave pleasure or changed experience. But all were part of purchase patterns that tell us something about backcountry consumers.

Alcohol

Every general merchant in Virginia invested the majority of his capital in textiles, but rum alone brought most customers into a store. Nearly one out of ten sales in Hook's store was rum, most commonly sold in small units, and a customer could buy a bottle (generally a quart) or bring one in for a refill.

Hogsheads, casks, or barrels that held between 100 and 130 gallons stood second in the list of rum sales. Customer Peter Donald may have run some kind of tavern business, which may explain his large purchase, and the other two men who purchased rum by the hogshead may have been planters or other merchants. Hook complained to Ross when the rum supply looked to be running low, rightly pointing out if another big sale came his way it might leave him unable to fill the daily demand for rum by the bottle at the store.

If the typical rum purchase was a quart bottle, perhaps for immediate consumption, and the second, a large cask to be hauled away and tapped, a third variant involved buying several gallons on a single trip. Simmons Everett bought a total of eight gallons on the four visits he made to the store on November 19 and 20, 1771. He also purchased powder and shot, a tin quart, allspice, and twelve pounds of refined sugar.

Everett presents a challenging first puzzle in matching purchases and buyers' motivations and uses. He appears in several unrelated documents, the details of which confound rather than clarify. In January 1769 he lived with Col. James Callaway near the Bedford County Courthouse in Bedford.[13] In June 1770 he signed an agreement to serve as John Murphy's overseer, but he did so with the stipulation that he not be barred from practicing his trade as a shoemaker. In November of 1771 he purchased eight gallons of rum and a rather large quantity of sugar at John Hook's store. Was the sugar to combine with rum for punch drinking? Or was a November purchase of alcohol to supply John Murphy's slaves, perhaps at harvest time? Or perhaps he ran an unlicensed tippling house. Or perhaps the prospect of spending long hours toiling over leather during the winter months simply made him want to drink.

Hook also stocked other kinds of alcohol, especially brandy and porter. Brandy, often made locally with fruit, ran a distant second in the alcohol sales. The fifteen purchases of brandy brought in £6; by contrast the 273 sales of rum grossed £91. Another fifteen customers bought porter (most often in quantities of two dozen bottles).

As Hook's records show, alcohol greased the wheels of the backcountry store trade. Although Bedford County lacked the variety of places to buy alcohol that existed in communities closer to Chesapeake Bay, Hook's customers did have other options.[14] Taverns operated in New London, including one established by rival James Callaway in a separate building from his store.

When historians study alcohol consumption in the colonial period, they generally look to public spaces like taverns, themselves busy institutions that were patronized by travelers and locals and that served food in addition to alcohol. Moral outcry often dogged taverns, tying these centers of drinking with a whole set of vices in the minds of some. As one Virginia clergyman asserted in 1751, at taverns "Drunkenness, Swearing, Cursing, Perjury, Blasphemy, Cheating, Lying and Fighting, are . . . permitted with Impunity . . . as though . . . those Houses were enfranchised with unlimited Privileges; and neither subject to the Laws of Man, nor yet to the Inspection and Authority of God himself."[15]

Hook's store records tell a different story from that of the tavern. Perhaps these people drank on site, but Hook's store had no place for seating. That so many individuals (men and women) left the store with a quart of rum serves as a reminder that alcohol was an ordinary, unremarkable, ubiquitous part of everyday life. Distilled beverages remained less costly than coffee or tea. Drinking alcohol to excess might lead to rowdiness but seldom to crime or violence, and hence most people in the eighteenth century did not deem intoxicants as threats to social order. Nonetheless, excess drinking helped create the impression of loose and wild behavior in backcountry life. It also became evidence of ungodliness that called the evangelical religious to the backcountry.

Textiles

Merchants considered textiles their most "material" items. They also spilled more ink complaining about the low quality of textiles sent to them than anything else. For their part, most residents of Virginia accepted the British formulation of the "mercantilist doctrine." They labored to raise and export tobacco (a raw material) and bought cloth (a manufactured good) from Britain. Reporting to the Board of Trade in 1763, Virginia's lieutenant governor, Francis Fauquier, emphasized the necessity and importance of importing all "kinds of fabrics as well as shoes, stockings, gloves, ribbons, and all ornaments of Dress," adding that "the Imports daily increase, the common Planters usually dressing themselves in the manufactures of Great Britain."[16] Invoices detailing the merchants' wholesale purchases and merchants' letters to their English and Scottish suppliers attest again and again to the importance of textiles to a store's success. Providing an assortment of textiles and sewing supplies tied up between 40 and 50 percent of a merchant's store capital.

Of the two categories of "material" things—everyday cloth and items of fashion—Hook's shop overwhelmingly sold everyday inexpensive fabrics. Yet stacked on his shelves, probably wrapped in brown papers, lay goods offering color and drama and romance, the sensuous world of beautiful textiles. Unwrapping and untying their protective covers was probably as dramatic for customers as it was tiresome for merchants, who so often showed to those who did not buy.

Hook held the tiger by the tail. Textiles dominated his business and consumed a large part of his capital. He had to be up-to-date and fashionable, even though fashionable fabric added considerable expense, sold less frequently, and had an expiration date. The colonists were no different from their counterparts throughout Britain. To appear "dressed," an individual had to don certain clothing elements; even backwoodsmen might choose leather skins for pants and jackets, clothing that differed only in materials and details from that worn by most other working white men in the colony. To appear respectable—let alone fashionable—an individual had to meet a set of local conditions, ones established abroad and then tempered by the immediate location. Virginia merchants found themselves confronted with an especially annoying problem when suppliers either ignored their orders or sent shoddy or old-fashioned goods.

Hook voiced profoundly felt exasperation at his lack of supply. Without the right quality and quantity of cloth, his shop would fail. He devoted about 40 percent of his purchases in the autumn of 1771 to textiles and 10 percent more on clothing items such as shoes, hats, and handkerchiefs.[17] That he devoted fully half of the store's business to covering and ornamenting the body or softening and warming the home raises three important questions. What kind of textiles were these? Were they merely practical coverings or did they satisfy a wish for style or color? What do the purchase of such coverings tell us about life in Bedford County?

Traditionally, historians have asked different questions. Historians of economy and technology discuss the cost or importance of, say, British woolens or burgeoning mills but seldom delve into the details of use or preference. For some historians, the endurance and strength of the myth of the prevalence of homespun cloth makes it difficult to even consider that most textiles in the southern colonies were purchased from countries across the Atlantic, particularly Scotland, northern England, and Germany. Other forms of evidence have also misled the historians' eye. Clothing made up only 3 percent of consumer wealth in contemporary inventories and surviving textiles are rare.[18] In recent years curators and women's historians have explored textiles and dress. Other historians interested in women's contributions to the culture have explored the household production of cloth.[19]

Hook's records bridge these academic chasms in another way. John Hook vended thousands of yards of British goods, but he also sold equipment to process fibers for home production and even accepted partially processed materials in payment. His records show that various aspects of the stages of textile production were part of an immense—albeit sometimes mysterious—flow from fibers to finished products to fashion.

Quite simply, Hook's customers purchased yards upon yards of manufactured textiles. A shipment in January 1772 to Hook from the English port of Whitehaven included goods with a value of more than £1,000 and illustrates the wide variety of textiles and clothing accessories Hook stocked. Any customer coming to New London just after the new shipment had arrived had plenty of choices to make at his store alone. Twenty-five grades of linen were available—more than a thousand yards in total—priced from 10 pence to 3 shillings 6 pence per yard. Specific named fabrics were there for multiple uses: inexpensive white and brown sheeting, hempen rolls, checks of linen, cotton, superfine cotton in checks, and half-inch crimson furniture check for upholstery.[20]

Hook's fabric stock included the sensory delights of fashion—sky blue, purple, pea green, and yellow-drab durants; purple and China blue chintzes; and pink, blue, black, and green alamodes—and he had written his supplier in November that the shalloon was wanted for women's winter gowns. His supplies included myriad buttons and sewing notions. A woman could buy stays, ticks, and other devices of fashionable bondage of the figure. She could leave with fantails or hats of beaver, black satin, or colored silk; old-fashioned or new-fashioned satin bonnets; velvet bonnets or velvet hoods. Around her neck she could clasp two-row large wax necklaces or three-row small wax necklaces. She might select from the two dozen fans or the netted green silk purses. Hook offered more than a dozen scarlet cloaks and satin or silk cloaks. For men, Hook stocked a wide range of hats, stockings, shoes, and buckles of pinchbeck or steel.[21]

Hook's customers purchased all the raw materials of dress, trimming, and accessories that was required to be attired according to the standard of a British colony. They could also choose materials in a semifinished state like breeches and gown patterns, to be stitched for a close fit on a particular person. Hook also offered two broadcloth suits with all the trimmings.[22] Orders by other merchants are sometimes more precise, although that might be because some mixed requests for their own clothing. In either case, their detail is telling. Charles Yates ordered "Good Cloth of grave colours to make four suits Cloaths with compleat trimmings—they are to be of diff. Patterns." Jones and Bragg's 1769 invoice specifically included linen for four shirts, cambrick and muslin for ruffles, and "light summer wear for Suits with trimmings; not gaudy and the patterns to differ."[23]

Because it was a new partnership, John Hook had no time to place an order with Scottish merchants for autumn delivery, so he personally selected goods from Ross's commodious Petersburg, Virginia, warehouse. Invoices indicate what came into the store, and daybooks tell what sold. Hook's customers purchased twenty-five hundred yards of textiles between the four fall and winter months of September and December 1771. Linens constituted nearly half of the purchases, woolens one quarter, and worsteds and cottons a small but significant number of sales. Only two textile purchases were for silk. Because linens were the most common type of fabric he sold, Hook offered them in a wide range of qualities, from very fine to rather coarse (table 3.6).

Osnaburg, an inexpensive, unbleached, and long-lasting linen, served as a multipurpose fabric for clothing and household use. Named for a region in Germany, this coarse fabric figured prominently in Virginia merchants' correspondence, most often accompanied by demands for more of that "material item." Many Virginia merchants preferred German-made osnaburgs to the English-made ones, but their English and Scottish partners had trouble enough simply getting and keeping any supply.[24] John Hook warned his partner in 1773 that unless he got a bale of good German osnaburg and a

TABLE 3.6. Sales of Textiles at Hook's Store, 1771

Item	Count	Percentage of all textiles sales
Cotton	86	13.8
Linen	270	43.5
Silk	2	.3
Woolens	139	22.3
Worsteds	48	7.7
Unspecified	77	12.4
Total	622	100.0

Source: John Hook Daybook, 1771, Library of Virginia.

large quantity of another inexpensive fabric called rolls immediately, business would suffer.[25] Osnaburg drove the ship of the store trade; customers bought that sturdy fabric twice as often as the next most common fabric.[26] Hook may have offered many different kinds of textiles, but one-third of all the yards of fabric stocked in his store in 1771 were osnaburg.

Partially because Southerners commonly purchased coarse linen in large quantities, some scholars have concluded that osnaburg was the accepted material for slave clothing and that the loosely fit basic attire of that undyed linen was a virtual uniform that made slaves easily recognizable.[27] Hook's records, however, provide convincing evidence that there must have been other customers and uses. The customers who owned the largest number of slaves and those who purchased the largest quantities of osnaburg were not congruent groups. The reverse was also true; William Mead, for one, was the only large slave owner to purchase osnaburg from Hook, but he only bought nine ells. Wealthy planters like Mead with large numbers of slaves likely had their own relationship with a merchant in England and could order large bales of osnaburg without retail markup, which female slaves on their own property then would sew into clothing. That they did not make the major biannual purchases of cloth for their slaves at John Hook's store is not surprising.

If this fabric, the most common linen sold in Hook's store, was not destined for the backs of slaves, then who used them and for what purpose? Hook's records provide convincing evidence that many in the free population also wore the familiar undyed utilitarian textile. The advertisement for runaway servant Samuel Milburn describes him as "ordinary clad" and specifies that he wore an osnaburg shirt. Moreover, of the white servants whose clothing was described in these advertisements between the years 1760 and 1770, 40 percent wore or carried away at least one osnaburg shirt. Nearly

TABLE 3.7. Sales of Clothing at Hook's Store, 1771

Item	Count	Total value sold (pounds/shillings/pence)	Item	Count	Total value sold (pounds/shillings/pence)
Bonnets	11	6/18/02	Hose	77	18/08/06
Breeches	1	1/10/00	Knee buckles	16	0/11/08
Buckles	39	6/13/06	Mantles	2	3/00/00
Cardinals	2	3/00/11	Pumps	7	2/19/11
Cloaks	2	1/18/10	Ruffs	3	3/19/11
Coats	3	3/05/06	Shoe buckles	10	0/14/06
Coat straps	14	0/11/04	Shoes	29	16/17/03
Gloves	6	0/13/04	Stock buckles	2	0/01/00
Handkerchiefs	127	20/16/04	Stockings	7	1/14/04
Hats	132	35/10/05			

Source: John Hook Daybook, 1771, Library of Virginia.

half of the trousers—loose pants worn by laborers—whose clothing was described in these were also of this coarse sturdy fabric.[28] Schoolteacher Devereux Jarratt likewise wore osnaburg when he arrived at a new job in Albemarle County in 1751 and continued to do so until his employer loaned him enough money for two shirts of checks.[29]

That many Virginians had working attire so similar to slaves—and so different from the colorful elegant dress of the elite—seemingly speaks loudly of the social chasm separating rich and poor, but the store records demonstrate that the situation was even more complex. Those who had no slaves bought two-thirds of the osnaburg, but they also bought the same percentage of the far more expensive broadcloth. Fabrics specifically identified as cotton and linen were equally represented in the purchases of people who had no bound labor, followed by shalloon, broadcloth, sheeting, and plaid.

Clothing items and accessories also played a significant role in sales at Hook's store. As with textiles, he mostly sold common items but kept a ready stock of finer examples. During his first four months in business he sold 132 hats and 11 bonnets. He also imported and sold 29 pairs of shoes, 9 pairs of pumps (slipper-like, single-soled shoes that might be used for dancing), and 127 handkerchiefs. He offered winter outerwear known as cloaks and cardinals for about £1, equal to the estimated annual per capita expenditure by Virginians in those years, and he sold only 2 of each (table 3.7).[30]

Foodways

Basic groceries and implements for cooking and serving food formed an important part of Hook's business. Ranked in order of money spent on them,

TABLE 3.8. Sales of Groceries at Hook's Store, 1771

Item	Count	Total value sold (pounds/shillings/pence)	Item	Count	Total value sold (pounds/shillings/pence)
Allspice	9	8/09/03	Nutmeg	8	0/11/06
Chocolate	6	0/15/6	Pepper	15	1/05/04
Cinnamon	3	0/05/09	Salt	55	19/17/04
Coffee	26	0/01/03	Sugar	113	26/16/11
Ginger	1	3/05/07	Tea	16	3/16/05
Molasses	22	5/09/07	Wafers	1	1/00/00
Mustard	11	0/01/06			

Source: John Hook Daybook, 1771, Library of Virginia.

the staples in greatest demand were sugar, salt, coffee, molasses, tea, pepper, allspice, nutmeg, and chocolate. During his opening months in business, customers spent a total of £20 on fifty-five pounds of salt. Salt had multiple uses, but with winter coming was most needed for preserving foodstuffs—especially meats and vegetables. Many of Hook's backcountry customers also had a sweet tooth: he sold £26 worth of sugar and £5 of molasses. Baking called for sweetening agents as well as nutmeg, cinnamon, ginger, and salt. The spices he sold had long histories in the cooking of meats, but customers no doubt also used sugar and spices in popular hot drinks like punches and toddies (table 3.8).

Finally, the growing enthusiasm for three nonalcoholic hot drinks—tea, coffee, and chocolate—offered a harbinger of changing ideas about sociability and meal structure. In this trend Hook's customers exhibited distinct preferences. Their purchases of coffee (twenty-six) vastly outstripped those of tea (sixteen). Chocolate came in at a distant third, less than a quarter of the coffee sales (six).

Hook also sold far more objects pertaining to drinking than to eating. Bottles and measures ("bottle," "quart," "pint") led the list that also included several mugs and a single glass. Seven expensive teakettles sold at 5 shillings each, and two coffee pots at half that price. Hook sold knives and forks but no plates or other flatware. He also offered basins, bowls, and porringers, all of which could hold semiliquid meals like stews and soups that might be cooked in the saucepans, fry pans, skillets, or pots Hook also carried in his store. He stocked boxes and other protective containers to store expensive grocery items such as sugar or pepper. Of the expensive mortar and pestles on his shelves, John Hook sold four, which brought in a total of £6 (table 3.9).

In summary, customers turned to John Hook's store for basic items related to dressing, eating, and socializing, and these items were his top-selling

TABLE 3.9. Sales of Foodways Objects at Hook's Store, 1771

Item	Count	Total value sold (pounds/shillings/pence)	Item	Count	Total value sold (pounds/shillings/pence)
Basins	5	3/01/03	Mortars/pestles	4	6/02/08
Bottles	36	1/05/10	Pans	6	0/13/10
Bowls	4	1/01/03	Pepper boxes	5	0/02/04
Cocks	4	0/12/03	Pints	8	0/12/7
Coffee pots	2	0/05/04	Porringers	4	0/01/03
Dishes	8	3/12/03	Pots	13	7/03/11
Frying pans	8	1/14/07	Quarts	14	1/05/00
Funnels	1	0/01/02	Saucepans	6	0/12/10
Glass	1	0/05/00	Skillets	3	0/05/04
Graters	5	0/02/10	Spoons	2	0/08/00
Grindstones	6	1/18/08	Sugar boxes	2	0/06/03
Half pints	3	0/01/11	Teakettles	7	3/13/00
Jugs	4	0/09/00	Ticklers	1	0/00/07
Knives/forks	14	4/19/5			

Source: John Hook Daybook, 1771, Library of Virginia.

ones. Alone, none of the commodities stand as particular markers of up-to-date social activities by the middling sorts. Nor do they demonstrate that their buyers had any clear concern with the latest fashion. The gross categories used thus far in this analysis cannot capture the more nuanced system of meaning and expression of a given object. A hat is not merely a hat; it is a particular kind of hat that is desired and available. Hook stocked multiple grades and qualities of even simple items such as handkerchiefs, and through these buyers could demonstrate taste, knowledge, even status.

Second, these common items were not expensive compared to larger investments. The average slave listed in inventories of Bedford County estates during the early 1770s was valued at almost £50, but the average purchase in Hook's store was only 6 shillings. One value was one hundred times the other. Yet the prices paid at the store were not insignificant sums. A quart of rum, the most commonly purchased amount, cost 1½ shillings. Customers earned 2 shillings credit for a day's work in Hook's garden, or 6 shillings for every two raccoon skins, yard of Virginia cloth, or eight chickens brought to the store.

Still, these are small sums compared to many other inessential but enjoyable expenses of the elite. Hanover County planter Richard Morriss paid 2½ shillings for a haircut in November 1771. Special pleasures and events were even more costly: Thomas Jefferson paid 7½ shillings to attend a play in Williamsburg in 1771, and William Ennals spent 5 shillings to see the fireworks in Annapolis a year later and 45 shillings to buy a new wig the year before.[31]

Backcountry residents did not live in a region untouched by the niceties of everyday life. The popularity of sugar demonstrates that already one foreign commodity had replaced molasses and honey for baking and for sweetening beverages like tea, coffee, and punch. Not coincidentally, Hook also offered the other ingredients for creating these drinks at his store. The sales of coffee and tea illustrate that the consumption of exotic and imported hot beverages had become increasingly commonplace in everyday life.

Yet, the store records also contain some surprises. The absence of sales of plates and other flatwares may signify the endurance of a simpler backcountry cuisine, the basis of which was semiliquid foodstuffs that did not require careful attention for long periods of time but could stew slowly over low flames during a long day outdoors. Or the absence may suggest problems of supply (perhaps the shipment containing plates had not arrived). Or, it may suggest that people living in this region relied on other kinds of, or another source for, plates.

One of the most detailed invoices for goods delivered to John Hook's store in 1772 listed several boxes of books (table 3.10). Many of these volumes were religious work—James Hervey's *Meditations and Contemplations,* Robert Russel's *Seven Sermons,* Bibles, New Testaments, catechisms, John Bunyan's long-popular *Pilgrim's Progress.* His backcountry customers could buy primers, spellers, and *Fisher's Arithmetick* to educate their children. These same Virginians also wanted to read novels, issues of the *Spectator,* and books about English exploration and discoveries. They still considered themselves British citizens, ones who shared the concerns of both the now and the hereafter.

Tucked amidst those books lay volumes with blank or lined pages— books for writing and jotting or more precisely for capturing the rise of consumerism itself in the rational and methodical system of accounting. John Hook sold account books—hard endboards held together with thread, generally covered with linen or leather filled with the most basic paper—commodities that could give voice to the drama of everyday purchases.

TABLE 3.10. Invoices of Books for Sale, 1772

Quantity	Item	Description	shillings/pence	LSD
ERF [box marking] Box No. 11				
4	Reams Writing Paper		6/6	1.06.00
4	do fine do	writing paper	10/.	2.00.00
0.5	do do post	fine post paper	16/.	0.08.00
5	quires Callender do	calendar paper	./5	0.02.01
1	hundred of fine quills	175 received	3/.	0.03.00
1	doz copper plate books		6/.	0.06.00
2	Yorricks Sermons (3 vol)		7/6	0.15.00
1	Langhorns do. (2 vol)		6/.	0.06.00
3	Fordyces do.		2/6	0.07.06
1	Family Instrustor (2 vol)		6/.	0.06.00
2	Sherlock on Providence		2/6	0.05.00
2	Herveys Meditations		1/9	0.03.06
2	do Dialogues		5/.	0.10.00
1	Tatler (4 vol)		12/.	0.12.00
1	Spectator (8 vol)		12/6	0.12.06
4	Economy of Human Life		./6	0.02.00
2	Golden Verses of Pythagores		2/.	0.04.00
1	Roderick Random (2 vol)		6/.	0.06.00
2	Tom Johns (3 vol)	Tom Jones	7/6	0.15.00
2	Joseph Andrews		2/6	0.05.00
2	Dudgeons Works		2/6	0.05.00
2	Yoricks Sentimental Journey		3/.	0.06.00
1	Thomsons Seasons		1/3	0.01.03
2	Paradise Lost		2/6	0.05.00
2	do regained		2/6	0.05.00
2	Visitors (2 vol)		5/.	0.10.00
4	Coll. Of Songs		2/.	0.08.00
2	dicks on gardening		15/.	1.10.00
1	Sett Hawey's Com'try		63/.	3.03.00
1	do Pools Notes (2 vol)		50/.	2.10.00
1	Johnstons Dictionary (2 vol)	Johnson's	10/6	0.10.06
2	Baileys do		5/6	0.11.00
1	Burket on ye. New Testament	Burkitt	25/.	1.05.00
2	Flavels Works (8 vol)		17/.	1.14.00
2	Shaft[e]sburys Charactersticks (4 vol)		8/6	0.17.00
2	Erskins Sermons (4 vol)	Erskine	8/.	0.16.00
6	Confessions of the Faith		1/10	0.11.00
4	Bostons 4 fold State		1/4	0.05.04
3	do on the Covenant		1/.	0.03.00
8	Pilgrims Progress		./11	0.07.04

TABLE 3.10. (*continued*)

Quantity	Item	Description	shillings/pence	LSD
3	Ambrose Looking		2/6	0.07.06
2	Fishers Cate'ms	catechisms	2/4	0.04.08
9	Russels Sermons	8 received	./5	0.03.09
4	Fishers Arithmetick		1/8	0.06.08
12	Dyches Spelling Books		./8	0.08.00
12	psalters		./5	0.05.00
24	primmers		./1½	0.03.00
12	Horn Books			0.01.01
2	doz'n small historys		5/.	0.10.00
8	doz'n Pryaer Books		1/6	1.10.00
2	fine 4 to Bibles Guilt	quarto Bibles gilt	15/.	1.10.00
3	Common do do	common Bibles gilt	6/8	1.00.00
12	do do	common Bibles	1/9	1.01.00
3	little do	little Bibles	2/10	0.08.06
12	New Testaments		./7½	0.07.08
2	Gazetteers		3/10	0.07.06
2	Lady Marys Letters		2/.	0.04.00
6	Octavie Paper books	9 received	1/.	0.06.00
9	do do	6 received	1/4	0.12.00
3	Fol. Do		6/.	0.18.00
1	Large Ledger		28/.	1.08.00
6	Pocket books		1/3	0.07.06
3	doz'n Mother Cate'ms	catechisms	./7	0.01.09
6	do Common do	catechisms	./3	0.01.06
2	discoverys of the English in am[erica?]		2/.	0.04.00
2	butlers Hudibrass		2/6	0.05.00
2	do Analogie		2/6	0.05.00
1	Amelia (2 vol)		5/.	0.05.00
9	L Yds Striptd pack sheet		./7½	0.05.11¼
72	Fathom Rope		./2	0.01.03¼
	Packing		1/.	0.01.00
	Box		6/.	0.06.00
	Total			39.04.03½

ERF [box marking] Box No. 12

4	Reams Writing Paper		6/6	1.06.00
4	do fine do	writing paper	10/.	2.00.00
0.5	do do Post	fine post paper	16/.	0.08.00
0.5	do Brown Paper		7/.	0.03.06
1	Hundred fine quills		3/.	0.03.00

continued

TABLE 3.10. (*continued*)

Quantity	Item	Description	shillings/pence	LSD
6	Copper Plait Books	copper plate	./6	0.03.00
4	Fordyces Sermons		2/6	0.10.00
1	Family Instrustor		1/.	0.01.00
2	Sherlock on Providence		2/6	0.05.00
2	Herveys Meditations		1/9	0.03.06
2	do Theron & Aspacio	aka Dialogues	5/.	0.10.00
1	Spectator (8 vol)		12/6	0.12.06
6	Economy of Human Life		./6	0.03.00
2	Golden Verses of Pythagores		2/.	0.04.00
1	Roderick Random (2 vol)		6/.	0.06.00
2	Tom Johns (3 vol)	Tom Jones	7/6	0.15.00
2	Joseph Andrews		2/6	0.05.00
2	Dudgeons Works		2/6	0.05.00
2	Yoricks Sentimental Journey		3/.	0.06.00
1	Thomsons Season		1/8	0.01.08
2	[illegible]		5/.	0.10.00
2	Visitors (2 vol)		5/.	0.10.00
4	Collection of Songs		2/.	0.08.00
3	Amelia		5/.	0.15.00
1	Johnstons Dictionary (2 vol)	Johnson's	10/6	0.10.06
1	Plutarchs Lives (3 vol)		12/4	0.12.04
1	Burket on ye. New Testament		25/.	1.05.00
2	Flavels Works (8 vol)		17/.	1.14.00
6	Confessions of the Faith		1/10	0.11.00
4	Bostons 4 fold State		1/4	0.05.04
3	do on the Covenant		1/.	0.03.00
8	pilgrims progress		./11	0.07.04
3	Ambrose Looking		2/6	0.07.06
2	Fishers Cate'ms		2/4	0.04.08
9	Russels Sermons	8 received	./5	0.03.09
1	doz. Spelling Books	probably Dyche's book	./8	0.08.00
1	doz. Psalters		./5	0.05.00
2	doz. Primmers		./1½	0.03.00
1	doz. Horn Books		1/1	0.01.01
2	doz. Small historys		5/.	0.10.00
2	fine 4to Bibles Gilt		15/.	1.10.00
3	Com. 4to Bibles Gilt		6/8	1.00.00
1	doz. do do do		1/9	1.01.00
3	small do o		2/10	0.08.06
1	doz. New Testaments		./7½	0.07.06
2	Lady Marys Letters		2/.	0.04.00

TABLE 3.10. (*continued*)

Quantity	Item	Description	shillings/pence	LSD
6	Octavo Paper books		1/.	0.06.00
9	do do		1/4	0.12.00
3	Fol. Do		6/.	0.18.00
6	doz. Catechisms		./3	0.01.06
3	doz. Mothers do		./7	0.01.09
1	Large Ledger		28/.	1.08.00
6	Pocket books		1/3	0.07.06
1	doz. Com. Parchment do.		5/.	0.05.00
8	yds Striptd packs sheet		./7½	0.05.00
72	Fathom Rope		./1½	0.00.11¼
	Packing		1/.	0.01.00
	Box		6/.	0.06.00
	Total			24.11.02¼

Source: John Hook Papers, 1772, Duke University.

THE LEDGER

John Price saw Bowker Preston crossing the river carrying something in a "Sack Bag" on his horse. He knew that they were the company books of the ill-fated John Hook and David Ross partnership. How could he testify with such assurance? How could a book be read without opening its cover?

Analyzing the ledger as object, rather than reading its contents, offers yet another form of fresh evidence in the world of goods. The business partnerships of several people and the sale of goods on credit required careful record keeping. How that record keeping evolved into a particular form tells of technological changes in paper and bindings (makers) and financial practices and institutions (users).

An account book is at its heart simply a blank book. The phrase "blank book" originated in the twelfth-century practice of creating multiple-paged books to house valuable paper. Their owners could use them any way they chose. Out of that simple beginning, specialized book forms evolved, with different sizes, shapes, and bindings created to accommodate precise manners of use and forms of accounting evidence. Blank books came first; bookkeeping followed.[32]

Bound books of blank paper were widely available in the eighteenth century. Colonial printers in Annapolis and Williamsburg printed, bound, and stocked books. In a lengthy 1730 newspaper advertisement for numerous services, books, and book types, printer William Parks noted in passing his supply of "shop-books." When John Dixon joined William Hunter and advertised their stationery supplies and bookbinding services, they also listed "Ledgers, Journals, Day-books, and all Sorts and Sizes of Blank books for Merchants Accounts or Records, Blanks of all kinds for Merchants, County Clerks, etc."[33]

General merchants also stocked blank books in their stores. In 1772, for example, Hook ordered twenty-seven different types of blank books; fifteen octavo paper books, three folio paper books, one large ledger, and six pocket books. The large ledger cost Hook an extraordinary 28 shillings, almost five times the amount of the folios. Smaller octavo and pocket books could be had for a shilling or so. He stocked small memorandum books to jot notes and other small paper books to list debtors—both could be tucked inconspicuously into a pocket or the corner of a bag. Hook's own surviving account books are common octavo and pocket-sized and either cloth- or paperbound, although some, such as his 1771–72 daybook, have lost their covers completely.[34]

To see whether this moves us closer to discovering a standard size that would help us understand how John Price could have come to the conclusion from afar that Preston's bag contained account books, it is necessary to assess them physically. Many archives simply catalog all bound volumes with names and numbers as account books so it is hard to generalize from their records. A survey of the contents of two major manuscript collections, however, revealed that middle and late eighteenth-century ledgers generally were greater in length than width than other bound books, with most being slightly less than fifteen inches long and nine inches wide.[35] The size of an account book was largely a function of paper size—that is, whether the paper was folded in folio, quarto, or octavo sections prior to binding. The octavo size—three times folded into long and thin sections—was well suited to recording the business of merchants, as it allowed for a certain set of data to be particularly arranged: a name could be written in on the top, a date, commodity, and price below that, running debits listed on the left side, and credits listed on the right. Vertical lines guided the writing so that information became standardized into certain forms. That ledgers continued to be filled with laid paper, a paper produced through a traditional paper technology using frames, when other paper types had evolved may indicate that lines embedded in laid paper lines helped in the demarcation of columns.[36] That need for order continued well into the nineteenth century: William Birch ended his early nineteenth-century advertisement for his Philadelphia stationery business with the note that he both made and sold an array of books "with or without cross pencil lines."[37] Only a few eighteenth-century ledgers in the repositories examined had embossed labels of "day-book" or "ledger." Most of the bindings were leather and boards, but some were made of paper and some had more extravagant vellum bindings.

The shape of the paper in the book in turn drove the evolution of certain financial mechanics—of keeping stock, single-unit pricing, total cost. The page size was such that there was only a limited space in which to write details describing the goods purchased. Late in the eighteenth century American merchants encountered difficulties as states began a decades-long transition to dollar accounting (two-part decimal numbers) and yet simultaneously continued to use the three-part English money designation (pounds, shillings, and pence). The books could not accommodate those both easily.

Even the type of writing used differed with each book type; in a day-book the writing is tightly clustered, sometimes just jotted notations hastily scrawled on a page. The ledger was filled at a more leisurely pace, with the customer's name often at the top of a page, dates of purchases arrayed below, and a greater empty white space left at the bottom of the page marking the prediction of future sales. Usually a junior member of the firm kept and cross-posted the books. Since the merchant might display these books to his customers, the ability to write well became proof of personal refinement and business regularity. In all these ways, and more, standardization of retail practices enforced ordered conduct among those who kept the books.

Finally, as ledgers increasingly became standardized in quarto size, specialized storage space for them was created. A long thin shelf or drawer, sometimes built vertically, sometimes horizontally, slowly became an element of choice in desk design, and the size of the slot or drawer corresponded with the common ledger dimensions (pl. 4). The planter who owned the Virginia desk shown in fig. 3.3 requested that a bookcase with two long flat niches that could hold ledgers be added to the desk built in Williamsburg by Peter Scott. A merchant probably requested the large number of ledger spaces, like the contemporary Philadelphia desk reproduced in pl. 4 has, so he could store a full set of accounts. Both furniture forms illustrate the importance of household and commercial accounting stored in bound books by the middle of the eighteenth century.[38] By the early nineteenth century, the functional combination of a thin central door to hold an account book, side drawers, and pigeonholes became far more common in writing desk interiors.

John Hook fought hard in his court battle with David Ross to keep control of his account books because they contained the essence of his business life. He stubbornly maintained that any court orders to surrender details of their business together did not entail surrendering the books. Their sight-

FIGURE 3.3. Desk and bookcase, attributed to Peter Scott, Williamsburg, Virginia, c. 1750. Black walnut, 90¾" x 44"x 23½". Courtesy, The Colonial Williamsburg Foundation. British émigré Peter Scott built a stylish desk for the planter William Basset in 1748 for £5 and added a bookcase on top some time in the next decade. The desk interior was fully fitted with a figured prospect door, arched pigeonholes over small drawers, and two document doors ornamented to imitate fluted pilasters. The bookcase added five stacked small drawers on left and right side of the interior with a center section of two drawers side-by-side under two long slots. This combination added a place for ledgers as well as plenty of room for small folded papers like bills and letters. Adjustable shelves for books of many sizes were located above. The household account book that recorded its purchase descended in the Basset family along with the desk.

ing (on a bed, in a bag) and their finding (with a divining rod or with assistance of slaves) were testimony to a mighty contest in which the books as objects served as prize. They could be read without opening because their shape defined their purpose.

Nonetheless, after a business had closed account books were curiously forgotten. If saved, they were seldom used and so ended up being tucked far away into a dusty corner or an archive. On opening such a book, a musty smell of time often wafts upward. The literary past is replete with Bartleby Scriveners and Bob Cratchets, men who copied and accounted for money. Yet their account books, if they survive, are but orphaned reminders of what may have been former greatness. Early nineteenth-century essayist Charles Lamb paid poetic homage to the abandoned books of the South Sea House. He had no love of accountants, no skill at figuring, but the "great dead tomes . . . with their decorative flourishes, and decorative rubric interlacing their sums in triple columniations, the costly vellum covers" moved him.[39] Yet, in the end:

> The moths, that were then battening upon its obsolete ledgers and day-books, have rested from their depredations, but other light generations have succeeded, making a fine fretwork amongst their single and double entries. Layers of dust have accumulated (a superfoetation of dirt!) upon the old layers, that seldom used to be disturbed, save by some curious finger, now and then, inquisitive to unveil some of the mysteries.[40]

FOUR

Living the Backcountry

Styles and Standards

ENGLISHMAN WILLIAM EDDIS traveled to the backcountry of Frederick County, Maryland, in 1771. It was "impossible to conceive a more rich and fertile country," and he predicted a great future for the backcountry region. He attributed the success of the early settlement to hardy German immigrants whose "habits of industry, sobriety, frugality and patience were peculiarly fitted" to carve out a civilization in the wilderness.[1] Eddis described a "natural" progression as people moved into a newly settled land. At first new settlers lived simply, building rudimentary houses, eating a basic diet, and satisfying their "utmost ambition"—to create a moderately successful life in a new place. But as stores began displaying goods for their view and as people gained wealth, they wanted to enjoy comforts. When they had neighbors, they wanted commodities to show and share. Farmers and their wives imagined new necessities and found their rude lives wanting. Those hardy pioneers soon demanded finer furniture, furnishings, and lifestyles. As Eddis put it, "as wealth and population increased, wants were created, and many considerable demands, in consequence, took place for the elegancies as well as necessaries of life."[2]

William Eddis told a simple story of the way the retail trade both followed and led consumer demand in recently settled societies. Yet, for him the action took place all in a timeless minute. He did not say how life changed. Moreover, he was not nostalgic. Nineteenth-century writers bemoaned the end of simplicity, the valor of an earlier Revolutionary generation, but Eddis merely described an inexorable process: "wants were created." His assertions raise myriad questions. Were residents merely awaiting the opportunity to view goods, the affluence to buy them, or the neighbors to impress them with? Was the New World just some incipient Anglo-American consumer society, where certain objects were immensely desirable? Did the merchant move in to capture that demand? Or did he help create it? Eddis collapses the whole story of backcountry consumerism into action without agency. He never asks: what creates a want, a desire?

Historians are often no better than Eddis in explaining the rise of con-

citation?

sumerism in America, and some share Eddis's assumption that it can be accounted for by a centralized driving force. According to that model, members of a community concurred about certain ideals and wants in more established settlements along the eastern seaboard. There greater wealth "naturally" led to certain behaviors and desires. Refined behaviors spread because the entire hierarchy—rich and poor—aspired to own more luxury goods.

The backcountry experiences of Bedford and Franklin county Virginians do not fit that model. The region had a mixed economy; there was no single pursuit of a slave-based tobacco agriculture that unified experience and aspiration. Society was linked vertically (high and low) and horizontally (through community, ethnicity, and religion). Some lifestyle choices were dictated by religion and ethnic background rather than by any professed standards of living. The geography of the area both linked and separated people, as varying communities clustered across rolling hills and in mountain pockets. This multiplicity was the very essence of backcountry character, a character that became deeply embedded in backcountry material culture.

At its heart, the practice of material culture seeks patterns and, in the best cases, identifies the patterns that explain. Often this effort requires analyzing multiple forms of evidence because "patterns imply intentions and carry toward meaning."[3] Patterns also provide a way to uncover context. In the case of backcountry Virginia the scholarly effort to discern the ways life was defined and patterned uses tools drawn from anthropology, history, folklore, and material culture. The task involves organizing and ordering a number of texts and exploring their possible meanings. It is an easy shorthand to use phrases like "John Hook's world" to discuss a *situation*. That is certainly valid, but a broader cultural analysis uses texts—words, landscapes, and objects—to understand *place,* a place made by and lived through people and their relationships.

This chapter thus goes to a place and uses three broad texts to interrogate evidence of action and meaning. The first section looks at making things and considers how stylistic patterns and family ownership of furniture tell us about the flow of information, cultural standards, ethnic identity, and relationships. The second examines housing and uses ideas of modish and vernacular housing as a method to examine identity claims. The third section assesses the divisions between the top and bottom of the social hierarchy and the ways in which social systems were built on local relationships that were sometimes rowdy, explosive, even brutal.

Together, the overlapping patterns that emerge from these three sections reveal the complex set of choices available to the inhabitants in a place of cultural blending. One could buy a better tool or a set of plates at John Hook's store. A different choice was to invest in more land or improve one's house, and one traditional historical tool has been to assess a region's relative wealth by looking at distributions of capital-producing assets like land or slaves. Consistent data is only available after British independence, when the state of Virginia instituted regularized county taxation of land and personal property. Unfortunately, that very political watershed makes the choice of units of study more difficult: in those same years the state government redrew county lines several times, and John Hook left the active Scottish tobacco trade and moved across county lines to became a planter/merchant. Hence this detailed assessment of place must encompass two counties in order to examine two types of investment, namely that of land to farm and that of slaves to labor.

Postwar Bedford County mainly lay in the rolling Piedmont, and in 1782 the land ownership there tilted toward the middling sorts. The most common holding size ranged between one hundred and two hundred acres, and almost three-quarters of the holdings were less than four hundred acres. The scant evidence of small farms—holdings of less than one hundred acres—suggests that many of the poor may have been tenants on larger parcels of land (ch. 3, table 3.3).

Slaves had been present in the county for many years. In 1755 blacks constituted 143 of the approximately 500 adult males. In 1783 the county had 7,150 tithables (5,497 white and 1,653 black). The high percentage of blacks in 1755 suggests wealthy slaveholding colonists were among the earliest settlers.[4] That by 1783 the county's white population had grown fourteenfold, but the number of slaves only elevenfold indicates a shift toward a more middling white population unable or unwilling to acquire slave labor. At that later date only about 30 percent of families owned slaves. Another 20 percent owned fewer than five. Only 4 percent owned more than ten slaves.

Slightly south and west of Bedford in 1783 and across the river lay the new Franklin County, in which one-third of the population was poor—anywhere between grinding poverty and hand-to-mouth below subsistence living. 60 percent of the population had a modicum of land, horses, and cattle, and only 5 percent constituted the economic upper tier. An astonishing 363 out of 689—more than half—of Franklin County taxpayers did not own land and three-quarters did not own slaves. In that county the middling part of the population was large, and a resident there could rent land and a few slaves and still move forward (table 4.1). These developments challenge the historians' traditional view of Virginia's rural social order.[5] The presence of slaves provides a rough index of both the wealth of an owner and his need for certain kinds of labor. Franklin County ironworks aside, most slaves in the region performed agricultural labor. But the Bedford/Franklin region developed an agricultural system surprisingly different from that of some of the

TABLE 4.1. Slave Ownership in Franklin County, 1786 and 1799

Number of slaves	Percentage of taxable households	
	1786 (n = 718)	1799 (n = 1,326)
0	76.7	83.8
1–5	17.5	13.6
6–10	3.3	1.6
11+	2.4	1.0

Sources: Franklin County Personal Property Tax Lists, 1786 and 1799, Library of Virginia.

neighboring regions. In the Piedmont region *south* of the James River (known as the Southside), large tobacco plantations and widespread slave ownership were the norm. Six out of ten families owned slaves, with a mean of five slaves per household.[6] In Bedford County only three out of ten families owned any slaves. Residents of the region sporadically considered agricultural alternatives to tobacco. John Hook encouraged them to cultivate viable crops for export such as hemp but was disappointed in the result. Some of his customers, even slaves, grew cotton. When farmers began to diversify crops late in the century, they turned to wheat and corn. Hook's customer base expanded to include independent small landowners living in arable pockets of land—the "hollers" or "knobs" or "gaps"—in the mountainous terrain. From the beginning, these men and women planted small crops, raised livestock and even made hats, presumably from animal skins.

Hence the Bedford/Franklin region slips through the fingers of those who attempt to characterize it in larger regional socioeconomic terms. The region lay in prime tobacco country, but tobacco was an extraordinarily labor-intensive business and not many residents owned slaves. It was a rural place on the supposedly open frontier—yet more than half the people living there rented land and not all of them even owned a horse. It was a "key to the backcountry"—yet the region represented a new kind of "back," one far away from the fall line of major rivers and, by the fourth quarter of the eighteenth century, no longer subject to frontier conditions.

Identity: Religion and Ethnicity

The Bedford/Franklin region attracted Virginians, Germans, Scots-Irish, English, and other immigrant groups. The things these groups made and used are important in understanding how people from differing backgrounds communicate identity and group membership in differing ways. Although

ethnicity never remains static and group boundaries are temporal, perme-
able, and evolving, it is important to determine, first, whether functional,
useful markers of identity existed in the backcountry, second, if and how
they worked, and, third, if and when they were challenged or rejected. Of
course, objects can mean different things to different people, but an understanding of what an object means to a group in general is necessary for
people of that group to arrive at their own interpretation.[7]

Markers of ethnicity highlight what sets of ideas people brought with
them from other places or formed with similar people in a new place. In the
Bedford/Franklin region, German, Scots-Irish, and English immigrants did
things in distinctly different or particular ways—whether they were making
furniture, cooking food, or playing music—because those methods seemed
matter-of-fact to them. Doing things in a particular way is essential proof of
a person's position in a culture.[8] This idea of doing things a certain way re-
lates ethnicity to consumer goods: people from the same ethnic group pos-
sess a shared preference for specific goods.[9]

Religious membership and ethnic identity were intimately intertwined
in the Bedford/Franklin region. Nonconformity to the Church of England
united many of Franklin County's early settlers, especially the numerous
Quakers, Presbyterians, and Baptists who had moved to the edge of the
colony, hoping to avoid prosecution for refusing to financially support the
official church. While some decided to push on, in their search for a place
of religious freedom and prosperity, others put down roots and remained
in the county. In the ensuing years numerous ethnically linked separatist
religions flourished, so much so that the Church of England remained all
but unknown.[10]

Some of the earliest settlers were Quaker, and they prospered. Records
of the South River Monthly Meeting reveal that the Quakers belonged to
all the social strata and participated in official county life through taking inventories and serving as militia officers as well as perhaps through involun-
tary appointments to government.[11] Some of the biggest names in the region would be Quaker ones; the Lynches, for example, gained fame for
both founding a town (Lynchburg) and an infamous extralegal action
("lynch law"). Neither seems a particularly pious point of celebrity.

German Baptists, also known as Dunkards, Mennonites, or Brethren,
had traversed the area for years, moving between their settlements in Pennsylvania and North Carolina. By the time of the Revolution they had decided
to establish a permanent settlement in Franklin County and built at least
two churches. Most of these "Primitive Baptists" bought land in the ten-
mile wide fertile valley that stretched fifteen miles along Bedford County's
Blackwater River and Maggodee Creek to near the Floyd County line. In

1793 the state legislature recognized the importance of these Germans by granting them permission to build two towns, Germantown and Wizenburg.

English settlers, too, swelled the ranks of religious nonconformists and reformers. The region became a hotspot of Baptist activity; at least seven churches were established in Franklin County alone between 1761 and 1790. The number of Methodists probably equaled the Baptists. In contrast, despite the early prevalence of the Scots-Irish, Presbyterianism did not flourish until the nineteenth century. Perhaps because their numbers were low, Anglicans and Presbyterians even shared a single church building beginning in the 1750s.[12]

Hence some of the earliest settlers were contrarian in profound ways. They refused to follow certain government rules. Many came to oppose slavery vociferously, and some freed their slaves as soon as they were able. Their contrarianism has a special resonance with respect to social relationships and the world of goods. These groups often saw themselves as outsiders, naysayers, as independents who eschewed the standard path. They also had personal and group identities that had visual (clothing, for example) and material (meeting in houses rather than churches) components. Finally, opposing other groups often strengthens ethnic or religious group affiliation, for one way to oppose is to differ. Some practiced ethnic isolationism. The beliefs and practices of all five could produce significant disincentives to buying into the world of goods.

Such considerations compel us to ask how an overlay of store-bought goods from an Anglo-American fashion system performed in such a different social context and how the residents of John Hook's world established society and navigated change with material things.

Making Things: Backcountry Furniture

The makers of things and the things they make constitute primary historical evidence. Decorative arts scholars who tackle this evidence often borrow tools from art history to study an object's style. The terms and special language they use may seem arcane, but their focus on descriptions of forms and ornament is an effective method by which to identify patterns. Those art historical concepts can also allow scholars to move from individual details to larger patterns.

For example, much late eighteenth-century backcountry furniture is baroque in important ways. "Baroque" in a traditional sense is a historical tag for a style or epoch, a period that came after the Renaissance but before the Enlightenment, and the term is often applied to the art, architecture, and music of that time. Some of its principles include exaggeration, monumental scale, and surfaces that reach, often sensually, into space.

But the *Oxford English Dictionary* offers a useful secondary adjectival definition of baroque: "irregularly shaped; whimsical, grotesque, odd." In the nineteenth century art critics borrowed the word "baroque" from Spanish jewelers, who probably coined it to describe misshapen pearls or things of unknown origin, and applied it to the florid designs popular in Europe especially during the early and middle decades of the eighteenth century. Just as the word "baroque" can describe the form, scale, or mass of objects made in backcountry Virginia during the later part of the eighteenth century, so too can it describe the irregular shaping of the furniture that emerges in those areas in which the inhabitants ignored or refused to fully adopt Anglo-American cultural patterns of goods and behaviors. In comparison to London furniture, backcountry Virginia furniture often looks out of proportion, skewed, or "not quite" right because its makers were both reinterpreting a style and using local materials.[13]

A tall clock made in the far southwest region of Virginia (now Pulaski County) provides a vivid example (fig. 4.1). Sebastian Wygal, son of an affluent German-speaking Swiss immigrant who lived on the wagon road to Tennessee, commissioned this clock around 1809. According to family tradition, clockmaker Peter Whipple provided the works and cabinetmaker Peter Rife the case. The clock case especially exhibits a duality of intent: on the one hand, the eagles, urn shapes and stringing emphasize the value of classical order and fine workmanship; on the other, the inlaid organic, twisting floral ornament and "F-holes" like those used on gun stocks emphasize a playful and creative spirit that valued showmanship.[14] Artisans Whipple and Rife and consumer Wygal somehow agreed to reshape established aesthetic patterns in ways that honored local preference.

While few backcountry pieces are as visually arresting as this clock, the basic idea of exaggeration of particular elements constituted a common practice. A chest from Piedmont North Carolina, probably Randolph County, which resurfaced in Rocky Mount, Franklin County, displays an exaggerated skirt on the frame case, a feature that appears on many other backcountry forms (fig. 4.2). A chest of drawers (pl. 5) constructed in the small hamlet of Woolwine in Franklin County earlier in the nineteenth century displays similar verticality and overemphasized skirt detailing. Multiple lines of small scratched x-marks, suggestive of inlay or carving, ornament the top of its case.

The furniture traditions of eighteenth-century Franklin or Bedford remain as yet unstudied. Individual pieces, however, do reveal extraordinary information.[15] For example, an undated portrait of James Steptoe, long-term clerk of court for Bedford County, shows him seated at a desk (fig. 4.3). The chair that he sits in strongly resembles those that his good friend Thomas

FIGURE 4.1. Peter Whipple, clock mechanism; Peter Rife, clock case, Virginia, probably Montgomery (now Pulaski) County, c. 1810. Mahogany and mahogany veneers on cherry. 108½" x 24" x 13". Courtesy, The Colonial Williamsburg Foundation.

FIGURE 4.2. Chest, Piedmont North Carolina, probably Randolph County, 1800–1830. Black walnut and yellow pine. 26" x 43½" x 15". Courtesy, The Colonial Williamsburg Foundation.

Jefferson had directed his slave artisans at Monticello to make, chairs that reinterpreted a French fashion (fig. 4.4). While furniture in portraiture is often fanciful, this rather uncanny resemblance suggests an itinerant painter visited Steptoe's office and faithfully depicted a real environment.

Objects similarly survive in Franklin County and illuminate the multiple strategies of consumption that eighteenth- and early nineteenth-century Bedford/Franklin residents pursued.[16] They also show how style can be used as evidence. Because they are linked to specific families, they serve as especially rich sources of historical ideas. Case pieces such as chests and cupboards, both of which represented substantial investments when originally purchased and both of which tended to be passed down from generation to generation within the family, constitute especially valuable evidence. And as a method of study, holding one kind of form (here, large storage pieces) as a constant facilitates our attempts to isolate variables (such as style).

Col. John Smith, who lived near Hook at Hale's Ford, owned a corner cupboard probably made between 1780 and 1820 that was later recovered from a smokehouse on his plantation (pl. 6). At first glance, it looks little

FIGURE 4.3. James Steptoe (1750–1826), Clerk of Bedford County, undated. Oil on canvas. Bedford County Courthouse; photograph, Ann Smart Martin. The unidentified painter displayed keen awareness of up-to-date artistic conventions and depicted Steptoe in a significant setting. The map intimates the sitter's worldliness; the portrait of Jefferson alludes to his ties to the well-known statesman. Steptoe's pen is at the ready, and a book—not an account book, he is no mere merchant—is in his hand. The "neat and plain" style of the desk suggests it originated in Virginia; however, the chair shows a strong French influence, even if made locally.

different from a host of cupboards made in the early nineteenth-century Piedmont. Its doors resemble house doors, having raised panels rather than inset glass. The highly figured pine has a reddish wash. It sports a strong dividing section (waist) with molding and pronounced bracket feet. The architectural cornice displays dentil molding and an exaggerated, almost

FIGURE 4.4. Armchair, Monticello, Albemarle County, c. 1790–1815. Cherry. 34" x 23¼".
Courtesy, The Colonial Williamsburg Foundation. John Hemings, Thomas Jefferson's
slave, probably made this chair using one of the George Jacob–designed chairs that Jefferson had imported from France as a model. While the back is distinctively different, the
upswept arms, leather seat, and simple, albeit tapered, legs are suggestive of the chair in
Steptoe's portrait. If the chair in Steptoe's portrait is a faithful stylistic copy of Jacob's
original chair, then Hemings's version exhibits both greater flair and visual appeal.

stepped pediment. Its maker understood part of the standard classical vocabulary. But he also decided to augment it with his own little fillip: a swag
connects each rectangular dentil point.

In form and decoration Smith's cabinet closely resembles a half-dozen
others found in the northwest corner of the county, an area settled by
Dunkards, which suggests the same maker produced all seven. Availability
of both the more expensive black walnut and painted pine demonstrates that

he likely offered two price levels to his customers. Raised panels do constitute decoration, but the unidentified maker did not offer any particularly
fancy decorative options such as a special paint scheme or inlay that other
expressive, perhaps even more skilled, cabinetmakers did, so perhaps like
many backcountry artisans, he spent more of his time doing multiple kinds
of general woodworking.

A second cabinet likely belonged to John Utley Wade (pl. 7). Born in
1739 in Goochland County, Wade married Alice Woodrum in 1763 and relocated to Franklin County about 1788, purchasing property there in 1792.
He died in 1798 at the age of 59. About twelve years later his 22-year-old son
Bradley married Rachel Lemon and in about 1820 probably built himself a
cabin at Shoat's Gap where the cupboard was found.

Like John Smith's cabinet, Wade's has raised panel wooden doors. Its
top and bottom cupboards are equally sized, and it has nearly all of its original hardware, including its key. An attractive cupboard of walnut, it contains a surprise inside, a purposely elegant interior designed for the display
of household wares. Originally all cupboards protected and contained objects, but expensive doorless ones with molded and shaped interior shelves
became a fashionable at the middle of the eighteenth century. The blind
front door on this cupboard is a curious feature that raises three fundamental questions. First, assuming shaped shelves are an expensive feature, why
pay for them and then hide them behind full wooden doors? Second, was
this cupboard built when the shaped shelves were most in vogue in eastern
Virginia or later, the shelves perhaps being a tradition that simply hung on
in more conservative rural societies? Finally, was it made in Franklin County
or carried westward by John Utley Wade when he left his own rural home in
the Piedmont and later inherited by his son?

A bit of sleuthing builds on close analysis of these and other features. The
hardware is imported and of English style, not made by local blacksmiths.
The shaped shelves suggest a skilled cabinetmaker. The closed (rather than
open) front may indicate that the cabinet was intended to be placed on a dirt
floor, and the wooden door (rather than one made with glass panes) may indicate a wish for sturdiness or the greater expense of glass. A hole had to be
cut in the Wade cabin roof to allow the cupboard to fit in it, suggesting it
probably was not made for that building. Finally, such major pieces of furniture often were acquired or moved at points of transition in the life cycle
(John Utley Wade was first married in 1763; Bradley Wade married in 1820).
While other sources for the cabinet are possible (such as their wives, Alice
Woodrum Wade and Rachel Lemon Wade), it remains probable that the
cupboard, likely of British style and influence, originated in the rural rolling
Piedmont home of John Utley Wade.

FIGURE 4.5. Cupboard, Franklin County, c. 1780–1800. Walnut. 77" x 44⅝" x 18". Photograph courtesy of the Blue Ridge Institute, Ferrum College, Ferrum, Virginia. My thanks to Ralph Arthur for his assistance.

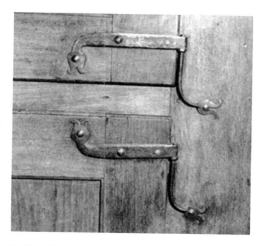

FIGURE 4.6. Detail of the forged hinges on cupboard in fig. 4.5. Photograph courtesy of the Blue Ridge Institute, Ferrum College, Ferrum, Virginia.

Finally, a pair of cupboards illustrates German heritage. Once owned by the Flora/Naff family of Franklin County, these two cupboards fit flat against the wall. Made of walnut, with simple, elegant lines, their main ornament comes from large decorative hinges. A local blacksmith fabricated these rat-tail hinges and added tulip finials, a favored motif in Germanic iconography (figs. 4.5 and 4.6).[17]

The well-documented migration, settlement, and family relations of the Naffs and Floras intimate the reasons behind the conservative choices they made in their furniture. Joseph Flora and his family emigrated from Palatinate Germany. They landed in Philadelphia in 1733 and moved due west to Lancaster County, where they joined the "Dunker" Conestoga Congregation. Thirty-four years later, in 1767, the eldest son Jacob purchased land in Frederick County, Maryland, where his sister Catherine and her husband Jacob Naff (also from the Palatinate) joined him. The siblings moved together to Bedford County, Virginia, in 1782 and purchased 150 acres of fertile land on Maggodee Creek, not far from Boone's Mill and John Hook's second plantation. Within a decade, Naff's brother Sebastian also settled in Franklin County. The Naffs and Floras lived near other German Dunkards. Jacob Naff spoke and read German; his son, Jacob Jr., spoke little English and read it with difficulty; in the next generation, Isaac, who became a preacher, spoke both languages with ease.[18] The Naffs shared with other German settlers in colonial America a reputation for conservative values and honest relationships as well as a preference for solid, substantial furniture.

The Smith, Wade, and Flora cupboards as well as Steptoe's chair and the

Woolwine chest of drawers offer physical evidence of cultural choices made by each artisan and consumer—whether to replicate, differentiate, simplify, exaggerate, or hybridize stylistic ideas in the world of goods. Just as close examination of stylistic attributes of furniture pieces can uncover links with particular makers or particular consumers, so too can it illustrate the five basic cultural choices backcountry people made in their relationship to the world of goods.

- Differentiate—keep apart. The Flora family cupboards illustrate how people *kept apart*. The prosperity of the widespread German community allowed loosely related family groups like the Floras to remain more insular and to choose furniture with distinctly Germanic elements.
- Simplify—reduce to essentials. The Smith cupboard presents a simplified architectural order—the dentil molding *refers to* a larger set of classical details. The additional tiny swags are also neoclassical details, but ones that do not "correctly" belong between the moldings. The artist simplified, stylized, and reinterpreted a set of ideas. The purchaser and the unidentified artisan were up-to-date in simplified backcountry terms.
- Exaggerate—a correlate to simplify, in which a single concept or factor is featured in an overblown way. The gigantic skirts on the chest and chest of drawers demonstrate this.
- Hybridize—create something different that blends the local and the Euro-American. Steptoe's chair exemplifies this. Thomas Jefferson took French ideas and recast them as Virginian, foregoing the ormulu mounts and fancy imported materials of the most expensive French pieces. A second level of reinterpretation occurred at the craftsman level when John Hemings made the chair, drawing on his own experience as an enslaved African American, although one specially trained as an artisan craftsman.
- Replicate—buy into the world of goods. The Wade cupboard illustrates fashionable objects made in more established areas that could be brought intact into the backcountry.

As a set, these five attributes—differentiation, simplification, exaggeration, hybridization, and replication—provide just one way to organize analysis. They also allow us to frame a set of wide-ranging questions during our search through far-ranging evidence.

Housing: Objects for Living

The most useful scholarly framework for understanding buildings in eighteenth-century America approaches them in terms of performance, intent, and audience, allowing them to be separated into two categories: the "modish" and the "vernacular." The former term refers to being "of the mode" or fashionable. The latter, "vernacular," has many definitions but in its purest sense refers to a type of architecture that is uninformed by academic principles and is rooted in the local. A house in both categories expresses differing degrees of what is appropriate, aesthetically pleasing, and a good value in a particular place and time.[19]

The idea of "modish" applies to the very plan of the town of New London, for the town leaders used small urban places scattered throughout Virginia as points of reference when they formulated the initial regulations. They drew from them notions of lot size and massing as well as the minimum requirements for houses. These rules also affected what individuals chose to build; they explain in part, for example, the twenty-eight- by thirty-foot wood frame house John and Elizabeth Hook built in 1772.

The floor plan of Hook's house lays bare the ambitions of the new merchant in town (fig. 4.7). A corner fireplace heated each of the two commodious rooms on the first floor. At 840 square feet, the footprint was almost three times the legally prescribed minimum size for houses in New London and nearly equaled that of the newly constructed Presbyterian church along nearby Otter River.[20] Visitors could not step directly into either of Hook's heated rooms, instead they entered a large passage that transected the house from back to front. While a passage was a relatively modish addition, Hook's passage was not a central divider but rather was on the side of the house, an expedient more often used for houses set on narrow lots.[21] Stairs led up to a second floor that may have had one or more finished chambers. A closet underneath the stairs provided secure storage; five windows allowed good lighting to the ground floor rooms. The house may have had a cellar, although not a bricked one. While further details of interior finishing are unclear (accounts for building materials do not distinguish between those bought for the house and those bought for the store), Hook went beyond the basics. He acknowledged David Ross's concern about the cost of building both a house and store with the assurance that he "would not be more expensive in the guildings [gildings] than what is necessary, except a little in the "Dwelling House," which was an expense he would bear himself.[22] One of those expenses came when he embraced the modish notion of including a passage that prevented direct entry into private rooms. Hook chose an up-to-date house, a house of the mode.

When Hook offered the house for sale fourteen years later, he termed it a "valuable tenement": a "very convenient" dwelling house with a good kitchen, garden, and all the "usual office houses for the accommodation of a family." The yard had a stone-lined well and nearby lay ten acres of

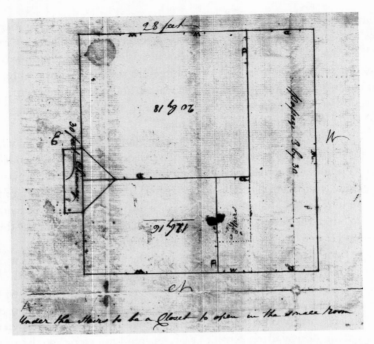

FIGURE 4.7. John Hook, New London house plan, c. 1772. Hook Papers, Duke University. Hook wanted to impress passersby and visitors alike, so soon after arriving in New London he designed the very large house (most cabins in the area could fit in its back room alone) that he and his bride Elizabeth moved into a year later. The multiple windows, side-passage entrance, and corner chimneys are all signifiers of his modish intentions.

fenced pasturage and two hundred acres of land for firewood. A storehouse and counting room as well as a large lumber house also sat on the one-acre main lot.[23]

When John Hook decided to move to his plantation in 1782, he once again drew up detailed drawings and notes (fig. 4.8). What kind of house a rich merchant like John Hook built is not especially significant; there were other rich merchant's houses. This dwelling is more important for what it reveals of the mental process Hook went through when designing the house. He chose not to rely on community standards but instead reached out to a regional group of specialists who could build in a newfangled way. He wanted a much larger house—forty-six by eighteen feet—bisected by a hall or passage with two large heated first floor rooms and an eighteen- by sixteen-foot cell with chimneys to the back. He likely intended the four spaces to be a hall, passage, dining room, and sleeping chamber. This design resembles that used by another backcountry elite, William Cabell of Nelson County in 1784.[24]

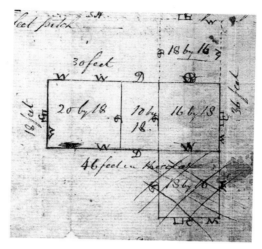

FIGURE 4.8. John Hook, Hale's Ford house plan, c. 1783. Hook Papers, Duke University. A decade after building his first house Hook strove to design an even more up-to-date home but struggled with where to place an eighteen- by sixteen-foot room in the core of the house. The new room likely was a dining room, and he had few local precedents to guide him. Dining rooms were modish spaces in which to carry on new polite social practices. Hook also had to find a way to design the new room so that it effectively related to the other rooms that formed the core of his house.

    Hook had 1,116 square feet on the ground floor and an upstairs room floored at the level of the eaves that was lighted by six small windows, three in each gable. He could access that overhead space by two sets of stairs (both equipped with banisters and rails), one rising from the passage and the other from the back chamber. He wanted eight windows on the ground floor and four in the cellar. He specified eight doors and cases and materials for two cellar doors, two closet doors, a "bowfat," and two closets. Indeed, next to each chimney he wanted a closet or buffet, a relatively modish French-inspired term. He directed that chairboards—a form of architectural trim to protect chairs and walls—be added to "C." (chamber) room and passage.
    Concerned with the functional parts of his new plantation, he stipulated a bulkhead entrance to the cellar in the back of the house. The separate kitchen, measuring sixteen by sixteen feet, had to have a stack of chimneys at one end; the smokehouse, at nine-and-a-half square feet, was to be built with a common square roof. He confidently wrote his instructions for the cellar, directing that it be dug four-and-a-half feet deep, with an eighteen-inch stone wall, and measure twenty by forty feet running north and south down one side of the house and under the back room. Ever attentive to detail, he wanted the excavated dirt thrown out to molder on the hill in preparation for rolling down to the brickyard. Planning ahead, he wanted a twenty- by fifty-

foot shed erected to shelter the bricks, a building that could later serve as a still house. He even made a note to have three wheelbarrows made for rolling the dirt to his brickyard.

Hook recognized that his skills did not lie in building. He needed a pair of professional sawyers and for the cellar wanted an individual "that understands framing stone." He made a note to enquire of bricklayer Joseph Lewis of Rockbridge, hundreds of miles to the north and west, to write Mr. Brown in Halifax or Pittsylvania, and to ask his storekeeper Holt the name of the man who built Colonel Cowle's no-doubt stylish house back east. Hook had decided that Cowle, the father of the second Mrs. Mead (a woman of refinement and wealth), owned a home to emulate, and Cowle's builder had the necessary knowledge to build such a home for Hook.

A side-by-side comparison of the plans for Hook's two houses provides clues about how Hook thought out his second house. The front facade of the New London house had a gable entry with side door and two windows. He initially replicated that arrangement on the east side of the Franklin County house, which might have allowed him to swing his second room from the back and put it beside his passage, but that created an unbalanced facade. He solved the problem by eliminating one of the windows in the large twenty- by eighteen-foot room, which he neatly crossed out in his Franklin County plan.

That decision, however, led to an unbalanced number of windows in the front and rear facades. In the ensuing sketches he explored shifting the extra core room, the chamber, to various places. His instructions also reveal that he remained uncertain about how the closets could be included and he even suggested that, if necessary, the wall be moved two feet out to make an inside chimney and closet on one side. Finally, at the very bottom of his memoranda, he acknowledged that the whole plan should be altered (if possible) so that the windows could face northward, a problem he had struggled with in his sketches.[25]

Hook also had another house built, probably in the 1780s at Burke's Fork and perhaps for an overseer. There is no extant plan, but he requested the roof be of "14 feet pitch, 9 feet below and 5 above [torn] the posts" and that the structure have two doors. He further specified that it be made of large logs of hardwood—white oak, locust, or chestnut—the bark removed inside and out. Only twenty by sixteen feet, the building could have fit in one room in Hook's plantation house.[26]

John Hook's structures provide a text of three different buildings built by one man in slightly more than a decade. Each of two houses he built for himself was large, even ostentatious, in local terms. He had the first structure built when he strove to affirm his importance as a merchant in a highly competitive business climate and no doubt provide a dwelling suitable for his bride, who came from a wealthy local family. To that house the mob came, threatening to destroy it and tar and feather him.[27] This same man who had made his fortune, despite the intense hostility of such customers and neighbors, built the second house in a nearby county soon after the Revolution ended.

Hook wanted his structures to last—even the one built for the overseer. In his own 1782 house Hook stipulated stone underpinnings, multiple brick chimneys, and carefully positioned outbuildings. He also wanted his house to impress those he invited inside. Built-in buffets or cabinets meant that Hook had porcelain and silver to display. He also hung a portrait of the king and queen of England in its rooms, perhaps to thumb his nose at the mob and the local elite that had encouraged them. Indeed the very size of Hook's house placed it in about the top 10 percent of Virginia houses advertised for sale in the eighteenth century.[28]

Hook wanted his new house to be both different and better. He did his house making on paper. He worried it out in his mind and tested ideas by sketching and drawing. He considered himself a member of the regional elite, and to this larger region-wide cohort group he turned for information. He wanted to replicate the lifestyle that he believed a host of wealthy merchants and farmers in the Anglo-American empire shared. Not all local people had the same desire.

Vernacular Housing

As new people poured into the Bedford/Franklin region, many chose to settle near friends, relatives, or countrymen and set up housekeeping in some version of a log structure. Over the past several decades elements in those structures have provided architectural historians with clues as to the makers' specific construction training. Among the most important evidence is the manner in which the makers processed or joined the logs. How logs were held together at the sides and corners was also a significant factor in the strength, longevity, and comfort of the house. The logs might be left in the round or hewn square; the corners might be notched with a V or dovetailed.

Architectural historians also examine room use and plan.[29] Nearly all vernacular houses in Europe had one or, more often, two rooms—a *stube* and *kuche* in Germanic society, a *hall* and *parlor* in English ones. Placement of specific features varied with each culture and affected the building traditions established in various locales across the colonies and nation, including Bedford and Franklin counties. The most visible external component was the placement of the chimney. The German version relied on a central chimney. That central stack allowed for a warm stove in the *stube* and a large but drafty cooking fireplace in the *kuche*.[30] The chimney on the more Celtic or English versions sat on the exterior, usually at a gable end, which kept the house cooler. When Virginians began to move their kitchens to separate outbuildings, room use distinctions based on heating and chimney placement faded.[31] This changed house plan enabled separation of work and respite, public and private. A more meaningful change came when householders decided to build homes with a central passage, a balanced facade, and stacked and compartmentalized spaces.

Finding an architectural footprint of ethnicity in the late eighteenth-century log houses of Virginia remains difficult at best. While certain tendencies separated German and Celtic or English building practices, those propensities had faded quickly on arrival in the colonies. Room uses became less clear; and in construction makers began using various kinds of corner notching. In part, this amalgamation occurred because building practices in the countries from which these immigrants hailed had already begun to meld into a single western European mode. On arrival in the colonies, these house forms continued to blend. Many immigrants built log houses. Many of these houses had both a more public and a more private space. Many houses allowed direct entry into domestic spaces. And the precise European antecedents of any one house are difficult to sort out.

Evidence for German housing preferences does exist. For example, Jacob Hickman, a German joiner or cabinetmaker, left detailed instructions in his will for the disposition of his estate in Franklin County in the spring of 1789. His wife was to enjoy his house, land, livestock, and all other effects except his "joiner tools" until his youngest son came of age. She was then to turn over the land to whichever child she desired, who must build her a house.

Hickman stipulated the details of the structure: "hued logs, Eighteen feet & fifteen feet and a shingled Ruff and Laid Above with Sawed Plank and two Windows, Eight Lights in Each and a Stone Chimney built in the middle." He left the precise location of the structure to the judgment of his widow but added that the site include one acre of good meadow, to be dunged every other year, and one acre of "Good Tendable Ground." She was to be given *housenfernsh* such as basins. Every year she could be given whatever fruit she pleased, twenty bushels of wheat, fifty pounds of beef, twelve pounds of hackled flax, hemp, and tow, and one pair of good shoes.[32]

Jacob Hickman was unusual in the careful instructions he left for the care of his widow. Of central importance is the house—a small log structure with two floors, windows and a permanent stone chimney built in the middle of it. By providing such precise instructions, Jacob Hickman gave his children no opportunity to cut corners in the care of their mother; his widow would live in the Germanic environment she had probably lived in her whole life. She would be provided with shelter, land to raise crops, and an annual allotment of food. The world of goods was unimportant; the only manufactured good that he thought necessary was an annual pair of shoes.

Hickman's instructions in 1789 suggest a house similar to those Eddis had encountered nearly twenty years earlier in backcountry Maryland—two rooms with central hearth. Hickman assumed that his wife would be comfortable and provided for in such a place, that his family knew what his brief words about a housing plan meant, and that a county court would know it too. His very assumption about understanding is significant—it constitutes an underlying principle of vernacular building practices, one based on local referents and local values.

As expressions of ways of thinking, acting, and confronting new situations, late eighteenth- and early nineteenth-century housing stock illustrates how Franklin County became a fertile intersection of differing ideas. Its merchants and wealthy planters lived in a world largely linked by particular knowledge of the new. Its other settlers relied on linkages stretching back to what they had known and grown comfortable with elsewhere. In between the two groups stood yet a third, settlers who mingled the old and new.

When William Eddis traveled to the backcountry in Frederick County, Maryland, he commented on what he saw, and one of the first things he mentioned was housing. That he termed the construction "rude" suggests he encountered log houses. Most such houses had two rooms, one for sleeping, one for "domestic purposes." A storehouse or barn may or may not have stood nearby. The outward rude appearance of the house and outbuildings matched the colonists' simple diet. These farmers did not complain about their food nor did they have plans for better housing. At this moment, as Eddis understood it, their "utmost ambition" had been met. All was well until stores arrived.

Eddis does not tell what might happen then, but his narrative fits into a larger notion of progress, and to him, the backcountry seemed poised for a change. The world of goods was arriving, and the standard of living would improve because expectations were changing. As an Englishman impressed with the polite grandees of tidewater Maryland, he envisioned an inexorable westward extension of English life and values. If civilized buildings followed, then a readable, recognizable hierarchy should likewise evolve. However, the backcountry evolution that in fact occurred would have left Eddis remarkably disappointed.

That early settlers chose to put up log-built structures is unsurprising. But by 1771 Frederick County's second generation had come to maturity and had the opportunity to rebuild or reclad their structures in frame or brick but chose not to. In Virginia's Lunenburg County south of the James River a

similar pattern had occurred many years before. There the plantation owners chose not to build manses of bricks and mortar, even those who had substantial holdings in land, slaves, or both.[33]

Much closer to Franklin County stands the example of Henry County.
A 1785 list of land and buildings in that county suggests few residents lived
in frame or brick houses. The Articles of Confederation had directed the
states to produce lists of both land and improvements in order to establish
their fair share of the burden of "common defense and general welfare." Presumably each Virginia county followed the new Virginia law to carry out
this directive; however, only a few such lists survive. The justices of Henry
County divided the county by militia district and received multiple lists,
most of which give name, number of white tithes, house and building materials, and associated outbuildings.[34]

The few surviving tax rolls simply make a distinction between dwelling
houses, dwelling cabins, various outbuildings, and "out cabins" and do not
denote form, size, or rooms or assign a house value. It is difficult to recap-
ture the meaning of local tax enumerators, but the categories of description,
such as "dwelling house" and "dwelling cabbin," indicate that a degree of
distinction existed.

In 1785 Robert Woods handled the taxation list for Capt. Owen Rubel's
militia district in what is now southwestern Franklin County, an area that
included the future Wade cabin. Woods gave far more detail than his peers
in other militia districts and included, for example, materials of house construction. Only the wealthy Peter Saunders lived in a frame house; the other
seventy-seven households resided in some form of log structure.

In Rubel's district, there were 460 residents, an average of six people per
household. The largest was William Ferguson's. Fourteen people lived in a
single log structure, and the household had only one outbuilding, a chicken
house. Daniel Ross also had a large household (thirteen persons), but he had
prospered sufficiently to build a chicken house, barn, and dairy. The most
common household size was three persons (22 percent), and more than half
had households of fewer than five persons.

Outbuildings indicate families had elaborated their domestic functions,
their care of livestock, or their craft activities. Forty-one percent of the
households had added a kitchen, 22 percent a barn, and 6 percent a dairy. Put
another way, fewer than one in two households cooked in an external building to avoid heat and fire, and only one in four had a structure to secure livestock and to store food and feed. Only two households had smokehouses for
meat preservation, and only two had stables. The remaining outbuildings
were for craft activities and small businesses. Capt. Rubel had a blacksmith
shop, a linen shop, and an ironworks. Benjamin Hize had a mill, both Bailey

Carter and Nathaniel Dickson operated smith's shops, and William Griffith had a hatter's shop. Only a few slave quarters are listed, which suggests that some individuals who had the capital to acquire bound labor lived side-by-side with them. In sum, by 1785 few of the households in this district were complemented by agricultural and domestic outbuilding structures associated with specialization of task, yet many of these householders had prospered enough to build specialized businesses and to carry out more efficient agricultural activities. Nonetheless, these people continued to live in log dwellings. Only Peter Saunders had built a frame house, and his slaves were also well housed in their own quarter. He had a barn and chicken house, too, and one of the two smokehouses in the district.

One small page included with Woods's loose tax papers contains additional information about three households. Henry Lyne had a twenty- by sixteen-foot log dwelling that had a shingle roof. Four men—two who may have been unrelated—lived there. Lyne also had eight "cabbing houses." As he was not taxed for slaves, the cabins may have been rented out. John Pelprie also had a log dwelling house with a shingle roof (in which he, his wife Betty, ten children, and a daughter-in-law lived) plus four "out cabins." William Quarles, his wife Judah, six children, his mother, and a Betsy Burnett, perhaps an unrelated individual, also shared life in a small house.[35]

The "lists of souls" in new Henry County indicate that many local residents had similar structures—probably of log. There were some real distinctions, on the other hand, in how they lived. In some families, five or six members from multiple generations lived in one or two rooms along with slaves. Outbuildings might have allowed agricultural and cooking tasks to be done outside of the small cabins, but few householders had built a full complement of them. That the most common household size was but three members suggests a family life just beginning or ending, or unrelated people living together. Perhaps, as Eddis suggested about the residents of Frederick County in 1771, all of the expectations of the residents of Henry County had been met.

The Henry County tax list is the only truly systematic record of housing—and occasionally people—close to John Hook's world. But it is limited to a geographical sector more mountainous than Hook's and largely populated by Scots-Irish settlers.

Evidence drawn from some of the folk building traditions in that area suggests that those residents relied on similar basic house forms: a single-room hall plan, a two-room or hall-parlor plan, and variants that incorporated a more modish center hall.[36] These forms also included "dog-trot cabins" or "breezeway houses"—two small cabins joined by a central space. Yet variety existed in terms of construction and finish. The Marshall House, built

near Hat Creek in the far eastern edge of Bedford County, had only one
room and an overhead loft. But the care in its building rebuts any notion of
a quickly thrown together, temporary structure. The builder carefully fitted
pit-sawn logs together with notching and used full dovetails at every corner.
He built it so tight that he needed no chinking or daubing, and he covered
the logs with beaded weatherboard. Inside, he fully paneled the walls with
beaded edge planking.[37] It contrasts markedly with the Frederick Rives house
in Franklin County. Like many local houses, it began as a two-room structure; later the kitchen was moved to a separate outbuilding, which a narrow
breezeway connected to the house. Not tightly built, the Rives house has
mud and rocks stuffed as infill between framing members and an unplas-
tered but whitewashed interior.[38]

Although a single-room or a two-room house is significant in terms of
house size and lifestyle, so too is an understanding of the very flexibility of
these modules. Owners of the Marshall House, that simple one-room building with a well-finished interior, added on to the building as needed. Farther east in Campbell County stood the Wood House, which also began as
a single-room log cabin, this one finished on the interior with flat-paneled
wainscot, beaded ceiling joists, and either neoclassical or federal style man-
tels. About a generation later its owner added a rough lean-to that had a
separate chimney stack. At midcentury, the family built a second one-room
cabin quite close by and connected it to the earlier house with a passageway
(also sometimes termed a "hyphen"). Early in the twentieth century a fourth
unit was added to serve as a new kitchen. Only in the 1950s did the Wood
family build a new brick house, at which point they converted the old structure to agricultural outbuildings. A single family "made do" with their log-
built structure for a century and a half.

The Wood House stood far from the hollows and mountain passes of
Capt. Rubel's militia district in Henry County, but the point remains: houses
record both a single moment when people build as well as a long series of
later needs and abilities.

In the early twentieth century, Pedro Sloan placed his grandfather
Thomas Hale's one-and-a-half-story house in a long continuum, terming it
"very much like most all the rest of the buildings" in Franklin County. In it
one large room, twenty-four feet long and twenty feet wide, served as the
main living room and bedroom combined. An enclosed corner staircase led
to more storage and dwelling space. The kitchen, which also doubled as the
dining room, stood fifty to sixty feet away. Sloan's father had added another
room of similar size with an "entry six or eight feet wide" and a porch that
extended the length of the building. Like others, that single module house,
a form that householders persistently built well into the nineteenth century,
grew by accretion.[39]

Reaching an understanding of the nuances inherent in any building hier-archy requires consideration of the number of interior rooms as much as of the finishes of the walls and roof. Wealthy Israel Christian's two-story "little house" had a clapboarded exterior, a lathed and plastered interior that in-cluded a chair rail and washboards in 1773. It also had three lower windows with shutters, five dormer windows, five six-panel doors, and "small Cor-nish molding." The details recorded in a lawsuit brought by the owner give evidence that his structure had multiple rooms and floors, and ample light. This "little house"—a phrase suggesting a larger one did exist—would have demarcated Christian from most of local society.[40] In 1772 Capt. Thomas Madison placed an order with John Hook for one hundred panes of window glass, six brass locks and pair of hinges, and enough Spanish brown paint, white lead, and lampblack for a forty-four- by twenty-foot house. This house was large, perhaps even "genteel." It was painted, had multiple windows, and rooms that could be locked. Each element was a bit of architectural nicety, a nicety few could share.[41]

Traveler William Eddis also raised the notion of "expectation" in hous-ing when he wrote his 1771 account, and that concept has relevance to any assessment of backcountry Virginia. Many settlers chose a log house be-cause it could be built quickly and cheaply with a modicum of woodwork-ing tools and skills or because it could be finished quite nicely on the inte-rior and added to and quickly updated. Thus in evaluating what was an appropriate or "expected" house we must also ask two other questions: by whom? For whom? In Franklin and Bedford counties, a house with a mod-ish center passage was rare. Two-room structures were so pervasive that they probably occupied the middle of the local hierarchy of buildings, and if accompanied by several outbuildings they may have moved closer to the top end.[42] Regulations in New London required all householders to con-struct framed buildings, but the minimum size—320 feet of living space on the ground level—meant that these could be as small as a common cabin. Variety ensued. Some of the residents lived in drafty thrown-together frame houses; others had snug, warm ones. Some houses had finished interiors and glass windows; some did not.

After the Revolutionary War, the pace of housing improvement did accelerate in Virginia. Larger houses with specialized multiple rooms for public functions and private living became more common in the Bedford/ Franklin region. In this, merchants often led the way. John Hook built a substantial house. So did his rival, merchant Andrew Donald, who con-structed a large brick residence with a symmetrical facade in the late 1780s and ebulliently called it Fancy Farm. His very choice of name for the prop-erty carried special meaning, as "fancy" denoted a planned but playful aes-thetic engagement with the out-of-the-ordinary.

But the overall improvement in housing still progressed slowly. In 1807 a peddler visited Liberty, which became Bedford's county seat when Campbell County was splintered off. Of the twenty dwelling houses, he considered ten "Genteel"—most were of frame construction and just two or three were made of brick.[43]

Perhaps only later in the nineteenth century did a cabin in the woods connote "not good enough." It was then that Franklin resident Andrew Bailey remembered the shame he felt taking his new bride from her father's house to a cabin deep in the woods and how relieved he felt when he could provide her with an appropriate home and furnishings.[44]

The notion that a general hierarchy of building exists is flawed and must be redefined. Building hierarchy is local. It is nuanced. And it is confusing. Thomas Anburey observed in 1779 that most Virginia houses were still constructed of wood and had shingled roofs, and only the houses of the "better sort" were finished on the inside by lathing and plastering, and on the outside by painting and the use of glass windows rather than shutters. While some houses had brick chimneys, "the generality of them were wood, coated on the inside with clay."[45] Daniel Drake lived in frontier Kentucky between 1785 and 1800 and later recollected that initially "the best kind of houses" were cabins and "the hewed log house, with a shingled roof" came later.[46]

Some houses in backcountry Virginia fit the broader understanding implied by Anburey's phrase "better sort." Others did not. They quite simply followed an existing local hierarchy. Modish vernacular housing could be quite distinctive, like the houses of the merchants John Hook and Andrew Donald. But local and acceptable vernacular housing was mutable, and more and more people incorporated modish aspects into them, which in effect made these features everyday ones.

Choices about how to deal with interior and exterior surfaces often elicited very different responses from householders. In 1813 Francis Gray stopped at an Albemarle County tavern—a one-room unfinished house with a door that would not shut. But inside that structure was "no appearance of poverty"—rather there were well-dressed inhabitants, a "very good" bed covered with a "very good counterpane," and a large mahogany desk that occupied one side of the room—yet nothing to drink from but broken glasses.[47]

Taverns were not homes, but Gray's observations raise exciting questions about what the two-room log-built houses in Bedford/Franklin might have contained. In many farmhouses throughout the world, decoration or elaboration has long been an interior expression, not an exterior one, which means an outside can be austere, an interior soft.[48] If that model applies to backcountry Virginia, then beyond the single door and shuttered windows lay small consumer goods like ribbons and teapots—items that might enliven dark, unfinished spaces at little cost and high benefit. So too might be found other items from the world of goods—objects such as more chairs for entertaining visitors or a chest of drawers for carefully sequestering clothing or linens.

A Standard of Living: Household Furnishings

Probate inventories offer one systematic way to seek patterns in domestic interiors. Analyses based on the lists of household goods put together soon after a person's death have been the mainstay of material culture analysis for a generation, and for many became the genesis of the whole consumerism story. The flaws and biases of these documents are well known, but the data nonetheless remain the most important form of evidence on furniture and furnishings, and they provide the foundation for comparisons across regions. Wills and inventories represent individual cases in a particular time and place. Separately, they present people; together they reveal patterns. Both illuminate the region and the world of goods.

Edward Bright died in 1784, survived by his wife Mary Ann, his son, Charles, and five married daughters. In his will, he stipulated that Mary Ann retain full use of his 120-acre plantation until either she chose to leave it or died, at which point it would pass to his grandson Charles. The rest of his estate was to be divided between his wife and son; each of his five daughters was to be given 5 shillings. When the court-appointed men inventoried and appraised his estate, they carefully listed the results of his lifetime of acquisition. Slave Roger had a value of £45. Three horses, a dozen cows, and four hogs added £39. Thus his single slave and livestock formed about 70 percent of his whole personal estate of £121.

Bright's modest household possessions included two feather beds valued at £20, but his several trunks, a chest, and eight chairs had little value. He had no tables from which to eat. With such a large family to feed, it was not surprising that he had a good twenty-five pounds of pewter as well as earthenware and glass and iron pots. His five daughters may have spent many hours at the two spinning wheels and the loom while growing up, weaving coarse hemp for family use or resale, perhaps even at Hook's store where Bright had shopped.[49]

How do the furnishings of Edward Bright compare to those of his neighbors, friends, and superiors? The snapshot of county life gained from analysis of certain categories of goods in the Bedford county probate record for 1768–77 depicts a society in which Bright would have probably been regarded as comfortable. But comparing Bright to others in Bedford sorted out by wealth in probate records is one thing; placing the household equipment of Bedford County next to that in some eastern Virginia and Maryland counties reveals a rather shocking disparity.[50] Bedford householders

TABLE 4.2. Personal Property in Bedford County
Estate Inventories, 1768–77

Category	Total value of estate				
	£0–49 (n = 28)	£50–94 (n = 18)	£95–224 (n = 18)	£225–490 (n = 12)	£491+ (n = 4)
Slaves	0.0%	11.4%	31.6%	63.2%	75.7%
Livestock	44.4	46.6	33.6	20.8	12.1
Furniture	17.7	10.7	12.3	7.0	5.5
Linens: bed/table	0.08	0.3	0.7	0.2	0.0
Books	0.4	0.9	1.0	0.2	0.2
Cloth production	2.4	1.5	1.6	0.4	0.1
Foodways objects	5.4	3.7	2.8	1.9	1.0
Groceries	0.3	0.2	0.3	0.2	0.5

Source: Bedford County Will Book 1, 1763–87, Library of Virginia.

simply did not place a high premium on creating any stage with props for "correct" elite behavior.

Consumer goods did not make up a large part of household items in these Bedford County inventories; instead bound labor and livestock accounted for three-quarters of personal wealth (table 4.2). Second, households had simple furnishings. Only a third of the poorest households (estates valued at less than £49) listed furniture from which to eat in the more civilized manner—seated in chairs around a table. Moving into the lower middling ranks, only about half were so equipped; an average of about one table and four chairs meant that in many households few guests could be seated comfortably, families ate in shifts, or household members perched on chests and doorframes. In those same years, comparable households in eastern York County, Virginia, possessed almost a dozen chairs for friends and family. Those Bedford County residents who were relatively well off—in the upper middling and upper economic ranks—did invest in a few chairs and tables, but they too lagged far behind their eastern counterparts. None of the wealthiest households inventoried had the overall package necessary for the correct elite environment. While wealthy York County residents owned an average of nine tables and thirty chairs for multiple social functions, their Bedford counterparts had less than a quarter of these furnishings (tables 4.3 and 4.4). Only a handful possessed a desk at which to keep accounts or complete correspondence; none had prints on the walls or silver plate on his tables.

TABLE 4.3. Mean Number of Household Tables in
Probated Estates, 1768–77

	Total value of estate				
	£0–49	£50–94	£95–224	£225–490	£491+
Bedford County					
(n = 80)	1.0	1.2	1.1	1.1	1.2
York County					
(n = 96)	1.7	2.6	4.1	4.8	8.8
Somerset County, MD					
(n = 261)	1.8	1.9	2.7	3.8	5.6

Sources: Bedford County Will Book 1, 1763–87, Library of Virginia; Lois Green Carr and
Lorena S. Walsh, "Changing Life Styles and Consumer Behavior in the Colonial Chesapeake," in
Of Consuming Interests: The Style of Life in the Eighteenth Century, ed. Cary Carson, Ronald Hoffman, and Peter J. Albert (Charlottesville: University Press of Virginia for the United States Capitol Historical Society, 1994), table 6.

TABLE 4.4. Mean Number of Household Chairs in
Probated Estates, 1768–77

	Total value of estate				
	£0–49	£50–94	£95–224	£225–490	£491+
Bedford County					
(n = 80)	2.8	4.8	3.4	7.7	5.3
York County					
(n = 96)	5.1	11.0	18.2	17.1	32.5
Somerset County, MD					
(n = 261)	4.3	7.7	9.7	13.9	19.1

Sources: Bedford County Will Book 1, 1763–87, Library of Virginia; Lois Green Carr and
Lorena S. Walsh, "Changing Life Styles and Consumer Behavior in the Colonial Chesapeake," in
Of Consuming Interests: The Style of Life in the Eighteenth Century, ed. Cary Carson, Ronald Hoffman, and Peter J. Albert (Charlottesville: University Press of Virginia for the United States Capitol Historical Society, 1994), table 6.

The less expensive items that grace those tables fill out the picture a bit
more. Across the board, objects related to the preparation and serving of
food constituted approximately 2 percent of the value of personal estates inventoried in Bedford county. If slaves and livestock are factored out so that
the figures reflect consumer wealth only, that percentage remains relatively
constant in all four wealth groupings (table 4.5). This pattern also obtains if
the items are sorted into categories of cooking, dining, and utilitarian storage. The analyses thus indicate that these expenditures remained somewhat

TABLE 4.5. Consumer Wealth Devoted to Household Goods in Bedford County Probated Estates, 1768–77

| | Total value of estate | | | | |
Category	£0–49 (n = 28)	£50–94 (n = 18)	£95–224 (n = 18)	£225–490 (n = 12)	£491+ (n = 4)
Furniture	31.9%	25.5%	35.2%	41.1%	44.9%
Linens: bed/table	0.1	0.7	1.9	1.5	0.0
Books	1.6	2.2	1.0	1.1	1.3
Cloth production	4.2	3.6	4.6	2.4	1.1
Foodways objects	9.3	8.9	8.0	11.1	8.6
Cooking	3.6	3.2	2.9	3.7	3.2
Dining	5.6	4.3	4.8	6.4	4.6
Tea drinking	0.09	0.7	0.01	0.5	0.6
Groceries	0.5	3.0	0.8	1.2	4.4
Foodstuffs	0.3	0.5	0.6	1.2	4.0

Source: Bedford County Will Book 1, 1763–87, Library of Virginia.

Note: This table has factored out slaves and livestock and the values accorded each; for inclusion of those two categories, see table 4.2.

inelastic; the residents of Bedford County did not spend a greater proportion of their wealth on these items as their wealth increased. The exception is items related to tea drinking, which show up with markedly more frequency in households of greater wealth. Householders with greater consumer wealth also acquired more furniture and a great deal more bedding and table linens. Ceramics and related items are not an important index of wealth. Pewter was overwhelmingly the tableware of choice, with the addition of wooden wares and fine ceramics in a few households.

These backcountry folk did compare favorably to their eastern cousins in other ways, however. High incidence of knife and fork ownership indicates that some improved standards of eating had become commonplace. Even if ceramics had not replaced old-fashioned pewter and even if not all family members could gather around a table, old methods of scooping, pushing, fingering, and spooning one's food were passing away (table 4.6).[51] These households also contained quantities of books comparable to their peers in eastern society, suggesting an emphasis on literacy and religion. Half of the poorest households and as many as three-fourths of the more well-off owned at least one book, often a Bible (table 4.7). Personal Bible study was important in many dissenting sects.

Overall few of the decedents in Bedford County owned teawares. The several listings of teakettles suggest that many householders did consume

TABLE 4.6. Households with Knives and Forks in
Probated Estates, 1768–77

	Total value of estate				
	£0–49	£50–94	£95–224	£225–490	£491+
Bedford County					
(n = 80)	33%	38%	56%	75%	33%
Rural York County					
(n = 73)	25	30	20	70	93
Rural Anne Arundel County, MD					
(n = 181)	21	56	63	76	82
Somerset County, MD					
(n = 261)	51	69	77	80	89
Urban York County					
(n = 44)	10	20	40	80	64
Urban Anne Arundel County					
(n = 30)	56	0	75	100	100

Sources: Bedford County Will Book 1, 1763–87, Library of Virginia; Lois Green Carr and
Lorena S. Walsh, "Changing Life Styles and Consumer Behavior in the Colonial Chesapeake," in
Of Consuming Interests: The Style of Life in the Eighteenth Century, ed. Cary Carson, Ronald Hoffman, and Peter J. Albert (Charlottesville: University Press of Virginia for the United States Capitol Historical Society, 1994), table 1.

TABLE 4.7. Households with Books in Probated Estates, 1768–77

	Total value of estate				
	£0–49	£50–94	£95–224	£225–490	£491+
Bedford County					
(n = 80)	53%	76%	76%	60%	67%
Rural York County					
(n = 73)	33	30	53	90	79
Rural Anne Arundel County, MD					
(n = 181)	22	48	63	66	82
Somerset County, MD					
(n = 261)	56	82	84	90	96
Urban York County					
(n = 44)	30	80	30	100	79
Urban Anne Arundel County					
(n = 30)	67	68	75	100	83

Sources: Bedford County Will Book 1, 1763–87, Library of Virginia; Lois Green Carr and
Lorena S. Walsh, "Changing Life Styles and Consumer Behavior in the Colonial Chesapeake," in
Of Consuming Interests: The Style of Life in the Eighteenth Century, ed. Cary Carson, Ronald Hoffman, and Peter J. Albert (Charlottesville: University Press of Virginia for the United States Capitol Historical Society, 1994), table 1.

Note: This table includes both religious and secular books.

TABLE 4.8. Households with at Least One Teaware in
Probated Estates, 1768–77

	Total value of estate				
	£0–49	£50–94	£95–224	£225–490	£491+
Bedford County					
(n = 80)	3%	19%	7%	17%	33%
Rural York County					
(n = 73)	25	30	60	50	86
Rural Anne Arundel County, MD					
(n = 181)	28	40	57	83	85
Somerset County, MD					
(n = 261)	32	43	57	76	89
Urban York County					
(n = 44)	60	100	90	100	86
Urban Anne Arundel County					
(n = 30)	67	80	63	100	100

Source: Bedford County Will Book 1, 1763–87, Library of Virginia; Lois Green Carr and
Lorena S. Walsh, "Changing Life Styles and Consumer Behavior in the Colonial Chesapeake," in
Of Consuming Interests: The Style of Life in the Eighteenth Century, ed. Cary Carson, Ronald Hoffman, and Peter J. Albert (Charlottesville: University Press of Virginia for the United States Capitol Historical Society, 1994), table 1.

tea, and the inventories of the wealthy do list a few teawares, but in comparison with other more eastern counties this demonstrates a surprising re-
jection of tea drinking per se (table 4.8). In Bourbon County, Kentucky, near
the end of the eighteenth century, tea and coffee utensils populated more
than half of all household inventories. Indeed, in a popular series of letters
published in 1793 to promote settling in Kentucky, Gilbert Imlay waxed rhap-
sodic: "there are certain luxuries which the progress of society has taught us
to consider as necessary;" "sugar, coffee, and tea, belong to this class."[52] If the
"progress of society" had taught Bedford County residents to consider tea
essential, it is unapparent in the probate inventories.

The picture of the domestic interiors of Bedford County residents that
emerges from the inventories shows a society that had a view of its own
about what constituted necessary and proper goods. Even if the inventories
merely capture the behavior of an older generation, they illustrate that these
individuals had not bought a number of furniture forms or furnishings that
their counterparts in eastern Virginia and Maryland had chosen to purchase.
Not having many storage pieces may mean there was little to store; not having chairs may suggest a group of people who squatted on the floor, leaned
against a wall, or sat on chests. But Bedford County residents did indeed fol-

low some new social patterns—eating with knives and forks—even as they rejected others—serving tea with appropriate equipment, like a full set of specialized cups and saucers, slop bowls, strainer, milk pitcher, sugar pot, and teapot.

Hence in some ways Bedford/Franklin residents may have *simplified* customs. Not owning teawares did not mean that a household did not drink tea, only that it had not fully adopted the cultural system of tea drinking and the learning and leisure that the ceremony connoted. Admittedly, a teacup could *stand in* for the whole system just as a few classical ornaments on a cabinet could *refer to* the whole classical constellation; however, the overall absence of teawares from the estate inventories suggests that local residents had seen no reason to embrace tea drinking as a social activity.

Standards of Behavior

Evidence of patterns in household interiors also comes from simple ideas about the correct or acceptable way to behave in differing situations. In analyzing this evidence, we focus on what it was like to move between two differing sets of cultural expectations. In April 1821 Thomas Jefferson and his granddaughter Cornelia made the ninety-mile journey from Monticello to Poplar Forest in Bedford County. Cornelia found the trip arduous. Torrential rain had left the roads in terrible order, and she and her grandfather had been forced to spend one night at "horrid Old Floods" house. Convinced that Dr. Flood had slept on the sheets, Cornelia pronounced the counterpane relatively cleaner and pinned the top sheet down before rolling "hand, foot, and face" in her clothes so that her "skin should not be defiled by touching pitch."[53]

The journey from the refined world of Monticello to Jefferson's backcountry retreat at Poplar Forest well illustrates the difference between those worlds. Jefferson had begun building his retreat in 1805, although he had owned land in the county for several decades. He envisioned it as a place of seclusion, a place to escape the horde of visitors and the wearisome and expensive rounds of hospitality.

Myriad settlers had traveled the same east-west roads. Others had taken north-south roads along the mountains and valleys of western Virginia. The people, products, and ideas that moved along these arteries offer keys to understanding this place. Distance is not only measured in geographical but also in hierarchical terms; space is a matrix that distances people in both social and physical ways. The records kept by 28-year-old lawyer Richard Venable thirty years earlier in combination with the letters of Cornelia Jefferson Randolph demonstrate the shifts in cultural expectations as people moved between various worlds.

Venable, who lived in nearby Pittsylvania County, kept a diary in which he recorded his travels, meetings, and thoughts.

Tues 12 April
Dined at St. Venables with Mr. Jno Smith and James Henry esquire. Chated on Religion, Politicks, Philanthropy, etc.

Wed 13 April
Set out for D. Court at New London. Met with George Henry and Col. Patrick Henry at Porter's, came that night to Hunter's 35 miles

Thurs 14 April
Came to N. London with company aforementioned

. . .

Sun 24 April
Samuel Callands 40 miles. Respectfully entertained.

Mon 25 April
Came to Henry Court 38 miles. Great crowding it being Election Day [torn] the election was over and the hill was coverd with a thick and numerous crowd of people, Rudeness displayed itself in every form imagined. With flying hats and shouts of yay some expressed themselves—others by loud and voseferous quarreling would collect a crowd Others would collect a crowd by rolling out grog and proclaiming come and drink all the friends of—this is his treat. When all of the sudden [torn] a violent affray broke out as to overset grog, cryer and all.
   In making my escape [torn] of fray, I became a witness to a different scene. A large troop of read cheeked mountain girls surround the cake carts with their sweethearts, treating and caressing them in every manner which would be dictated by clownish fondness. Oh ye fair dames who live among these hills and mountains if you regard chastity and modesty as I hope you do, avoid such promiscuous crowds lest the ru[torn]deness of beasts and men [torn]

27 April—Attended Court, but little business done and that in the greatest confusion imaginable

29 April—To Callands store and down to Pittsy Cthouse 35 miles.[54]

Venable's legal practice in Pittsylvania County necessitated frequent travel through the southern Piedmont. The district court sat at New London, and he went there regularly with colleagues and friends. During the April visit, he acquitted a murderer, defended a burglar, and dined with friends. Head-

PLATE I. Type of goods stocked at John Hook's stores. Front, left to right: playing cards, razor, watch, and bone-handled cutlery. Middle: tinware box, brass candlestick. Rear: printed cotton, books, simple print in frame. Courtesy, The Colonial Williamsburg Foundation.

PLATE 2. Examples of eighteenth-century checked fabrics. Tan and white linen check fragment, original use unknown, late eighteenth to early nineteenth century, accession no. 1955-89; blue and white linen checks, each check 1⅛" square, original use unknown, probably eighteenth century, accession no. 1951-360, 1; blue and white linen checks, each check 2½" square, originally a mattress cover, probably eighteenth century, accession no. 1952-178, 1; blue and white linen check windowpane from set of bed hangings, late eighteenth to early nineteenth century, accession no. 1963-192, 1–11. Courtesy, The Colonial Williamsburg Foundation. Hook complained about the checked textiles he received from England in the 1770s, terming them well liked but expensive.

PLATE 3. Punch bowls. Left: Chinese export porcelain, overglaze paint, and gilding, c. 1750. Courtesy, Chipstone Foundation. Right: cast iron. Private collection; photograph, Ann Smart Martin.

PLATE 4. Desk and bookcase, Philadelphia, c. 1750. Carving attributed to Samuel Harding. Walnut. 110" × 40¾" W × 23¾". Courtesy, Chipstone Foundation; photograph, Gavin Ashworth. That the maker lavished ornament on interior elements such as the shell-carved drawers and arched pigeonholes indicates he or the owner expected it to be left open for view. The extraordinary number of niches for ledgers and small holes for bills suggests its original owner was a merchant.

PLATE 5. Chest of drawers, Franklin County, c. 1810. Poplar. 46" × 38" × 18½". Private collection. Note the exaggerated stylistic details and the shallow decorative cross-hatching (detail, below); both are common features on furniture made in the back-country in the late eighteenth and early nineteenth centuries.

PLATE 6 (left). Corner cupboard, probably Bedford/Franklin region, 1780–1820. Pine. 77" × 30". Private collection. The cupboard has a red wash that some makers applied over soft woods like pine to approximate the look of finer hardwoods, such as mahogany. This well-worn cupboard ultimately ended up in an outbuilding where it was used to store hams, hence the unusual staining.

PLATE 7 (right). Corner cupboard, probably Goochland County, Virginia, 1760–1790. Walnut. 82" × 45½" × 25". Private collection. All hardware, including key, is original.

PLATE 8. A Glasgow shopkeeper of the 1790s, artist unknown. Courtesy, People's Palace Museum, Glasgow, Scotland.

PLATE 9. Ribbon sample book, 1804–11. Courtesy, Herbert Art Gallery and Museum, Coventry, 1988. A note on the left page reads "Sold well every where except Liverpool. all returned from them," which suggests the vagaries of fashion and popularity could be quite local.

PLATE 10. Lewis Miller, *Negro Dance,* Lynchburg, Virginia, 1853. Watercolor and ink drawing. Courtesy, Abby Aldrich Rockefeller Folk Art Museum, The Colonial Williamsburg Foundation, Williamsburg, Virginia. Gift of Dr. and Mrs. Richard M. Kain in memory of George Hay Kain.

PLATE 11 (left). Small wall mirror, probably early nineteenth century. Courtesy, Abby Aldrich Rockefeller Folk Art Museum, The Colonial Williamsburg Foundation, Williamsburg, Virginia. Human figure on top with legs spread. A thin indentation around the figure's waist suggests that something hung there, perhaps a cloth flap on cord. If so, the intent was humor.

PLATE 12 (right). Looking glass, probably England, c. 1760–80. Mahogany. Private collection. This looking glass has a history of ownership in the New London region. Britain supplied most mirrors sold in the colonies prior to the Revolution. The rococo decoration on this is early and elaborate. It is likely similar to the mirrors John Hook kept in his high-end stock at the New London store.

ing home, he traveled south and west to the court at Henry County. The election fracas he encountered took him aback. Here was drunkenness, rudeness, cries of "yay," loud quarreling, even a fight. Having escaped this disconcerting scene, he saw behavior that perhaps disturbed him even more, rude louts caressing sweet red-faced mountain lasses.

Venable's diary illuminates the dichotomy between rich and poor, top and bottom, educated and unlettered at the end of the eighteenth century. He traversed the countryside to attend different county court days, staying with friends and colleagues. He paid close attention to housekeeping skills and marital relations, and he drank tea with the ladies ("[had a] mighty dish of chat with the old lady and the girls"). Occasionally, he stayed with clients: "Mr. Payne lives in a very plain way," yet the family operated with "harmony and industry." At home, Venable might spend the forenoon reading *The Spectator*, entertaining guests, or attending "singing school." He socialized at weddings and quilting parties; on the road he attended a play in Richmond and supped at a tavern in Williamsburg. He hungered for cultural information that arrived in letters, books, newspapers, and gossip. On a trip to the Franklin courthouse he visited with "living newspapers"— "found much scandal and misinformation in them—How wide the contrast twixt women."[55]

Social time could also be religious time. Venable heard and read sermons by a variety of preachers, often commenting on their skills in his diary. He attended one Methodist religious gathering where first one and then another in the congregation "began to cry out in religious rapture . . . while almost the whole congregation were filled with confusion and roaring." Marveling at how long the hubbub went on, he left them "in as much confusion and making as much noise as sometimes seen at a contested election of representatives."[56]

Venable's words provide powerful testimony of the evangelical revival that swept the region at the end of the eighteenth century. Professing Methodists, Baptists, and even Presbyterians split families, generations, genders, and structures in significant ways. For some who had found Christ, it was unbearable that friends and loved ones were destined to a fiery pit so they worked hard to convert them. For others, deep religious strictures only evoked disdain for the nonbelievers.

Acceptance of evangelical faith had an impact on material expressions of a social hierarchy. First, evangelism rejected the very competitive climate of conspicuous display that was one of the most important features of consumerism. People other than Quakers and Dunkards came to value plain clothing as signs of both humility and group identity. As pride was a sin, then overly fine clothing surely signified shameful worldliness. And in the eyes of some evangelicals, those who wore such goods were likewise shameful: "Instead then of vain, thoughtless company and frivolous conversation which abound in this world," advised one backcountry minister in 1811, "choose the people of God for your associates and your friends."[57]

Venable focused his lens on society from the position of an elevated outsider. His observations delineated the premium that members of the elite placed on gathering with their peers, even if a long distance separated them. The less affluent had different kinds of meetings—often large and rowdy gatherings that had little to do with rank and everything to do with faith. His accounts of various gatherings also shed light on one of the most puzzling aspects of backcountry people's behavior: a seeming predilection to a particularly brutal form of fighting known as gouging. In these heated contests, maximum disfigurement seemed to be the goal, most particularly the liberation of eyes from their sockets.[58] While fighting was common in eighteenth-century society, rough-and-tumble eye poking stood as a hallmark of backcountry life. All too often social slights or insults escalated to brutal violence—be it the gouging of eyes or the biting off of ears. Part of this reflected how the local society measured slights; if one's good name was the source of honor, the smallest besmirchment brought shame. At the same time, in a society that prized physicality as a skill essential in taming the wilderness, fighting prowess conferred rank in a different kind of hierarchy.[59]

British officer Thomas Anburey recounted one such story of brutality that he had heard while in Virginia. Several gentlemen and British officers had gathered to play billiards "when a low fellow, who pretends at gentility came in." Words were exchanged during the game until the low fellow insisted on a fight. Mr. Fauchee rose to the bait but stipulated the two should meet "in a gentlemanlike manner" as he did not know how to box. No sooner were those words spoken "before the other flew at him, and in an instant turned his eye out of the socket, and while it hung upon his cheek, the fellow was barbarous enough to endeavor to pluck it entirely out, but was prevented."[60]

Anburey voiced his horror at the "barborous custom" that was "peculiar to the lower class of people . . . especially those in the back woods." Although there was a law in force, "they are so little restrained by any laws the state can pass," that "this savage custom prevails." "I have seen a fellow, reckoned a great adept in gouging, who constantly kept the nails of both his thumbs and second fingers very long and pointed; nay to prevent their breaking or splitting, in the execution of his diabolical intentions, he hardened them every evening in a candle."[61]

Violent fights often coincided with court days in the Bedford/Franklin region. The muted legal response to them suggests the officers tolerated such fights because it was unlikely anyone would be killed. For example, James Board bit off part of the lip of Charles Divan "in an attempt to maim and disfigure," yet he was probably only charged in court because Divan interrupted and raged at the court for justice.[62] According to one resident fighting was the "prevalent vice"; it began with "serious quarreling," led to "revolting profanity," and ended in "a regular game of fisticuffs." A peddler visiting the area in 1809 wrote with disappointment: "very poor Court, no fighting or Gouging, very few Drunken people."[63]

Violence took many forms. In 1787, Thomas Jones, Thomas Prunty, and others gathered for a drink, probably in a tavern. Perhaps they were neighbors, perhaps friends, but the court records are silent on this detail. At one point Prunty offered Jones a drink from the punch bowl in a "gearing [i.e., jeering] insulting manner." Rather than receive the insult, Jones smashed the bowl out of his hand.[64]

Passing the punch bowl around was a shared ritual of drinking. It bonded the participants with one another, not only through the alcohol but also through the vessel itself. Even though more refined manners of dining and drinking in a domestic context required individual cups and plates and forks, the ritual of passing the punch bowl endured as an acceptable suspension of "manners" (fig. 4.9).[65]

In Jones's mind, the only proper response he could make when presented the punch bowl in an insulting manner was to smash the punch bowl, likely by throwing it to the floor. Smashing it was equally insulting for it encoded both a refusal of hospitality (sharing alcohol) and a refusal to put his lips where Prunty's had been.[66] This insult could not be borne, and Prunty brought a suit. Jones countered with his own suit. The jury, however, agreed with Prunty: Jones's refusal of the punch bowl constituted the greater social violence. The few words about group interaction in the court records thus reveal information about bonding and conflict, about behavior in an institutional setting, and about how a material object was encoded with cultural meaning.

Just a year earlier, in 1786, a group of men gathered in Franklin County were playing whist, a popular card game, when tempers flared. The words of a witness in the lawsuit recount the exchange. "There seems to be a fals Deal, that Mr. Wilson got a Kandle to Count the tricks, that upon Sarching, Wilson found a Card between Mr. Ingland's feet." A fight erupted and the ensuing melee spread to another guest who began hitting Willson's wife and son.[67] These men had initially been joined in a highly structured form of entertainment, one based on intricate rules of play and appropriate behavior. When a personal insult shattered those structured rules of sociability, oddly chaotic behavior ensued.

FIGURE 4.9. *Christmas in the Country,* Bentley & Co, London, England, 1791. Engraving. Courtesy, The Colonial Williamsburg Foundation. The idea of rural bumpkins in drunken debauchery and play resonated throughout the satirical literature and visual culture during the eighteenth century.

Other fights are captured in court cases. In 1770, George Callaway Jr. hired Adam Brown, his apprentice, and his slave to work at blacksmithing. One clause in the agreement stipulated that if Callaway caught Brown neglecting his work, "he may order him to his business" and "he shall go without Being offended at it & not to take it amiss." Two years later Brown brought suit, claiming that Callaway used clubs, swords, and fist to "beat, wound, and ill treat him so of his life it was greatly dispaired."[68]

The county court also handled a multitude of grievances between neighbors, many of whom believed if one's name was worth fighting for, it was worth suing for. James Pate was ordered to appear for slandering Elizabeth Finley who had not reached age 21. John Hale sued George and Robert Baber for slandering him with their accusation that he had "carnal knowledge of a Negro wench" owned by George Baber. Hale protested that their "repeating, proclaiming and publishing of which False, Feigned, Scandalous and Approbrious lying English words" had caused him to fall into "great Infamy and Scandal with several worthy persons" and put him at risk of court penalties.[69]

These kinds of disputes, common throughout Virginia society, also make a strong argument against any assertions that the backcountry had a wild or lawless culture. Although fighting, drinking, and scandal may have been common, observed boundaries of decent behavior between the sexes and races existed and people used the courts as arbiters in times of social disarray. Jones and Prunty did not engage in honorific brawling to settle their punch-drinking slight; they went to court.[70]

Evidence about fighting and violence also illustrates that the Bedford/Franklin region fails to fit the preconceived categories mentioned at the beginning of the chapter. It is the not-quiteness of the fit that tells the story; an evening of cards at home ending with violence against the host's wife, communal bonding over a punch bowl leading to insult, honorable reputation against sexual assault of a slave, the expectation of regular eye gouging at court day and disappointment when it did not transpire.

Contemporary residents of the colony and state did not know what to make of the backcountry. To the "civilized" folks of the Tidewater, backcountry people were ill-behaved, morally suspect, even abstractly incomprehensible. Edward Hooker was raised in Connecticut, educated at Yale, and studied law in South Carolina. He took a seventeen-day trip through the mountains with his friend, Reverend Lilly. They dined at the home of a mountain preacher. Hooker considered the one-story framed house "a comfortable size" and took note that it "was furnished in a way and inhabited by a family exactly corresponding to the stile of the people, whose minister it belongs to." Their meal consisted of "fresh pork, and sweet potatoes cut up and set in a large tin pan, without any bread or sauce, or any accompaniment, except salt." Of greater notice than the undressed, unsauced food were the eating arrangements: "A chest no higher than our knees served for a table:—the end of another chest served for a set for our kind host: while my fellow traveler and myself occupied the only chairs in the room."[71]

Hooker went on to say that "I have rarely, perhaps never, made a meal with more satisfaction." After prayer, Hooker climbed "in a coarse but comfortable bed, which was furnished with curtains of a coarse sort of gause." Hooker's host, like many other backcountry householders, had an awareness of style, but the materials he used were "coarse." His furnishings were multipurpose, "make-do," and to Hooker's eyes oddly awry. When Hooker returned home he took with him "some corrected notions of the Mountain people, who have not infrequently been represented as intolerably savage in their manners."[72]

Backcountry people had responded to the New World of consumer goods with all its attendant social behaviors in many different ways. The lens by which we see them most often gives a picture of how they were perceived by "cultivated" people back east. Still, on days of public gatherings, boys fondled the mountain girls or bit off the lips of rivals. Evangelical preachers roared at those who came to be saved. Court days resonated with profane and vulgar voices lodging charges and countercharges, together forming the "language of hell."[73]

Contemporary scholarship sees the backcountry as a particularly intriguing place where multiple ethnic and racial groups mixed, the distribution of land and labor was oddly skewed, and less "refined" behaviors were welcomed. Yet attempts to pigeonhole John Hook's world in the existing sets of historical categories fail. The region does not fit the descriptions of a tobacco culture. Indeed, few residents owned enough slaves to grow a large tobacco crop. Neither does it fit the notions of the frontier. Stores sold green satin hats, not coonskin caps. The scenes that emerge of backcountry life from the evidence reveal people who drew on European ideas, appropriating what was useful and renegotiating and reinterpreting the rest.

That the migration of so many other new peoples and ideas from differing places quickly upended any status quo in the backcountry, however, leads to another question: how did people craft *new* cultural systems with the world of goods in a different environment and social system? The people who settled in the Bedford/Franklin region did not choose the package of genteel behaviors and fine equipment that their counterparts further east had readily bought into. They chose what was important or useful to them and drew on goods, buildings, and related social behaviors that either reinforced old meanings or assigned new ones. "Backcountry" was a way to be.

THE WADE CABIN IN BACKCOUNTRY TIME

Every material culture scholar dreams of finding serious local historians and collectors who avidly track down a broad array of local material culture, keep it local, and record the history of the things they own. I found such historians in Francis and Laquita Amos who recovered the Wade cupboard. Their efforts have provided important keys to intensive scrutiny of a place in time as well as a wonderful story.

The Amoses retrieved the Wade cupboard more than a quarter-century ago from a circa 1820 cabin that Bradley Wade probably built and passed down through his family. By the twentieth century a newer second cabin stood near the original one; George Wade, his sister Betty, and Mary, a relative by marriage, occupied the older cabin, and brother Posie Wade lived in the newer one. Francis Amos served as Posie's doctor and during his visits relished hearing Wade talk about old times and the old family place. Although not a family member, Amos absorbed the amazingly extensive oral history of the Wades.

Amos had asked for "the right of first refusal" on the cupboard should the family ever want to sell it. And Margaret Ferguson Gonzalez contacted him when the family decided to clear out the cabin and its contents several years after the death of her great-uncle. The photographs that Amos took and the objects he recovered and kept together show the way that old and new things might be lived with and held in place for a very long time. My own meeting with Gonzalez enabled me to truly visualize the objects in the hands of people in a particular space. And her memories put the Wades in motion.[74]

Amos's visit represents one moment in time in the life of a building, a collection of furnishings, and an object—all are part of a cultural biography of objects in a market sphere marked by personal obligations and connections.[75] When Amos arrived family members had already moved some furnishings and sold a chest (which Amos subsequently purchased) to an antiques dealer. The photograph of the cabin's main room that Amos took on that visit shows much of the cabin's remaining contents—chairs, a treadle sewing machine, a bicycle, a textile—all in a jumble in the middle of the floor. New wood framing members stacked about suggest repairs were about to begin. But within that jetsam and flotsam of things lay extraordinary and early pieces of material culture that amounted to another set of cultural evidence for Franklin County. While the story begins early in the nineteenth century, in many ways it is still unfolding.

Measuring twenty-four feet wide and eighteen feet deep, the cabin was like most one-room structures built for more than a century in Franklin County (fig. 4.10). On the gable end sat a large exterior stone chimney flanked by a smaller window. An off-center front door and single window cut through the front facade. In the rear an attached room with fireplace and a side porch had been added in the twentieth century for Mary. Inside the house a steep stair climbed to a loft, the bottom few steps almost ladder-like. A stovepipe hole blocked off the fireplace, and an iron skillet hung on the wall by the fireplace. The freestanding corner cupboard stood in the front right corner (opposite the staircase), a location that put it in proximity to the kitchen, and windows to either side gave it the greatest available light. On the other side of the window sat a shelf two feet wide with a five-feet-high back of hand-rived, not sawn, wood. A later nineteenth-century clock sat on the shelf (fig. 4.11).

John Utley Wade may have brought the upscale corner cupboard, which he perhaps bought when he got married or maybe even earlier, when he moved from Goochland County in 1788 (pl. 7). His son Bradley was an

FIGURE 4.10. Wade cabin, Franklin County. Photograph by Francis Amos, c. 1980.

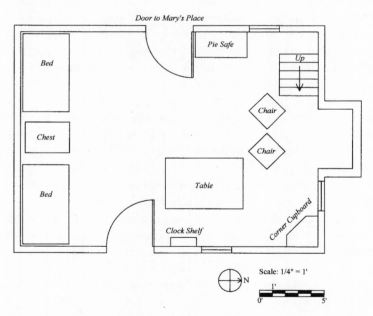

Door to Mary's Place

Bed

Pie Safe

Up

Chair

Chest

Chair

Bed

Table

Clock Shelf

Corner Cupboard

Scale: 1/4" = 1'

N

1'

0'   5'

FIGURE 4.11. Plan of Wade cabin and hypothetical furnishing plan. CAD by Christine Gesick; original drawing by Emily Pfotenhauer. Measured by Ann Smart Martin, Margaret Gonzalez, and Laquita Amos.

infant when the family arrived and but 11 years old when his father passed away. At age 22, Bradley married Rachel Lemon and went on to father five children. Land records suggest he built this structure about 1820, which means that at least three or four generations of Wades may have made this building their home.

As a child Margaret Ferguson visited Uncle George and Aunt Betty numerous times. Her memories of them paint a picture of two people who epitomized "farm self-sufficiency." They tended dozens of beehives. They kept a milk cow. They churned butter. They canned meat. They grew their own vegetables and grapes. Betty washed clothes on a washboard and hung the linens to dry on a bush. (As the niece remembers with humor, "they were a great example of the 'dirt won't kill you' philosophy.")

How did two, then three, twentieth-century adults use the tiny cabin space? Such congestion might have prompted friction, yet interviews with present-day men and women who grew up in one-room houses—known in architectural lingo as single-pen dwellings—show that close quarters do not necessarily lead to disharmony. To create their own intimate space, they used hanging quilts or found small corners or else they mentally segmented space.[76] Gonzalez recalls George and Betty's beds placed toe to toe on the southern end of the room separated by a small "nothing fancy" chest. The fireplace had a large hearth, with a swing arm trammel and a tin heater, and Betty and George kept a frying pan hung by the fireplace. They kept several splint-bottom chairs near the hearth and ate from them or while standing nearby, not bothering to use the wooden kitchen table, located on the south wall.

Like many houses in Franklin County, the cabin grew by accretion. The second cabin, attached to the first with a breezeway, dates from the later nineteenth century. When an older generation passed away, George and Betty moved into the original section, which still stands.

There were ancillary spaces and buildings that the family put to use. For instance, the Wades set up a hat manufactory in outbuildings. But these were protean spaces where use was dictated by need. George kept a deep layer of tobacco for his personal use on the partially floored loft of the cabin.

The Consumer Goods of George and Betty Wade

Oral history could perhaps tell us more about how the Wade family supported itself and to what extent they were integrated into the international economy, but the study of furnishings can add an entirely new dimension to the possible story. The poplar chest that sat between the two beds is a fine example of early nineteenth-century backcountry construction (fig. 4.12). It was built in a culture that honored solid craftsmanship and that valued proof

FIGURE 4.12. Chest with one drawer, Franklin County, early nineteenth century. Poplar. 20" x 40" x 23½". Private collection.

of construction, and so it was made with little attention to artifice: the dove-tailed corners are displayed, not hidden to make a clean surface. The chest has one unusual feature, a drawer with no hardware to assist in its opening, leaving it to be teased out by fingers pulling at the edges. At some point, the key to the chest lock broke (or was broken off), and someone curled the tip back and inserted it in a hole to pull open the drawer. That very step indicates that the need to secure the contents of the chest had given way to the wish for ease of opening the drawer. Its owner made do with what hardware was at hand. The action made manifest the then-current use—the *performance*—of the chest.

A chest with a single drawer represented an amalgam of ideas. Germans held onto their boxy, deep chests for storage long after their English neighbors turned to chests of drawers. Chests of drawers enabled compartmentalization, differentiation, and a more efficient use of space for belongings. This chest's lone drawer is a nod in that direction of spatial organization, and the chest's lock suggests that individual possessions were beginning to matter more and more.[77]

The Wades also used or kept a number of household goods that fall beneath the notice of inventory takers and do not appear on the lists of goods imported by merchants. One was a small iron fat pot to hang on a hook or a

FIGURE 4.13. Burl wood bowl and cast-iron chopper with hewn handle, Franklin County, probably nineteenth century. 7¼" x 10" (top). Private collection. The bottom of this durable bowl has a hole and a corncob stopper.

nail. It was the kind of low-technology implement used for hundreds of years to provide small-task lighting. Burning fat smoked and smelled and was difficult to keep lit, but it sufficed. A rusted hole had ended this pot's usefulness. Iron cooking implements like long-handled forks and spoons or spatulas for spearing and stirring were (at least partially) locally made. Other items that survived command attention even as they raise questions, such as the large bowl, ten inches in diameter and seven inches deep, carved from a giant burl from a tree. Marks on the interior surface suggest someone repeatedly chopped food in the bowl (fig. 4.13). But why have a round bowl for chopping, when a flat surface should do? Ceramic bowls were inexpensive and easier to keep clean.

Finally, a hollowed-out sourwood tree trunk, topped with a stretched skin and edged by a series of shoemaker's tacks, some of which are connected by silken thread string, puzzles the most devoted investigator (fig. 4.14). Posie Wade identified it as a "dunbull" or "bullroarer," an instrument that employed a drum-like tube to amplify the vibration of a string and create a low roaring sound. The oral history is most useful when considering this object. George, Betty, and Posie Wade's parents always kept the instrument atop their cupboard for easy access, so that they might summon family members who were hunting in the mountains or working distant fields, as its low roar carried much further than a dinner bell. They also used it to settle the bees in the family's hives. Its rather ancient Anglo-Saxon name is "dunbull."

These objects for living—cooking, lighting, and sounding—are disparate

FIGURE 4.14. Bullroarer or dunbull. Franklin County, nineteenth century. Wood, metal pins, fiber strings. 11" x 5½". Private collection.

parts of the world of goods. As scholars, we value them for their physicality, the evidence they offer, and the way they direct our attention to everyday activities. Because we can see a form, we can wonder about its use or its meanings. Reading material culture is not an art, not a science. It is at times a groping into the past with clues that are only readable through patterning. It is a scholar's confidence with ambiguity that comes from familiarity. It is only through the intensive study of a place, and perhaps through comparing it to multiple places and times, that we can use our clues to form meaningful ideas.

A final clue about the Wades is even more poignant because it is hidden. In an early photograph of George Wade in his cabin a clock sits on a shelf, a shelf that still exists. The shelf back is rough and large and the shelf ledge tiny, and the clock thus appears massive. Close examination of the shelf revealed that the ledge has shaped corners and bracket feet. The upper surface has a small lightly carved symbol (fig. 4.15), which the clock obscured. This one is a fylford or a fylfot cross, and it can be found on southern backcountry furniture, houses, even gravestones, and on some barns in south central Pennsylvania.[78] Its meaning is somewhat unclear, but in Pennsylvania Dutch

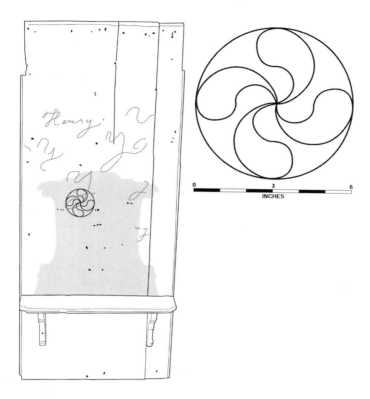

FIGURE 4.15. Left: drawing of clock shelf and backboard from Wade cabin. An eager writer scrawled the name Henry, along with several distinguishable letters (*y*'s). Small holes mark the placement of compass points to produce the swirling blades of the cross. The clock shown in George Wade's photograph and now owned by his great-niece is represented here by the shadow, showing where it sat on the clock shelf. Upper right: light sketching of fylfot cross. The slightly unsymmetrical fans and uneven scoring of the lightly carved lines show an unpracticed hand.

country it is a "hex" sign that wards off evil, an attribution that it did not have until the second half of the nineteenth century. A more generic iconographic idea is that it is part of a larger practice of blessing a house, a good luck sign. The small fylfot in the Wade cabin is not meant to be an ornament like others produced by marquetry or painting, such as found on boxes for spices and other valuables (fig. 4.16).

A second interpretation of these signs is that they are displays of work-manship, most specifically a play with geometry, compasses, and tools. Close examination of the shelf revealed the placement of small holes where the

FIGURE 4.16. Cabinet, central Piedmont North Carolina, 1780–90. Walnut, yellow pine, maple. 15" x 12" x 9". Courtesy, Old Salem, Inc.; Collection of the Museum of Early Southern Decorative Arts. Few pieces of furniture are decorated with just a single fylfot; most have the motif as a component of a larger more formal design, and as a rule these appear on tables and large case pieces, not small cabinets.

compass was centered. But the sketch is simplified. It is an off-center light scoring or tracing in wood. Lightly penciled near it is a name—only the first name "Henry" is legible. According to Francis Amos the Frederick Rives house in Franklin County also had a fylfot, and although on a mantel rather than a shelf, it too was an off-center sketch. Were these just schoolboy geometric drawings? If so, why did they take that particular form?

A symbol, a name, an object, a building—together they should tell a neat story. But the clues seldom add up neatly. Frederick Rives and his family were English and had come from eastern Amelia County. The Wades were early Scots-Irish settlers. Their corner cupboard is a fine example of earlier and English-inspired craftsmanship, probably from an eastern part of Virginia. Their cabin plan was common throughout the region for a century or more.

Perhaps the clues offer a particular corrective to the study of the world of goods. One of the advantages of living in a newly forming society that offered different possibilities is that more choices could be made.

The five actions described in this chapter—differentiate, simplify, exaggerate, hybridize, and replicate—are simply ways to imagine how the residents of John Hook's world, including the Wades, navigated through change using material things. At first, we are astonished by how little seems to have changed. With deeper analysis, however, it becomes clear that backcountry people did not just replicate what those before them had done. The Wade cabin and its partial contents teach us that backcountry people had many choices. They might not make a choice to replicate, to keep apart, to simplify, or to hybridize. They could choose to do all.

The backcountry was a transcultural space. By the end of the eighteenth century, the people who lived there or arrived there already had expectations that were hybridized or creolized. We persist in feeling a sense of baroqueness—not quite rightness—only if we keep hoping for neat boundaries and edges. This entirely different snapshot of the world of goods provides clear evidence of the way that traditional peoples used what was useful and changed what was necessary. We should not romanticize Franklin County. For every farming family like George, Posie, and Betty Wade, there are just as many families and individuals who went to town, went to college, maybe even brought back home new agricultural techniques learned at nearby Virginia Polytechnic Institute and State University.

Historical memory, oral history, and material culture are tough forms of evidence. Sometimes serendipity prevails. As I busily analyzed and wrote the Wade Cabin story, I had a note to myself that said "Pedro Sloan?" I was reminding myself to go find "The Way of Life in Turner's Creek Valley Sixty Years Ago" by Pedro T. Sloan, written in February 1943.

I discovered Sloan's typescript over a decade ago at the Virginia Division of Historic Landmarks in the "General Files" for Franklin County. It had, quite frankly, joined my personal version of the general files for Franklin County: a large file cabinet chock full of primary materials related to this manuscript. But I never knew what to do with the essay. Because it had been written in 1943, I doubted it held any material relevant to my investigations of the eighteenth century. Sloan wrote it at a time when Appalachian culture had gained celebrity and notoriety (as a land of hillbillies and moonshiners). Sloan's citation of a historian who had described a valley as "the land that time forgot" probably meant that the story was romanticized. As he began to describe the one-room twenty-four- by twenty-foot cabin owned by his grandfather, Thomas Hale, he admitted that a reader might consider the old-fashioned ways incredible, but he averred that "customs and ways of living were still in use here that had been abandoned in other states and in Tidewater, Virginia for one hundred years."[79]

The valley that he described lay in the "southwest corner of Blackwater District, in the mountainous section of Franklin County. The little valley extends east and west about four miles, and is about two and one-half miles wide between the tops of the mountains." Through it flows Turner's Creek, known as Ragland Branch in old deeds. According to Sloan the eighteenth-century settlers of the valley were Scots-Irish, and many of their descendents still lived there. Among nineteen different family names he listed three jumped out at me: Hale, Sloan, and Wade. The Wade cabin stood in Sloan's valley "that time forgot."

FIVE

Setting the Stage, Playing the Part

Stores as Shopping Spaces

Perhaps you may think me wrong in sending [an order] for so many fine
Goods espetially for Women, but I assure you they are much in demand, the
Reason of which is the People that goes down the Country for these Goods
generally is afraid of not bring[ing] those things which will please there
Wives and Daughters and often willingly forgettes them entirely, whereas
were the Articles that they Generally want in a Back Store . . . they could
see them themselves. I'm certain that they would look no further for them.

John Hook to William Donald, 1766

BY THE END of the eighteenth century, retail stores constituted the
most common nondomestic buildings on the Virginia landscape—in
towns, at crossroads, or on plantations.

The precise lines of triangulation connecting merchant, customer, and
artifact varied considerably and reflected the differences among the per-
formers, the setting of the stage, and the store's location in town or country.
The richest matron and the poorest slave both faced a merchant across the
counter in the store. To be consumers, wives stepped free from their husbands, slaves from masters, and girls from mothers, at least to a limited
degree, and entered into a distinct relationship with the merchant, the market, and the world of goods. But men, too, stepped out of their more comfortable business identities to negotiate the vagaries of fashion and consumer choice. It is in this sense that stores served as stages on which people
acted out larger cultural paradigms and developed new economic and social
scenarios.

Refocusing the lens one more time to examine the world of goods in the
backcountry leads to the study of the store. The building's form and finishing both shaped and responded to the dilemmas of social action in commercial life. The merchant had to display goods in a way that entreated purchase yet prevented damage, loss, or theft. In the process, he simultaneously
worked to limit access for some and to encourage the entrée of others. His

role was to make money. How he achieved his goal—and how well he performed—tells much about the larger world of Virginia society.

As consumers became more particular about the kinds of things for sale, merchants also competed by providing better shopping experiences. At the beginning of the eighteenth century, having goods suitable to the market served as a basic predictor of a merchant's success. A century later, a merchant needed to store, display, and actively present a wide array of fashionable amenities and luxuries to maintain patronage. He also had to provide an appropriate consumption arena—a fixed place of a recognizable form, one that controlled the access and movement of his customers but simultaneously released the powerful desires of consumption. The merchant took on a new character role, and a stereotypical figure thus emerged: the man behind the counter, willing to please.

The shift in business practices brings to the fore a multitude of questions because the physical environs of shopping remain largely unstudied. Did men and women jostle at a counter? Were objects for sale draped about or enveloped in wrappers? How did the Virginia experience compare to the highly ornamented and sophisticated world of London shopping? How did Virginia structures evolve? What did it mean for a store to be "completely fitted up"?[1]

This chapter examines stores as both buildings and consumption spaces and then considers the quality of the experience of shopping in the Virginia backcountry. Architectural fieldwork—visits to measure and draw store buildings that still stand—and documents such as floor plans, building contracts, and insurance policies as well as correspondence supply considerable evidence of the size of the buildings and the room arrangement; placement of windows, doors, chimneys, shelves, and counters; and interior and exterior wall finishes. Activity in store accounts in combination with information gleaned from data contained in myriad personal, local, and state documents provide an image of the customers and their family relationships. Although the two sets of evidence do not fit neatly together, the spatial study forms the backdrop for functional use and the relations between merchant and customer and the account-based study allows the scenes of travel and family visits to emerge. Together they illuminate the experience of shopping in John Hook's world.

Consumption Spaces

Vending consumer goods in Virginia required pragmatism. Although trade cards and prints intimate that London merchants mounted elegant displays in their stores, their counterparts in colonial Virginia quickly learned to keep goods covered to avoid devastating losses that could be inflicted by insects, rodents, and moisture. In 1720 John Bates's stock, for example, had lost considerable value because fabrics and clothing had been eaten by rats or moths, the drugget had suffered the depredations of both, and some handkerchiefs were "spoiled and rotten." Such problems may also explain why most of the first merchants in backcountry Virginia did not want much stock left at the end of each selling season.[2]

Merchants also had to be practical about organizing and sorting their myriad goods. James Robinson advised young John Turner to keep his goods in "proper order" and to take them down often and retie them, presumably in papers.[3] Yet more than one merchant complained that he and his assistants were all too "frequently called upon to shew [their goods] & hitherto have had as often the trouble of putting them up again."[4]

Over the course of the eighteenth century Virginia shopkeepers found solutions to the problems of security and access and storage and display. Three inventories of store goods, two with an accompanying plan or room size, provide rare evidence of the detail of goods, their organization, and their location. In combination, they allow an assessment of change over time and illuminate differences between rural and urban stores. As the decades passed, growing consumer desires tilted the balance toward greater access and display, and the process occurred more rapidly in urban settings.

In 1728, the appraisers of Richard Walker's store in rural Middlesex County carefully listed the goods for sale and defined seven spaces by name: "store loft," "below stairs," "under the shelves on the floor," "lower floor," "middle floor," "new house," and "dwelling house." Walker had stored some goods in an assortment of containers: casks, chests, crates, barrels, trunks, and boxes, many of them in the store loft. One of the store shelves held hose, hats, and eight pieces of fabric. Numerous books, shoes, ironmongery (tools and small metal goods), and small items like beads and spectacles, he had left "under the shelves on the floor." A single box on the floor contained a jumble of stoneware, glass, marking irons, combs, needles, pewter, sugar, and books. In the "new house" he had stashed assorted tools, metal chafing dishes, engineer rules, a hogshead of ship bread (hardtack), two boxes of pipes, and a loose assortment of earthen chamber pots, punch bowls, and other ceramics. Scattered in the rooms of the "dwelling house" were dozens of pairs of hose and gloves as well as pins and primers. The overall picture is one of chaotic combinations of objects and spaces.[5]

This early eighteenth-century rural store contrasts mightily with John Hook's in rural Franklin County seventy-three years later (fig. 5.1). The court-appointed commissioners prepared a detailed inventory of the store in 1801. That inventory in combination with evidence from the still-surviving building and a shelving plan that Hook prepared some years earlier for his New

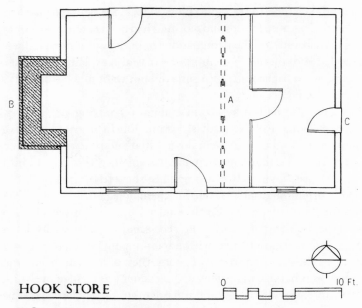

HOOK STORE   0   10 Ft.

A. Door location in original partition
B. Chimney 2nd quarter 19th century
C. Door early 20th century

FIGURE 5.1. Plan of Hook's store, 1783. Drawing, Carl Lounsbury; measured by Carl Lounsbury, Ann Smart Martin, and Meredith Moody, 1991. For this store Hook also stuck to the traditional commercial plan; he designed it with a store room and merchant's counting room. The northern wall faced the road, and a glass panel or "light" above the door and modillioned eaves served to announce to passersby and customers alike that this was no rude cabin. During the nineteenth century, a subsequent owner moved the building for use as a slave quarter, at which time interior walls and the fireplace were relocated and a door added. Subsequently a second structure was built and connected to this one with a breezeway, and the structure served as a tenant's quarters.

London store (fig. 5.2) offer strong evidence of how merchants organized and displayed goods in rural Virginia stores by the end of the eighteenth century.[6] The store room (that is, the room in which the goods were shelved) measured fifteen by twenty and had shelves on at least one wall. According to the inventory, he also had a section filled with pigeonholes (table 5.1). Ten contained 124 types of buttons, wrapped in protective papers. Two held razors, and others were filled with an extraordinary array of small consumer goods, from knives and forks to ribbons, nearly all wrapped in paper. Elsewhere around the store he had barrels of ginger, brimstone, shot, and pepper, casks of brandy and whiskey, and even a freestanding anvil. Hook kept

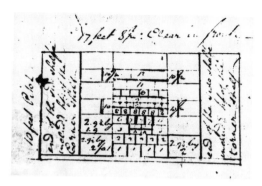

FIGURE 5.2. Shelving plan, John Hook's store, New London, c. 1771. Hook Papers, Duke University. The plenitude of storage for small consumer items like ribbons, buttons, and even knives and forks that are documented to have been in the small pigeon holes in a later inventory of Hook's store shows how important the smallest and most inexpensive items were to daily business. Goods like buttons and ribbons were inexpensive and were good for encouraging shopping because they might call for repeat visits to choose and buy.

breakable items mostly in trunks, such as the 41 different sizes of looking glasses, the glass goblets, the decanters, and the vials. Creamware filled three crates, and window glass two boxes. That the commissioners listed each of the textiles separately, and did likewise for the individual books and household goods, such as pewter, tin, and iron, suggests those items may have been stacked on shelves or hung in relative proximity to each other rather than stored in boxes. The two pair of small brass scales and weights likely sat on the counter, probably close to his few pounds of tea and indigo as well as the barrels of brimstone, pepper, and shot that Hook also sold by the ounce or pound. Boxes of chocolate, bags of ginger, and bladders of putty may have been on shelves near barrels of copperas or brown sugar, seed cotton in bags, bushels of salt, chests of tea, and tin candle boxes full of candles.

The snapshot of the contents of Hook's store presents an image remarkably different from the jumble recorded at Richard Walker's store many years before. While barrels and boxes probably lined the walls at both stores, the picture of John Hook's store is one of relative order. He had consigned small consumer goods to specific pigeonholes; he kept breakable items packed together. He also kept his immense array of fabric organized in a single group and perhaps stored it on the shelves.

In 1797 Richmond merchant William Parrott bought fire insurance. Less than a year later he died. The floor plan of the store in the insurance records and the inventory of the estate in the probate records provide a remarkably detailed record of a store in an urban area of Virginia at the end of the eighteenth

TABLE 5.1. "Sundry Articles Contained in Pidgeon Holes" in John Hook's Hale's Ford Store, 1801

124 papers buttons, different kinds, some broken
36 papers thread, different kinds, silk and twist
1 paper ribbands, different kinds, 6 bunches tape, 1 ditto bobbin
shirt buttons, 3 parcels thread, hat bands, 38 ps ribband
1 paper black silk handkfs, 4 papers ink power
40 papers pins, 2 bunches bent combs, 2 boxes wafers
1 paper tobacco boxes, 1 paper spectacles, 1 paper snuff boxes
1 paper nutmeg graters, 2 papers needles, 3 ditto thimbles
9 papers razors, 2 papers desk mountains
12 bundle pins, 2 boxes wafers, 3 papers ink power
1 paper sleeve buttons, 6 papers small buttons
4 papers bridle bitts, 6 papers scissors, 9 papers snuffers
6 ditto combs, 2 papers cupboard locks
1 paper sewing silk, 3 boxes wafers, 4 ps ribbands
1 paper sadle boxes, 4 papers spurs, 7 papers awl blades
4 papers cutto knives, 2 ditto pen knives, 5 ditto bridle bitts
11 papers scissars, 1 ditto knee buckles, 1 ditto saddle bosses
4 ditto screws, 1 bunch knitting needles, 1 ditto compasses
12 papers knives and forks, 4 ditto shoes knives
1 ditto nutmeg graters, 1 paper 2 foot rules
2 bundles gilt buckles, 1 paper of money weights
5 papers cubboard locks, 1 paper bridle bitts
2 ditto center bitts, 1 paper butcher knives
1 gun lock, 2 pr sheep shears, 2 papers wood screws
1 paper white chappel needles, 1 paper shoe tacks
1 ditto table butts

Source: Inventory of John Hook's Property Relieved by the Supersedens Issued from the High Court of Chancery, Sworn 16 January 1802, Ross v. Hook, U.S. Circuit Court, Richmond, Virginia.

century.[7] At thirty by twenty, Parrott's store room was twice the size of John Hook's. Shelves completely lined two walls and at least a part of another. Carefully grouped grocery items, followed by textiles and clothing, filled the east wall shelves. The far end of those shelves and the south and west wall shelves held stacks of less expensive but breakable ceramics and glassware. Shelves also ran across the front two windows, and one held a stack of glass plates. Bushels and barrels of foodstuffs—corn, salt, potatoes, preserved fish, and the like—stood on the floor to the west. Several casks of alcohol stood nearby. An ancillary lumber house (a period term for storehouse) contained large quantities of alcohol and additional sacks of salt and barrels of corn.

These three inventories illustrate the transition to spaces with specialized architectural fittings and the shift toward displaying goods in an orderly way. Although some rural storekeepers left objects in shipping crates in late eighteenth-century rural stores, the jumble and chaos that characterized Walker's early eighteenth-century store had by then vanished. In urban stores, the need to display goods dominated. Whereas Hook kept ceramics and other breakables in protective containers, Parrott stacked them on shelves for all to see and even placed some in the front windows to entice customers in from the street. Self-service shopping was hardly considered, and merchants still worked hard to protect (be it from rodents or sticky fingers), to show, and to sell their goods. Nonetheless, the balance on the scales had shifted from protection toward display.

The buildings themselves give further evidence of the growing importance of wooing, yet controlling, customers. Before the second quarter of the nineteenth century, most Virginians used the same building vocabulary for stores and domestic dwellings. Some standing stores became dwellings and vice versa. When offering real estate for sale some sellers hinted that a store could be transformed to a dwelling at small expense. As with houses, the size of a store building depended on its owner's wealth, location, or desire to impress. Interior space on the ground floor ranged from three hundred to one thousand plus square feet and included at least two distinct spaces: a store or sales room and a counting room or office.[8]

The placement of the building on the lot, its alignment to the street, the sizes of the two main rooms as well as any additional rooms, and the location of doors and windows differed from store to store, but one simple organizing plan of two core rooms predominated. In one version the gable end faced onto a street: a large front room served as the store, and the back one constituted the counting room. The fenestration is important: the placement of windows and doors signaled it as a purpose-built store structure. A central door and flanking windows pierced the gable end, and if the structure had an upstairs storage area, a hoist and upper door facilitated lifting boxes and crates in and out. Windows clustered toward the back of the side walls, lighting the back of the store room and the counting room. The intervening broad uninterrupted expanse of wall allowed for continuous shelving, even though it left an asymmetrical facade.

In the other version of the store plan, eaves along the long side of the building faced the street: the store room and counting room thus stood side by side, and in many instances each room had an exterior door. This allowed access to the office, even if the store room remained locked.

In both building types the store functioned as the heart of the structure. It was often square or nearly square and ranged in size from about two hundred to five hundred square feet.

John Hook opted to place his New London store at the edge of his two-acre lot and positioned the building so that the long side ran parallel to the street, which meant he did not have to use a front-back arrangement but could instead design the rooms in a side-by-side configuration (see ch. 1, fig. 1.3). The forty-two- by twenty-foot ground floor had three spaces: store, counting room, and storage room that Hook referred to as the "lumber room." The twenty- by twenty-foot store had a two-foot, ten-inch-wide counter across the middle of the room that confined shoppers to a space eight feet deep. The street side of the room had a central door and two equidistant windows. Opposite the entrance and several feet behind the counter lay a windowless ten-foot-high wall furnished with twelve shelves and fifty pigeonholes, ranging from four-and-a-half to twenty inches wide. Three tiers of cross-divided drawers, one of which served as a cash drawer, lay underneath the merchant's side of the counter and filled out the room's fixed storage spaces. An interior door located near the front wall on the public side of the counter opened into the eight- by twenty-foot lumber room; a second interior door, this one located slightly behind the counter on the opposite wall, opened into the fourteen-by twenty-foot counting room. The windowless lumber room had an exterior door that opened onto the street. The counting room had a street-side window, a gable-end fireplace, and both a door and a window on the rear wall.

The store had discrete zones: one for customers, one for the merchant. The counter and shelves framed the merchant and his realm. At the counter he measured out cloth, weighed commodities such as gunpowder, personally displayed the countless small items stored at his arm's reach behind him, hastily wrote and tallied up sales entries in the daybook, took in money, and made change. The propensity for small items to disappear from display on open counters can be seen by the small glass cases increasingly for sale. The most specialized stores included more specialized glass casing, such as the "three mahogany counters, with glass fronts, fit for a jeweller's shop" advertised in Charleston, South Carolina, in 1803.[9] Drawers underneath counters also allowed control of goods and money. The counter likewise served as a barrier over which a thief must reach to acquire his or her prize.

Hook, like many merchants, used architectural fittings to define zones of exclusion. A patron advanced merely to be stopped by the counter midway; only the customer's gaze could go beyond that barrier. Courthouses and Anglican churches also had exclusionary zones, but these were more often marked by railings and contained the symbolic elements of the power of church and state. In commercial enterprises like stores, the demarcated power was the world of goods.

The counter separated a physical space and a symbolic one. Philip Freneau's poem "The Village Merchant," which first appeared in 1792, recounts the travails endured by a young farmer who dreamed of becoming a merchant and envisioned a counter "behind whose breast-work none but he might stand." Only a "brother merchant from some other place" could broach his place of honor.[10] By the early nineteenth century "Life behind the counter" became a catch phrase for a shopkeeper's career.

Few standing stores contain their original shelving and trim. Ghost lines on the walls of the White Store, a structure probably built in the middle of the eighteenth century in Isle of Wight County, indicate that an elaborate system of pigeonholes and shelves covered the entire back wall. In King William County, the store at Marmion Plantation also had extensive shelving on the walls, and nails and hooks high on the walls suggest the shopkeeper hung many items for easy viewing. The counter, which disappeared along with the original flooring many years ago, likely fronted the shelves. The builder constructed that plantation store building much like a mid-eighteenth-century house; he sheathed the store room with unpainted vertical boards and capped the walls with crown molding. As with the White store and most others in Virginia, the Marmion Plantation store had no stove or fireplace.

The other major room in store buildings was the counting room or office, in which the merchant tended his account books, ordered new goods, handled correspondence, and entertained customers. The finishes used in most counting rooms paralleled those used on domestic interiors—lathe and plaster walls, some of them adorned with wallpaper, chair rails, and wash boards. Most had a stove or fireplace as well as good furnishings. Chairs, drinking vessels, and tea services all played a role in the wooing of customers.[11] The floor plans of various stores indicate that merchants paid special attention to regulating access to this space. Some gave it a separate entrance from the street; others preferred that the only entrance be through a door located behind the counter in the store room.

The counting room of Hooe and Harrison in Alexandria, Virginia, contained desks, tables, chairs, scales, money chests, and a bed. The equipment for writing included quires of paper, ink bottles, lead pencils, Dutch quills, paper cutters, and seals. Other items might include published treatises on trade and law as well as "compting House Candlesticks" (valued at an extraordinary £75.00) to aid work during the evenings.[12]

Ancillary structures and spaces often rounded out a store's setting. Some merchants had a need for (and could afford) extra storage and sleeping for shopkeepers, apprentices, or slaves and hence added extra rooms on the ground floor or an upper floor. Clerks often slept on the premises for security; either in the counting room or directly above. John Hook's counting room contained a bed. Additional structures often included sheds. Merchants also might add stables, warehouses, granaries, and log houses for storage of goods and for arriving slaves they intended to sell. Yet more elaborate sites boasted two stores—one to accommodate dry goods, the other to hold liquors and bulky wholesale items. Basic needs such as receiving customers and making sales; storing, unpacking, and/or displaying goods (both wet and dry); keeping books, conducting business; entertaining important clients; and receiving slaves or servants on errands or their own shopping trips dictated the use of space in all these commercial establishments.

Many merchants combined domestic space for their own families and storage space for goods in a single building. The Dudley Digges store property in Yorktown, for example, included a "commodious Brick store-house which has necessary Apartments for private family."[13] But precisely how the structure was divided to allow for these very different uses remains unclear. Given the labor required to move goods, many merchants likely used the ground floor of these buildings for storage and placed the family quarters upstairs, providing separate access to the latter by an interior side passage or an exterior alley door.

More is known about the shopping experience. Most store rooms matched the size of an ordinary Virginia dwelling.[14] The counter and an inside door controlled access to a merchant's goods and services. Light emanated through the windows, most of them located on just one wall; thus the store may have been relatively dark. On cloudy days, the merchant likely had to pull items from the shelves and pigeonholes behind the counter and carry them to the better-lit side of the room when trying to make a sale. The absence of a stove or fireplace left the space cold in the winter; the lack of cross ventilation made it hot in the summer. Customers invited into the counting room could sit, socialize, or haggle over both goods and financial terms. Those who did not make it that far still had the goods within their purview. While many items remained wrapped in papers or stored in hogsheads, boxes, or other containers, merchants enticingly placed a number of items on shelves in plain view.

Overall, a broad range of design options were available for Virginia stores, just as they were for Virginia dwellings. The early rural stores provided little more than shelter for the valuable stock of goods inside. Increasingly, however, merchants invested considerable money in these structures; stores and their related buildings ranged in value from £300 to £1,000 in the later eighteenth century. The size and interior finishes of these stores reflect permanency and year-round use as well as a need to store and display a vast range of consumer goods both to create order and convey a knowledge of fashion. Important business clients had to be courted. Storekeepers, clerks, or enslaved workers had to be housed. Store complexes with multiple ancillary structures may well have resembled little plantations.

By the third quarter of the eighteenth century, even backcountry stores tended to be purpose-built single-function buildings. That specialization also means that the act of consumption had become distinctive. For many Virginians the store building became as defining a place on the landscape as a house, church, tavern, and courthouse. Behind those doors lay a whole world—a world of color and fashion, hard-nosed bargaining, and impulsive decisions.

Between 1750 and 1830, market economics and consumer demand shifted dramatically throughout the Western world. Retail stores stocked more and different goods to please more and different people. The ability of consumers to see and touch and handle new things spawned new desires. How Virginia stores evolved as specific shopping environments tells us about the particular economy that produced them and the society that frequented them.

Virginia merchants relied mainly on exchanging their imported manufactured goods for customers' agricultural products. As the shift occurred from a tobacco monoculture to a more diverse market economy at midcentury and beyond, the number of petty entrepreneurs rose. Merchants could no longer readily judge a customer's ability to pay. In response to an expanding customer base that increasingly included people from differing economic groups, races, and genders, the merchants changed their stores and techniques. The need to display goods to entreat purchase yet control the goods to prevent loss and the need to allow access to people on the economy's margins yet still court patronage of the well-heeled continued to guide merchants in how they allowed the consumption performance to unfold. That slaves bought ribbons did not release them from bondage, that women bought teapots did not make the legal or household structure less paternal. This consumption, nonetheless, constituted a new social performance in an economic setting. Thus the dialectic of stage and performance continued to evolve. Incremental changes in form and fitting began to create an environment that encouraged shopping as a leisure activity, even in the eighteenth century. In the decades that followed, purveyors of goods would continue to peel back the skin of the building, insert multiple large windows filled with commodities, and add heating and lighting, thereby ultimately introducing the notion of shopping as entertainment and leading to a new triangulation of merchant, customer, and consumer goods.

Shopping as Action

Because few people in colonial America described the shopping experience, Sarah Kemble Knight's account of her trip between Boston and New York in 1704 provides a noteworthy opening commentary on the demeanor and behavior of rural people coming into a store. When a customer entered a store, the first question asked was not about the availability of the goods, but the merchant's gruff "is Your Pay Ready?" The answer allowed the merchant to establish the prices he quoted, based on credit arrangements needed or the kind of currency offered. The very question also established the power relationship. Knight's description of one customer, a "tall country fellow," is, like other characters in her journal, a bit of a comic sketch, yet it offers plentiful detail:

> He advanc't to the middle of the Room, makes an Awkward Nodd, and spitting a great deal of Aromatick Tincture, he gave a scrape with his shovel like shoo, leaving a small shovel full of dirt on the floor, made a full stop, Hugging his own pretty Body with his hands under his arms, Stood staring rown'd him like a Catt let out of a Basket. At last . . . he opened his mouth and said, have you any Ribenen for Hatbands to sell I pray. The Questions and Answers about the pay being past, the Ribin is bro't and opened. Bump-kin Simpers, cryes[,] its confounded Gay I vow; and beckoning to the door, in comes Jone Tawdry, dropping about 50 curtsies, and stands by him: hee shows her the Ribin. Law You, sais shee, its right Gent, do You take it, tis dreadfully pretty. Then she enquires have You any hood silk I pray? wh[ich] being brought and bought. Have you any thred silk to sew it wth says shee, wh[ich] being accomodated with they Departed.[15]

According to Knight, the poor country folk who entered the store generally stood "a great while speechless and sometimes don't say a word til they are askt what they want." Knight attributed this to the "Awe they stand in of the merchants." Customers were often indebted "and must take what they [the merchants] bring [out to the counter] without Liberty to choose for them-selves." Knight, a wealthy merchant's daughter, had little sympathy for these consumers, pointing out that they too often made the merchant wait long for his pay.

Knight's words draw stark attention to the nature of the relationship be-tween merchant and poor ordinary customer at an early date. She took note of the absolute discomfort, gestures of humility, body language, wonder-ment at the beauty of ribbons, and even that Jone Tawdry waited outside until her husband beckoned her (fig. 5.3).

Another account, which dates from seven decades later, alludes to the shopping experiences of the wealthiest families. Virginian Landon Carter tersely recorded in his diary an account of the shopping trip of his 24-year-old daughter Lucy. Written in his customary complaining tone, he noted on Saturday, October 23, 1775, "Lucy as usual is much in want of necessaries." She had planned to go to Blane's store but having heard that a better selec-tion existed elsewhere, she went there instead. Her father gave her 7 Span-

year ?

FIGURE 5.3. *The Chandler's Shop Gossip, or, Wonderful News.* Engraving. Courtesy, The Colonial Williamsburg Foundation. Depictions of store interiors are rare, and most of those that do exist show urban, more high-end places. The simple interior in this image accurately reflects that of many Virginia stores.

ish dollars to spend, and she returned in time for dinner with a fan, some ribbons, and "several such prodigious nothings," for which she spent much more than the cash given to her. Landon Carter's credit was good in any store, and so she could—and did—spend freely. As her father wryly observed, "I am trusted and that is her comfort."[16]

People of the Carters' stature reversed the power relationship between merchant and customer. Although merchants treated the Jone Tawdrys with disdain, they handled the Lucy Carters with the complaisance and deference owed to a social superior. As the daughter of one of the wealthiest men in the colony, Lucy Carter brought welcome business. Both purchased ribbons, but their personal comfort in the world of goods presents stark contrasts. Jone stood stock-still and wide-eyed in the shopping environment; Lucy, who had far finer things at home, did not. While shopping provided an enjoyable activity that took Lucy out of the house and allowed her to augment her already fashionable things, she did not take the same intense pleasure as Jone Tawdry in their color and visual appeal or any thrill in their ownership. For the rich, consumption was a different experience.

A third shopping scenario emerges from court records. In 1765 Elizabeth Hog, daughter of a wealthy planter, gave a deposition to the Augusta County, Virginia, court concerning an incorrect billing for a ribbon acquired when she and a friend, Priscilla Christian, daughter of a merchant, stayed in Staunton for the opening of the fair three years before. Her testimony paints a vivid scene in which a more modern form of trade—an accounting of goods in debt—came squarely up against a customary fair-day gifting obligation.[17]

The 24-year-old Priscilla asked Elizabeth to accompany her to Mr. Crow's store, which lay across the street from the courthouse, to get a fairing (an inexpensive gift or tribute purchased or presented at fairs). Elizabeth initially demurred; however, when Thomas Crow, standing on the doorstep of his brother William's store, waved his hand, beckoning the girls to come over, she relented. At about the same time, Crow's sister-in-law called him out of the store, and as he passed by the girls, Miss Priscilla asked him if he was going to give them a "fairing." "Stay till I come back," he replied. So they entered the store. Priscilla promptly made the same demand of Joseph Bell "who was then within the counter." After giving no reply for some time, he took from the shelves "two pieces, or bolts, of ribbon, and told her to take her choice." So he cut off a yard and gave it to her, but Priscilla then asked if he would give one to her friend Elizabeth, which he did. Soon after Priscilla asked if he would not give them a fairing from Thomas Crow, so he took off two yards from another bolt of ribbon and gave each of them one. The persistent Miss Priscilla had done a good day's work and soon afterward the two of them departed.

Poor Elizabeth. She subsequently stopped at the store to pay off her account and met with owner William Crow: "on hearing the articles read over with which she stood charged," Elizabeth noted with surprise that the list included a yard of ribbon. She objected, stating she had never bought a yard of ribbon in the store, yet Bell had charged it to her along with a yard of linen that she had bought that same day. She told William Crow (the plaintiff) that Joseph Bell (the defendant) had made a present of a ribbon to her and Priscilla.

All three examples illuminate the lines of triangulation among merchants, customers, and objects. All contain a story of shopping. All present women as consumers. Because women, too, had roles on the stage of consumerism, their scenes raise issues of power in a world legally dominated by men. According to evidence in the novels of eighteenth-century English writers, shopping had become gendered behavior, a constructed role. Author Henry Fielding's tales suggest that as a male activity, business by nature was both orderly and systematic, and that women by nature were inconstant, weak beings who could not resist the bedazzlement of things and smooth seductive words of shopkeepers and who thus became profligate spenders.[18] The spreading perception of the trickster merchant and the easily beguiled woman prompted author Daniel Defoe to scoff that such a notion was the stuff of "a ballad and a song." He pointed out that men could be just as "impertinent as women" and added that "it would be a terrible satire upon the ladies, to say that they will not be pleased or engaged either with good wares or good pennysworth, with reasonable good language, or good manners" but need "long harangues, simple, fawning, and flattering language . . . to set off the goods and wheedle them in to lay out their money."[19]

Benjamin Franklin's writings offered the colonial equivalent to the rhetoric of English literary figures. His Anthony Afterwit pursued an increasingly expensive lifestyle that led to ruin; his Poor Richard complained of "silks and satins that put out the kitchen fire." In the columns of the *Pennsylvania Gazette,* anonymous shopkeepers and customers sparred, most of the accounts claiming merchants used trickery and fraud to seduce the inherently weak women to buy more goods than needed. But merchant and household accounts and contemporary diaries and letters indicate that women found shopping a serious and time-consuming duty. They considered shopping a utilitarian duty (to fulfill needs) that involved searching for value ("a good pennyworth"), building relationships (shopping for relatives and friends), and cementing business cooperation (wives of factors shopping for wives of planters). Shopping thus was a task, prerogative, duty, weakness, and pleasure for women and often performed by them.

Despite the close connection between women, domestic economy, and shopping, women figure little in historians' accounts of the eighteenth-century Virginia retail trade. Most of them present the store as a male realm.[20] Some attribute the absence of women to legal restrictions and inheritance patterns, perhaps because few women held separate accounts in stores during the eighteenth century and beyond.[21]

Account books provide a record of purchases, not documentation of store activity. Excluded from notation in all account books are many people who entered and left the store without making a purchase. Merchants had little reason to note those who came to socialize or shop for recreation. Similarly, neither Hook nor his competitors cited persons who left disappointed in the hunt for an item. Nor did they note whether wives, children, or slaves accompanied the customers. Also absent from the ledgers are the names of those who dealt solely in cash; however, the daily notations of cash taken in suggest that at least one person each day paid Hook in hard currency at the time of purchase. Finally, in transferring entries from the daybook, Hook, like other merchants, sometimes recorded a person's multiple visits in a single day as one account entry.

The ledger entries thus do not reflect activity that did not need to be accounted for in some way. That is a key understanding. Although broad questions abound, store accounts can only answer them in limited ways. For instance, any assessment of how busy a store was requires framing careful questions. On an average day during 1771, fifty items were charged on various accounts at Hook's store. Dividing the number of named customers by the number of days covered in the account book yields an average of ten customers a day. But a day-by-day analysis demonstrates that the customer visits to the store varied widely in the autumn of 1771. On some days, only a few people stopped by to make small purchases. On other days, Hook was out of the store, and because he had no assistant, he had no business.[22] On multiple days fifteen people came and purchased goods or paid cash on their accounts.[23] Does that make the place bustling or lonely?

An analysis of Hook's accounts on the daily level of business allows a nuanced view of how a store system worked, and how actual people used the store over a longer period. In combination, his daily record of sales and his correspondence from those same days detail the flow of goods in and out of the shop. The purchases of his more regular customers provide a micropattern of everyday store activity, one that shows shopping to be a male activity, a female activity, and a family activity. Following the objects and households simultaneously also animates the actions of women and, to some extent, slaves.

A Daily Calendar of Shopping

David Ross and John Hook's new store had a slow beginning. Even though Hook had traveled to Petersburg in the summer and selected goods, there had been a long silence from his new partner and a mere trickle of goods. Ross had been caught in Norfolk during a horrific epidemic of yellow fever and had been sick for several weeks. During his illness, no one stepped in to supervise the shipping of Hook's goods. Indeed, rivals Alexander Stewart and Robert Donald had even "enticed away" the wagons that Hook had arranged, which prompted the once again well Ross to hire new wagons at his own expense.[24] The letter Hook received from Ross, outlining his renewed efforts, cheered Hook. He had heard that Ross was dead, and the rumor fit the unexpected long silence from Petersburg.

The lack of goods in Hook's store coupled with the fact that it was a busy agricultural time probably explains the relatively low number of purchases in September and early October. By the end of October, the daily activity began to build, and the wagons filled with goods likely arrived on October 19 and October 22.

Hook's relief proved short-lived. On October 26 he complained in detail that the charges on the invoice included many goods that had not arrived. From London he was missing delft and stoneware dishes, looking glasses, lampblack, even mop heads and buckle brushes. From Whitehaven, he was missing nails. He had only one hogshead of rum and no tar; he needed sheeting, shoes, saddles, cutlery, Irish linen rolls, and German osnaburg. Hook directed Ross to order rice and candles from Norfolk and noted he had six or eight hogsheads of tobacco ready to be shipped. He added a postscript to his long missive: "writg Paper much wanted."[25]

During the next two weeks, transportation problems plagued the shipments, and Hook bitterly grumbled that his competitors received shipments, but he did not. Finally, the supply logjam broke. On November 7, Hook received at least four more wagonloads of goods. During the second week of November, goods poured in from Warwick and Rocky Ridge, and quantities of butter and tobacco that Hook had amassed at the store flowed eastward.[26]

On November 26, the largest shipment of goods finally arrived. On the same day, the Bedford County court swung into session. The busiest autumn days at John Hook's store coincided with court dates. The meeting of the court provided an important occasion for social and business gathering. Hook's store stood across the street and only a few lots away from the courthouse in New London. The first day of the session the number of people buying doubled and the number of purchases quadrupled. The following day the purchases stood at three times Hook's average business. In all, Hook made 429 sales between November 26 and 28. In just those three busy days, Hook made 13 percent of all sales for four months.

William Pollard's wife visited Hook's store on the 26th. Perhaps he had court business in New London, and she accompanied him to town. On that single visit, she purchased three-quarters of a yard of calico, twenty-five sewing needles, a bottle of mustard, new clothier's cards, powder, shot, and wrapping for guns. Her husband came in on November 30 and purchased a silk handkerchief for his son, more gunpowder, and a necklace, perhaps a gift.

The transaction posted to William Pollard's account on the 26th bears the annotation "per spouse," which places Mrs. Pollard in the store in a precise way. The accounts run up by the store's most frequent visitors have similar notations and by tracing these individual and family identities and their purchase activities, additional micropatterns emerge.

Thomas Stevens's account recorded the most visits to Hook's store in New London in the fall of 1771. Multiple family members came to the store, including his spouse and his sons Thomas and Robert. Beginning at the end of October, someone from his family came to the store at least once a week. In early and again in late December, one of the Stevenses came every day. The family members purchased a wide array of goods. On November 4, Thomas chose nine checked and printed handkerchiefs. Five days later his wife left with four pairs of yarn stockings. Son John visited twice in the next week, each time buying a quart of rum. Mrs. Stevens bought two yards

ribbon on November 18, and two days later she picked up sugar, the outstanding balance of several pounds of sugar purchased on October 29 and
November 5.

The list churns on: two gallons of molasses, one dozen needles, more yarn
hose, many quarts of rum. On Christmas Eve, son Thomas purchased two
gallons of best rum. On Christmas Day, son Robert bought a half-pound of
tea. Their Christmas celebration did not last long—the next day Mrs.
Stevens picked up five hundred pins, and her husband selected three tailor's
needles. During the last week of December, Hook began crediting Thomas
Stevens's account for tailoring services: making a pair of breeches and clothing for another two men.

Thomas Stevens's name also appears often in the larger records of Bedford County. According to tax records, he owned three slaves but no land in
1782. He also has charges beginning in mid-October of 1771 in Dr. Peter
Donald's account book for tavern fees and a rather large bill for medicines.
He paid his bill by sundry miscellaneous credits and through Daniel Robinson's cash payment.[27]

Each of these shines a separate spotlight on the life of Thomas Stevens.
His family seemed to spend freely. Large quantities of alcohol flowed on his
account, as did tea and coffee. He bought tools of the tailoring trade—such
as pins and needles—but also finished items like handkerchiefs, stockings,
and shoes. The one contemporary source of Bedford County life that also
mentions him—Dr. Peter Donald's account—tells us little beyond that he
enjoyed company at the local ordinary and that someone in his sizeable free
and enslaved household needed costly medicines.

Josiah Carter also visited Hook's store with frequency. Like Stevens, his
account reflects a network of relationships and a number of visits. Thirteen
times he came alone. Once he accompanied his wife, and once she came
without him. Once Joseph Leftwich accompanied him; once he sent Leftwich in his stead.

As with Stevens, his purchases escalated in mid-November. He came
more frequently, and the number of purchases expanded. On his first visit
Carter purchased a gilt trunk as well as cotton and clothier cards for processing fibers. On November 18 his wife bought pins, ribbons, notions, and
textiles. Three weeks later, on December 9, the couple arrived at the store
together to purchase a number of household goods for cooking—pewter
dishes, tea kettles, iron pots, a mortar and pestle for grinding spices, a coffee
pot, and a keg of butter—as well as a pair of sad irons to press clothing. Like
Stevens, Carter may have celebrated the Christmas holidays with spirits; indeed his only rum purchases came between December 24 and 30.

Bernard Gaines was another kind of active customer. Little is known
about him, but his store records suggest that he dressed well. His account

received multiple credits, and he frequently placed orders for other people. To a greater degree than many customers, he used Hook's store as a petty bank and as a forum for barter exchanges in which no cash ever changed hands. Nine different people were involved in his web of store relations: John Wood, Thomas Jones (both of "Falling River"), and Mrs. Jane Frankling (location unknown) sent cash to his credit. Cash went the opposite direction when Gaines was debited for cash loaned to several other people. "Men's best pumps" and plated shoe buckles were part of a different kind of exchange—not cash but consumer goods—as those items were charged to a Mead by another man. An exchange of expensive rifles and saddles were also part of the book credits involving Gaines. Finally, the teenaged Nicholas carried home worsted hose on Christmas Eve charged to Gaines's account.

While the Stevenses, Carters, and Gaineses represent frequent visitors, the more typical customer made purchases at the store an average of three times during the last months of 1771. They, too, were a varied group. Micajah Terrell, one of Bedford County's earliest and most influential citizens, had married the daughter of Charles and Sarah Lynch, who themselves had arrived and settled by 1752. Sarah Lynch was an ardent Quaker and the first South River Quaker meeting met at her house. Following the 1782 splintering off of Campbell County from Bedford County, the court meetings of the newly formed county took place at Terrell's home, which suggests he had a large house located east of New London.

When Micajah shopped at John Hook's store in 1771, he probably had six children at home—sons ages 16, 14, and 10, daughters ages 14, 12, and 3. He purchased four pruning knives—three sized for a boy's use. The purchase in combination with the biographical data brings the customer to life—a man at work with his children. He only bought work essentials—along with the cutting knives, he bought thirty pounds of bar iron and a knife.

During his three visits to Hook's store Guy Smith also bought knives and ordered a bushel and a half of fine salt. His sister Betsy came to the store two days after Christmas to deck herself out in a white silk bonnet and two yards of plain lawn. This is probably the same Elizabeth Smith who married John Hook in late February and bore his daughter seven months later.

John Hook's late 1771 store accounts record multiple webs of relationships and kinds of visits; however, most people did not leave such a varied record of consumerism. Individuals who had a single charge against their account were responsible for half of the recorded visits. Put another way, half of the visitors to whom Hook extended credit did not return to the store that autumn. People who made purchases two or three times at Hook's store comprised another quarter of the visits. Less than 3 percent of Hook's customers visited the store more than a dozen times in those months.

Hook's 1771 accounts suggest that stores were points on the landscape that linked women to merchants, their families, and even unrelated men in multiple ways. Because men did go out on the road more often than women, they sometimes picked up items on women's accounts. One Thomas Richards charged green tea to Mrs. Ramsay's account. When visiting the store to make his own purchases, Colonel Callaway picked up silk thread and fine calico for Mrs. Elizabeth Thorp. Women sometimes charged goods to an individual with an entirely different name. Isbell bought on the credit of Thomas Bruce. James Patterson's account was charged for brown sugar per Elizabeth Boyd. "Miss S. C." chose textiles and sewing goods and charged them to Alexander Gordon. Hook's 1799 accounts at his second store also indicate that spouses or multiple generations came to the store together. Thomas Robinson brought his wife who bought textiles and notions for sewing and household goods like a pepper box, sauce pan, and cards for combing cotton; he purchased rum and a bottle. Henry Brown accompanied his daughter to buy women's gloves and a checked handkerchief.[28] George Cock arrived with his daughter and bought a woman's blue satin bonnet. Brown's and Cock's daughters bought clothing accessories, just the stuff of rapid fashion change.

Elizabeth Read's account spotlights one woman's relationship to multiple family members and their purchases. It illuminates how a set of seemingly random purchases fit together and raises issues about the personal circumstances of a family and how purchase decisions linked friends and family. It also demonstrates how crossing into widowhood suddenly catapulted a woman onto center stage in the world of consumption.

The small account book for Hook's Falling River store in May 1773 documents that Elizabeth Read personally visited the store at least once. On May 17, she bought twenty ells of best German osnaburg. She sent William Park two days later for a pair of small H-shape hinges. Multiple people named Read held their own accounts at John Hook's store. Her sons had visited the store multiple times during the preceding two weeks. On May 4, Adzonadab Read and his spouse picked out three large basins of white stoneware and one small one. Three days later William Read borrowed a small amount of cash on the account and also bought two tin pans, one large pewter basin, and two white stoneware basins. On May 11, Daniel Read purchased salt and brandy. Two days later Adzonadab returned, this time with a cash order to his favor on William Hutcheson's account. Again he bought basins, these being designated specifically as washbasins (four small and two large), and one mug. On May 16, eldest brother William paid the account with a hogshead of tobacco (grown at "bobbling brook"), which the storekeeper immediately credited to David Ross, Hook's Petersburg partner. On this same visit Abraham Read, who was debited a few lines down in that day's account for six ells of osnaburg, may have accompanied his uncle William. Only after the hogshead of tobacco had been credited to the account, did Elizabeth come to the store to make her purchases.

Elizabeth Read could trade on her own account and stand liable for debt because she was a widow. John Read's will was returned to county court the week following her visit. The half-dozen Reads with accounts recorded at the Falling River store were her sons and a grandson. As per custom, John Read gave his wife the use of his plantation and estate during her life. His land, lying on both sides of Falling River, was to go to his sons William, Adzonadab, and Daniel upon their mother's death. The mill had immediately passed to them (William was given "quiet possession"). John Read left his moveable estate to his daughter Elizabeth Simmons and to Thomas Read's children, including Abraham.[29]

The purchase of multiple basins by Adzonadab (ten) and William (five) may reflect a seasonal need for dairying equipment or have related to some aspect of mill operation. Or perhaps the pans were new to the store, went home with one brother, were admired by another brother or his wife, and resulting consumer interest rippled on throughout the family. Although the account books do not provide answers to why the Reads bought these goods, the ledgers do reveal familial relationships and purchases and, with the help of multiple records, open out tiny transactions.

Although the period following the death of a husband could be one of great fragility and lack of security, it could also be one during which a woman might experience more freedom and authority than she had before. Elizabeth Read was widowed and went shopping—or at least finally left a record of her shopping. Women often used this freedom to increase expenditures on consumer goods or make improvements to their domestic environments—specifically rebuilding, updating, or redecorating their houses.[30]

An entry in a young woman's diary makes the family trips to the store more comprehensible. During 1797, Frances Baylor Hill of King and Queen County filled her days with sewing, visiting, riding out, and walking with other young people, many of them women. She described a visit to the store as a family affair: "One day 'Papa, Mama Patsy, & myself went to Walkerton dealing Mama got Betsy & Patsy muslinetts got needles thred [sic] I got a handkerchief for myself & one for Sister Nancy, saw 4 or 5 gentlemen in the store staid there about two hours.'"[31]

The store experience for Hill parallels the pattern apparent in Hook's accounts. Multiple family members went, and the women bought textiles and clothing. Frances shopped for herself and others. But her family did not just go shopping, they went "dealing," and they spent a long time in the store building. Men outnumbered women, and none of those women was likely to have an account in her name.[32] Evidence in the account books suggests that Hook's stores served more as a center of community life than a rough and tumble world of men and commerce—and increasingly so into the early nineteenth century. Some youngish women—identified by the appellation "Miss" or "per daughter"—traveled to his store. Katie Thomason and Betsy Jones, for example, both appeared at Hook's Hale's Ford store on January 17, 1799, but on quite different errands. Betsy Jones purchased whiskey, brandy, and a quart bottle on her father's account. Katie Thomason bought handkerchiefs and pins, fine fabrics like taste and muslin, even a scarlet cloak, charging some to her father's account and some to her brothers' accounts.[33] The two girls had traveled to the store together, seemingly without parental supervision.[34] This fits a wider pattern in late eighteenth-century Virginia, as many parents allowed their daughters to travel in pairs, groups, or sometimes simply accompanied by a servant.[35]

Hence, one additional way that stores took on special meaning for women was in the evolving notion of shopping as entertainment or pleasure trip. On December 25, 1771, the Misses Elizabeth and Esther Thompson went to John Hook's store. One returned home with a silk bonnet, the other a piece of silk gauze.[36] A similar sense emerges from Lucinda Lee's activities while visiting cousins in Westmoreland County in 1782. After an early morning horse ride, "Cousin Molly" at breakfast suggested they ride to a store in a nearby town. The three girls went in the chariot, "and left the two Married Ladys by themselves." The storekeeper they visited was the brother of the fiancé of one of the girls. They did not go to acquire goods; rather it was an entertaining diversion, part of the sociability of visiting.[37]

The Thompson girls' Christmas visit or Cousin Molly's party are early examples of a seed that reached full bloom in the following century. In 1836, seventeen-year-old Eliza Barksdale wrote of a day's visit by the three "Miss Marshalls" to the home she shared with nine siblings in Charlotte County. The girls trooped down to Capt. Williamson's store "to look at his new goods" and were treated with "candy, plunbs and Almonds." They all walked in the evening to an ivy cliff, gathered bouquets of flowers, and walked through the street, "one before the other, about two yards apart, making a string of seven ladies including a servant."[38]

The delights of a large group of girls tumbling down to look at new store goods, treated with candy by a merchant, gathering flowers, and strolling in a long chain through the streets (slave included) captures what is both old and new in rural Virginia. They were briefly free of paternal authority but chaperoned nonetheless. These outings signified rural pleasures that linked girls and the world of goods in new ways at places where women were increasingly welcome. Ultimately, the idea of consumption would be reconstituted as a solely female task.[39]

Hook's account books, much like the many documents that historians used to dismiss as "ephemera"—commonplace books, household accounts, jots and scrawls of money paid and money due—show women as remarkably vital economic and social players, even in backcountry Virginia.

The evidence that families went in groups to stores offers a new slant on everyday activities. That women came—across creeks, down mountain passes—with daughters, sons, friends, and spouses to stores widens the understanding of women's lives. So too does the apprehension that teenage girls used shopping as entertainment. Young women moved across the landscape and did so often without an adult. Once in a store, they learned about cost and value—"a good penny's worth," a merchant might say—but also what was new and desirable. They practiced the roles they would take as wives.

A store building offered a special space. The merchant held sway there— at his bulwark behind the counter. His assistant, if he had one, unwrapped goods and handed them down; wrapped them up and put them back, likely as the merchant cajoled and flattered his special customers. The wealthy held the ultimate power; the power to choose something or leave empty-handed. Others needed cash or its equivalent in hand or the largesse of credit.

Thus far this study has examined business systems, sales patterns, and shopping experiences. What remains is the most ephemeral and inexplicable part of consumerism. What did people desire and why? How would we know? What can object studies teach us that studying patterns and numbers has not? We now know that the store's portal opened for women, and the next chapter turns the spotlight on yet another group of consumers.

RIBBONS OF DESIRE

Poor Elizabeth Hog. Her friend Priscilla was a rather pushy flirt and one fair day she went in search of "fairings." When Elizabeth went to pay off her account, she had been charged for a yard of ribbon. She objected because she had never bought a yard of ribbon in the store; the ribbon charged to her had been presented to her by the shopkeeper in response to a traditional fair day demand—even if Priscilla rather than Elizabeth had made the actual demand.

We know too little about colonial fairs and their customs. But it was the concept of a fairing that set this customer-merchant relationship askew. A fairing is a present given at or brought from a fair. Its more general form is a complimentary gift of any kind. A third more particular definition identifies it as a cake or sweet sold at a fair.[40]

The pairing of the two words—ribbons and fairing—suggests a move-

ment had occurred in the meaning of desire. The idea of a fairing dates back
to the sixteenth century; before stores became everyday facilities, the fair
served as a locus for the exchange of goods and a site of community gathering, merriment, happy consumption, and gifting. An inexpensive gift from
the fair—a memento or a token—was perhaps extraordinary when consumption itself remained distinctive. A token from the fair might signify a
rare instance of sovereign consumption, an uncontrolled purchase to express
attention, to foreground desire.[41]

A fairing's particular meaning often depended on the relationship involved, as one could seek a "fairing" for one's self or others.[42] But the idea of
the fairing seems to have most common potency as a kind of courting gift
from a man to a woman, a gift that sparked doggerel and common song.

THE FAIRING

As Roger the ploughman a lusty young swain,
Was whistling and trudging it over the plain,
He met black ey'd Susan, whose dull maindenhead,
Long had tir'd her more than the pail on her head.

Dearest Susan, said he, well met, in good time,
I've a favour to ask, if it is not a crime,
Will you go, pretty maiden, with me to the fair,
And I'll give you a fairing to stick in your hair,

The damsel reply'd as she struggled to go,
I ne'er grant men favours, I'd have you to know,
To teize me and follow me, no longer dare,
I want none of your fairings to stick in my hair,

The lovers walk'd on 'till they came to a grove,
Where no one could see but the arch god of love;
He laid her down gently, she was not aware
Of the fairing he gave her that stuck in her hair.

Ye lasses of Britain who sigh and look wan,
And pine all your life-time in secret for man,
While frolick and free and goodnatur'd you are,
You'll never want fairings to stick in your hair.

*CALLIOPE, OR THE AGREEABLE
SONGSTER. . . . , 1775*

As the poem suggests a mere ribbon carried intimate connotations. It
had become a metonymic device. The offer of a ribbon teetered on the edge

between custom and transgression. On the one hand, it was a sexual advance—the promise is to go to the fair with the giver. The fair was a site of pleasure, the pleasure of consumer goods that offered fancy, exoticism, colors, textures, wonder, and sweetness. It is also a destination. Away from the eyes of chaperones, the man and woman moved into location between home and fair, where there were simply many places for sexual play. The final two stanzas make the ribbon/sex connection absolute.

Yet, in a second way, the fairing fits into the nexus of obligation and promise in which gifts secured relations. Gifts, tokens, and fairings belonged to a ritual exchange in which courtship proceeded through various precise stages.[43]

It was easy to conflate the object, custom, obligation, and promise. Ribbons—relatively narrow widths of woven fabrics with selvage edges—had multiple uses. Some involved physically situating the ribbon on intimate places on the body. Others involved more visible uses, trim, both functional and decorative, on clothing and hats worn by men and women. That multiplicity of use is also specified in several Virginians' millinery orders itemizing the particular intended uses for the items. London merchant John Norton and Sons sent one such order to Catharine Rathell of Williamsburg on January 31, 1771. Among the many types she requested, she stipulated two "pieces of very handsome Black & White Second Mourning Ribbon," three "pieces of Black plain edged Sattin Ribbon for tieing hair," and one "pice of Love Ribd for to tie in Boes Stomachers & Sleeve Knots."[44] The phrase "love ribbon" referred to an actual particular commodity, one recognized on both sides of the Atlantic as an item used to attach items to undergarments and sleeves—ties to the closest parts to bodies (fig. 5.4).

Further research reveals additional links between ribbons and sexual promise. Ribbons or tapes framed bosoms by tugging breasts forward and up in stays. They have parallels to the busk, a small wooden stick that held the upper body straight from bosom to waist. It, too, was embellished and gifted as a sign of love made precise by its physical positioning. Both women and men used ribbons to hang a miniature portrait of a loved one around one's neck. Such a portrait could be suspended beneath a costume and brought forth to share, thus taking the form of hidden / not hidden liminality.[45] And women might also tuck a ribbon in her bosom and later remove it for bestowal on a suitor.

But ribbons are also an index of whirling change in fashion, or more precisely, a signifier that the retailer or wearer was "in the know." Retailers and customers relied on multiple systems of information to convey a ribbon's style and to make a selection from a vast possibility of choices produced by several towns in France and especially Coventry in England. A sample book

FIGURE 5.4. Robert Laurie after John Collet, *The Rival Milliners*, London, 1772. Mezzo-tint engraving on paper. Courtesy, The Colonial Williamsburg Foundation.

of Coventry ribbons marketed between 1805 and 1811 holds multiple hand-bound pages, each side of them covered with approximately twelve swatches of ribbon, and some of them carry marginal notations as to what types sold well and in which towns (pl. 9). Retailer Catharine Rathell pinned a snip-pet of silk ribbon to her July 22, 1772, order to ensure she received more of a specific pattern. A Boston merchant followed a more precise method, which suggests he had a catalogue of sorts. He ordered ribbons using a numbering system, requested specific types (such as "Black Taffety"), identified a func-tion (such as shoe ribbons) and a grade ("Quality").[46]

Merchants who operated stores far from style centers had to walk a fine line between replenishing an existing locally popular item and obtaining newly fashionable ones—and do so with a six-month or longer lead time. John Hook's choices for his new store assortment in 1772 show a mixture of preference and open order. Hook wanted twenty dozen assorted fashionable ribbons priced by the dozen and three particular ribbons ("pink," "double satin," and "colors") priced by the yard or piece. The fashionable assortment came in at 6 to 8 shillings a dozen and the others ranged from 6 to 8 pence each, making them all inexpensive treats. In sum Hook chose not to differ-entiate his ribbons into high- and low-end choices.

The popularity of particular ribbon colors, sizes, and patterns was im-portant news that women readily shared. For example Abigail Adams, while living in London, wrote a newsy letter to her niece Lucy Cranch Greenleaf describing the dress at a ball she had recently attended. In a single paragraph Adams mentions ribbon trimmings six times: large bows on hats, white satin petticoats trimmed with black and blue velvet ribbon, wreaths of black velvet ribbon spotted with steel beads, on and on. In the late eighteenth century ribbon trim—both its color and the uses to which it was put—was as significant as the textiles.[47]

Some colonists, however, considered ribbons emblems of fashionable excess. Quaker Ann Cooper Whitall confided in her diary at midcentury, "Oh the fashions and running into them." Young men had adopted the habit of wearing their hats up behind, and "next it's likely to be a ribbon to tie their hair behind." Even worse, many girls "have their necks set off with a black ribbon, a sorrowful sight indeed!"[48]

Literary and visual sources have allowed an untumbling of the multiple meanings and uses of ribbons. We could stop there, and many do. But it is the second layer, the second wave of enquiry that makes a material culture analysis so potent. That enquiry asks why ribbons succeeded as metonymic displacements. One answer lies in their very materiality. They were small, slight, easy to hide yet likewise easy to display. They decorated, looping color around a package or a body part. They had multiple uses; they attached one thing to another and they updated a gown or a hat. They enabled female expressiveness in a standard domestic practice. John Mair's mercantile guide, published a number of times in the eighteenth century, categorized them as petty wares, "a grouping of needles, pins, combs, fans, thread, tapes . . . laces, beads, ferrets, &."[49] His categorizing shows them to be slight, inexpensive, personal items for adornment.

Another answer looks to long-term history. Like many truly potent "hot" consumer goods, their meaning came from their having been an exclusive item of the upper classes that was ultimately offered at a broad range of price levels—they became everyday and commonplace, luxurious and extravagant. Tea is the classic example of the pattern. It began in Europe with royal use but by the mid-eighteenth century came in finely made and high-priced choices and in simple, low-grade ones. It could retain that sense of luxury even as it was boiled over and over and served in a cracked mug.

The history of ribbon use has not been studied as intensely as tea. Certainly in a mythological sense, the power of ribboning goes to its symbolic use in heraldry, as an award for distinction. On a maypole as well as on a tambourine, ribbons represented the rays of sun. In later costume they adorned early seventeenth-century male garments, not sewn in flat, but hanging off as a kind of fringe, mirroring the earlier uses. They had a ceremonial function in their past. Their slow disappearance from male attire came as part of the long-term process during which the bright plumage that had comprised men's attire was replaced by somber envelopes of suit coats.

By the eighteenth century, ribbons more commonly embellished a wide assortment of women's attire although sewed flat, not left flowing. Nonetheless, ribbons that a wearer wrapped flat around neck, leg, or head harkened
to a past use that linked the individual to high style, even courtly, dress. A
blue ribbon is still a symbol of high honor.

Simple inexpensive items like ribbons are part of a culture, and they have
a past. They hence illustrate a core concept of material culture analysis. By
taking a consumer good and pressing forward and back through economics,
art, and literature—and through forms that are considered "high" and "low"
or "major" or "petty"—scholars can reach desire. Another bawdy song, also
titled "The Fairing," makes that transformation even more explicit. Its narrative focus is not on gratification of desire but the experience of it. This
damsel met a shepherd who invited her to the fair. He promised her no
harm, just an entertaining walk with a story to "charm her" and a gift of a
ribbon. The wary lass was tempted; she had "dream'd of a fairing to come
from a fair." The desire overwhelms her; she "long'd e'er so much for a gift
from the fair." She warned him to behave; another young man had promised and disappointed her the year before. But when they reached the stile
to cross, he would "scarce be said no" but pressed her "soft lips, as if there he
would grow." She ran away crying, promising herself she would never go
again for a gift to the fair.[50]

The Scots-Irish had a notorious wedding custom in nineteenth-century
New Hampshire that was called "riding for the ribbon." Parties of male
friends of groom and bride raced at top speed to the bride's house to secure
a ribbon-bedecked bottle of whiskey. Securing the bottle was securing the
bride, and surely a ribbon wrapped around a bottle—perhaps even body
shaped—had sexual meaning.[51]

Desire—wanting something—can take many forms. Few objects in the
eighteenth century may have been as insidious as a simple ribbon. Is its desire sexual? Material? Did men desire ribbons because they stood as potent
symbols for female sexuality and provided a mutually understood path toward conquest? Was female desire cast in terms of their fashionable (i.e.,
material) qualities because of the effect they had on men or because of their
own sexual desire? What does it mean that sexual desire is connected to the
desire for a commercial consumer object? Ribbons—either moderate or extravagant—were consummate desirable things that had value.

SIX

Suckey's Looking Glass

African Americans as Consumers

R ICHARD STITH'S SLAVE Suckey purchased a looking glass and a ribbon at John Hook's store in February 1774. She paid for them by supplying four pounds "cotton in ye seed." When I first encountered the record
of her purchase in a tiny account book, I neatly entered it into my large database of store purchases: I categorized the object as an item of "personal
adornment" and noted that the buyer was female and a slave. As a quanti-
fier I felt comfortable with my numbers and words. As a material culture
scholar, I began to muse. Why did Suckey choose a mirror? What does a
mirror do? Does it matter that Suckey was both part of an emerging Anglo-
American consumer culture and part of the African diaspora?

So I followed the active agent, the enslaved Suckey, to explore possible
reasons why a slave might buy things and to determine if others were consumers like her. More importantly, I followed the objects she purchased in
order to consider their range of meanings. Finding the answers to my questions required exploring multiple cultures in the trans-Atlantic world, and
they revealed new ways of thinking about a specific place and time.

This chapter examines enslaved men and women as players in the world
of goods. It turns the spotlight of our stage on the slaves and explores their
actions as presented in the formulaic narrative of bookkeeping. It also uses
evidence found in and on objects, objects like those Suckey and other slaves
purchased, to reconsider aspects of the lives of these otherwise little-known
men and women. It looks at slaves and market activity as a series of behaviors linking people, physical movements through public and private landscapes, and material things. Three crucial aspects are assessed: How the
slaves provided the goods or services that gave them the credit needed to
purchase consumer goods; what motivated them to engage in this kind of
entrepreneurial activity; and whether the purchase represented a desire to
improve their level of comfort or an expression of their heritage or religion.

The experience of slaves in the retail trade presents a profound paradox.
Slaves could appropriate commodities even as they could be appropriated as
commodities themselves. The same account books bearing their names as

173

customers could also record their sale to a new owner; a single merchant could both serve them and own them. The ability to purchase consumer goods put slaves on the same performance stage as poorer whites, and it allowed them to make choices—however limited.

Markets and Market Culture

Recent historical scholarship has dramatically reshaped our understanding of the ways in which slaves in the New World participated in market culture for themselves.[1] By the middle of the eighteenth century in Virginia, masters generally supplied slaves with food and clothing that met basic needs. Slaves also had free time, although the amount varied (and reflected the temperament of the owner, the stage in the crop cycle, and the location of the plantation), as did the slaves' energy to use it. In sum, slaves worked. What they did, the degree to which they worked for themselves as well as their owners, what they consumed, saved, and bequeathed, all formed the basic pattern of their lives. The two overlapping circles—work for master and work for self—set the boundaries. The work for self extended far into slave culture—it was initially a way of providing better subsistence but it ultimately became a way of obtaining access to both cash and consumer goods.[2] Indeed the introduction of cash into the rural plantation economy changed the lives of slaves as much as it did the lives of planters by creating hierarchies ordered on wealth, status, and power in slave societies.[3] Successful acquisition of commodities and consumer goods by slaves was a basic determinant of larger changes within slave society and how the Anglo-American culture viewed the slaves.

Most slaves gained access to the world of goods by selling their own surplus agricultural commodities, such as poultry and vegetables. Those slaves who came from West Africa were no strangers to market sales and market relations; the Yoruba expression "aye l'oya" (the world is a marketplace) is a constructive metaphor for what one scholar terms "the dynamics surrounding transactions, the pushes and pulls, the actions and reactions, the negotiations of living life."[4] In the New World region that stretched from the Caribbean to the lower South, black men and women became the de facto suppliers of foodstuffs for a broad cross section of the urban population, both white *and* black.[5]

That economic system is not so well documented or understood in Virginia. The sheer quantity of market regulations passed at the local level implies a strong African American presence existed in the marketplace. Norfolk appointed a committee in 1764 to examine the problem of "slaves . . . selling Cakes &c and small Beer at the market and other public places." Nine years later, Norfolk banned "Indians, mulattoes or negroes Bound or free from selling any kind of dressed meat, Bread, or bakes, or retailing any kind of Beer or spiritous Liquors"; however, the 1783 repeal of the law suggests that slaves and other marginal entrepreneurs had become too important in the supply of food to be prohibited.[6] Later eighteenth-century regulations throughout the state tried to control slave activity, most commonly through the requirement that the owners give written permission for slaves to sell foodstuffs, in order to prevent the sale of stolen foods.[7] In the opening decades of the nineteenth century, such economic activity by slaves likely increased; Henry Fearon noted during his 1817 visit to the Washington, D.C., market that "Negroes are the chief sellers."[8]

Slaves also frequently sold poultry from their yards and produce from their gardens to their owners and others. Between 1805 and 1808, Thomas Jefferson's granddaughter Ann Cary Randolph kept a small account of slaves who sold products to the plantation kitchen at Monticello. Her records show that slaves supplied the household with a multitude of products, especially eggs, but also poultry, vegetables, fruits, nuts, and even brooms and baskets.[9]

Among the slaves who entered the marketplace in central Virginia, men outnumbered women approximately three to one. Age also played a significant role. The most active traders were either quite aged or were childless young adults. Few of the traders had children under the age of 10, which suggests that families with young children consumed what they grew or that childrearing swallowed up the time needed to produce surplus goods to market.[10]

Another local account illustrates how these small transactions might vary from plantation to plantation. Jane Frances Walker Page lived in Albemarle County in the opening decades of the nineteenth century; she, too, purchased food from slaves, keeping a record of each transaction. Of the twenty-eight sellers, most were women, and Page labeled a third of them "old." As at Monticello, most of the purchases revolved around the slaves' poultry yards, but in this instance it involved meat, not eggs. Nor did she purchase (or perhaps have the choice of) an immense variety of foodstuffs. Page's form of payment varied. For some she gave small amounts of cash; for others she bartered consumer goods.[11] In combination, these two examples indicate the fluidity of slave participation in the market.

Public markets linked both plantation and urban exchange systems in critical ways. Freedom to travel—to see family members, to carry produce from their owners, or to vend their own foodstuffs and poultry—was another element of the relationship of slave to owner. Some slaves were given permission to travel extensively. According to the recollections of one former slave who lived in Franklin County during the nineteenth century, the plantation's mistress gave her slaves Saturday afternoons free, and any of them could go to Lynchburg: "Merry parties on foot followed the farm wagon, which was loaded with tobacco, brooms, nails, baskets of fruit and vegetables in season, and various articles of domestic manufacture contributed by the women, such as yarn, woolen cloth, sometimes a piece of rag carpeting or a patchwork quilt. Small pigs in boxes, with baskets of eggs and chickens, completed the outfit."[12]

Market days were times to travel, to sell and buy, to see and be seen. So much so that in 1810 the town of Alexandria directed its constables to disperse the slaves from the Sunday market at nightfall. Most specifically, this duty required the officers to "see the negroes from Maryland go over the river, to prevent the riotous play of boys of every description, and of negroes on that day, and if country negroes, to cause them to leave town."[13]

Slaves quickly developed an awareness of the value of goods, and that knowledge of urban market prices quickly spread throughout a region. For instance, in Prince William County Spencer Ball's slave Dick raised corn and watermelons on his truck patch and kept chickens, ducks, turkeys, and geese. He recognized the plantation mistress's largesse, noting she "always gives me the price of the Alexander market for my stock."[14]

Gaining knowledge of and practice in vending produce, poultry, and home production in turn allowed many slaves to become petty entrepreneurs. That activity brought them the cash necessary to purchase consumer goods and in some instances property.[15]

The nature of slaves' access to consumer goods and the items they chose to buy remain largely undocumented, testimony to the uneasiness and ambivalence that such slave activities produced among whites and how difficult it was to keep legal or customary boundaries. Slaves could and did appropriate the commodities from their owners. Early in the eighteenth century, illicit trade between slaves and poor whites provoked Virginia lawmakers to insist that slaves obtain the written permission of owners to trade for goods, a legal nicety many purchasers ignored. George Washington worked to identify local whites who actively received stolen foodstuffs in the vicinity of Mt. Vernon. He even tried to prevent his former carpenter's daughter from opening a store, arguing that "her shop wd. be no more than a receptacle for stolen produce by the Negroes" and adding that all too many shopkeepers "support themselves by this kind of traffick."[16] Williamsburg mayor and merchant John Holt accused fellow storekeeper Joseph Fischer of such illegal activity in the March 1754 Hustings Court. Fischer demanded that Holt produce evidence of any "Negro of reputable character . . . who would only say, I had ever let a negro have any spiritous liquors without the leave or order of the master or mistress, or any person whatever in less quantity than a pint. No one merchant that sold rum in this town," he averred, "was so cautious of letting any Negro be supplied with rum, without a written or Verbal leave as myself." Such scrupulous adherence to the letter of the law had earned him ridicule, and he pointedly recalled that in one single day two slaves that he had turned away went directly to Mr. Holt's and were served.[17]

In combination, the records pull back the curtain to reveal the performance of slaves as consumers in the retail trade. The sale of poultry, vegetables, and other products of slave labor put petty cash in their hands or allowed them to barter with merchants for consumer goods. They freely entered stores, some with cash in hand, others with commodities, perhaps some with notes from their owners, permitting such activity.

Slave purchases in Virginia figure in a small number of business papers and court cases in the colonial period. Many of these are represented in the ledgers used by business owners to record an array of marginal people who were able to pay for small purchases by bartering goods and services. During a youthful stint as a store clerk in Virginia, Andrew Bailey hid a little disreputable business from his employer by "keeping a ticket account on what we called 'Memorandum Book' for negroes."[18] Anne Frame of Berkeley County, like many other merchants, kept a book labeled "ledger for blacks."[19] John Hook just called his "mercantile ledgers" or "petty ledgers" and included in them the petty accounts of both black and white customers whose transactions did not fit into normal store accounting practices. Merchants Thomas Barbour and Benjamin Johnson, who operated a store in the Piedmont region of Orange County, kept accounts with slaves under the slaves' own names in the 1780s.[20] Approximately a half-century earlier, William Johnston, who kept a store in Yorktown in the 1730s, listed in his account book the names of nine slaves who traded field peas for consumer goods. Colonel Byrd's slave Witt traded four pecks of peas for a felt hat. Billingsley's Will exchanged three bushels of peas for a coverlet. Thomas traded seven and a half bushels of peas for fabric, a handkerchief, and a knife and fork. Negro Daniel made the largest number of purchases, including rum and six yards of quite expensive fine chintz. Johnson made no notation of how Daniel paid for his purchases, but the fabric alone was equal to eighteen bushels of peas in trade. George chose an ell of garlix (a multipurpose fabric often used for aprons), a linen handkerchief, and even a small quantity of lace. These purchases, all by males, overwhelmingly took the form of textiles for clothing and household goods.[21]

An occasional reference to slave purchases appears in other merchants' records. According to the Glassford and Company accounts for its Colchester store in the 1760s, "Negro Sue belonging to Mr. Grayson" received payment in cash for chickens, fowls, and cabbages. Other slaves, like "Negro Jack," had extensive similar accounts, but even more intriguing is the long list of

store goods traded for foodstuffs with no name designated or cost recorded—
in essence, a return to a barter economy in which no cash changed hands.
Extensive exchange of goods for small quantities of foodstuffs fill this ledger:
rum for oysters, yarn stockings for migrating fowl, textiles for eggs, powder
for crabs, a "woolen felt hat no. 1" for chickens.[22] The identity of these food
suppliers is unknown, but many of the foodstuffs exchanged with the storekeeper could be grown in small plots or fished or hunted in spare time. The
exchange of fruit for thread and a thimble or strawberries or greens for ribbon suggests the involvement of women.

Anne Frame kept a series of account books between 1798 and 1812 at her
store in what is now Charlestown, West Virginia, and she traded extensively
with slaves. The "Black Ledger," which commences in 1802, lists 114 individuals, only 4 of whom she specified as "free" and only 6 of whom she identified as women. Frame posted most of these expenses to one of two other
ledgers and listed only amounts of debit in this one. Intriguingly, under the
name "Washington's Thomas," Frame noted amounts posted to "daybook
white one" and "black daybook," a purchase of several yards of blue coating,
and cash in payment respectively.

Mrs. Frame's store, probably founded by her late husband Joseph, had
extensive stock. She probably sold at both wholesale (to other merchants or
peddlers) and retail (for example, to Rebecca Wallace a "Dressed Bonnet,"
yards of fine satin, a necklace, and a pair of gloves). Anne Frame carried on
her business at high volume. From her large stock, Davenport's Daby selected chocolate, an almanac, penknives, and pepper and paid with a pair of
shoes, sweet potatoes, a fowl, flax, and carriage of goods. Nat at Mr. Read's
chose two strings of beads; Rutherford's Peter a fiddle string; and Rutherford's Adam a quire measure of paper. The few slaves with paid accounts
dealt mainly in cash; the others traded apples, potatoes, broomstraw, corn,
soap, shoes, beef, and geese. The payment from "Hannah at Grove's" even
included cash "order from master."

Several of the slaves who made purchases at Frame's had ties to Battaile
Muse in Berkeley County. Muse managed multiple large western tracts for
George Washington and several of the Fairfaxes. Muses's slave Isaac, Washington's slave Thomas, and Fairfax family slaves Robert and Sinty all went
to the store. Some slave customers were also craftsmen: Will was a weaver,
Frank a hatter; others were waggoners or worked "at the Mill." Their activities suggest slaves had greater freedom if they lived on estates with absen-
tee owners or if they worked in more industrial settings.

The merchant constructed a business system that attempted to separate
white and black customers as a way of accommodating both the world of
goods and the world of slaves, but that system nonetheless often ended up

blurring the racial identity of the buyer. Anne Frame kept separate daybooks for blacks and whites yet by mistake occasionally penned entries in the wrong book. During the 1770s John Hook included the petty economy of blacks and whites in the same accounting frame, although he broke it out into separate books thirty years later. Nearly every other eighteenth-century Virginia merchant simply integrated slave transactions into their larger bookkeeping system. Perhaps the increasing level of slave economic activity in the early nineteenth century prompted ad hoc solutions that separated the records of black and white consumers. As agriculture continued to diversify and customs of slave liberties evolved, the store activity of slaves accelerated. More plantation stores appeared in the antebellum period through which planters sought to further regulate consumption activity by centralizing it in their own control and using it for incentive as well as punishment.

Slaves as Consumers: John Hook's World

Court records in combination with John Hook's store ledgers for 1773 to 1775 and 1805 to 1808 link slave families within the world of goods in new ways. For example, the detailed inventory of Hook's property in 1801 and in 1809 after his death that the protracted court battles between Ross and Hook necessitated show that in both instances the court-appointed inventory takers enumerated Hook's slaves, often by age and family grouping, and sometimes added a noteworthy physical description. Although slave kinship in the antebellum South could be real or fictive, groupings of women and children or men, women, and children, recur in the multiple inventories of Hook's estate.[23] Those same inventories also include a much larger mass of men and women who did not receive any such distinction.

Armed with this study's deep and broad information about relationships and purchases, the knowledge of slaves as consumers highlights those flexible arrangements for slave's labor and time in a local context. This microcosm can then be understood in terms of a regional pattern of the upper South and an Atlantic world that not only delivered goods but also slaves to build the economy that drove the machine of commerce.

Hook's 1773–75 petty and mercantile ledgers record purchases made by thirteen slaves. The petty ledger notes small debts that Hook occasionally posted to a larger ledger (no longer extant). The mercantile ledger noted exchanges of a vast range of goods, services, and foodstuffs for consumer goods. Most transactions in both books involved small amounts—only 12 shillings per capita on average, as compared to 18 shillings for white men per visit and over £1 spent by white women.

Yet among the most popular commodities the customer groups exhibit nearly identical purchasing patterns. As with the whites, rum was the overwhelming choice of slaves; it provided an escape from the grueling workaday world, a means of socializing, a medicine, and a caloric supplement. Slaves also purchased sweeteners, perhaps to provide a bit of flavor to an otherwise repetitious diet, and the molasses at least had nutritional value. Inexpensive mirrors were popular, as were ribbons, hats, and textiles. More surprising, better quality textiles made up a higher percentage of slave purchases than those of any other subgroup in this population.

Payments listed for these purchases demonstrate the remarkable willingness of the merchant to accept slaves as active economic players in their realm. These slaves enter Hook's record-keeping system because he extended them credit—the merchant assumed that they were "good" for the amount due. It is unclear whether or not Hook was disappointed—perhaps these customers' payments were acknowledged in other ways—but most slave accounts remained unbalanced at the end of books. Suckey, for one, purchased her goods in February, and Hook credited her for partial payment ten months later.

The slaves who did pay most often used the value of their own time and labor. Suckey paid for her mirror and ribbon by supplying four pounds "cotton in ye seed." Hook credited the accounts of five other slaves, including Harry, another of Richard Stith's slaves, for bringing in raw cotton. The onerous task of picking seeds out of that fiber raised the value of a pound of cotton fourfold, enabling London, George Caldwell's slave, to purchase clothing, rum, sugar, and even a necklace.

Labeled as the "blacksmith's ledger," another small book kept by Hook's storekeeper at Hale's Ford details the purchases made by thirty-five slaves between 1805 and 1808. Unlike the group of slaves coming to his New London store thirty-some years earlier, Hook owned fully half of these customers, and they lived on his three working plantations at Hale's Ford, Maggoty Creek, and Hunt's.[24] Two others were slaves Hook had rented to a neighboring planter. There is only one woman's account in this group. In contrast to the ad hoc group of slave purchases drawn from general ledgers recording both black and white populations in the 1770s, these accounts focus a lens on a slave economy embedded in a store trade. These men grew crops and provided services to pay for consumer goods. That alone provides fair evidence that they had both the land and time to cultivate gardens or crops for personal use. Like those on plantations throughout the South, these slaves could visit Hook's store across the turnpike from the home plantation or could stop by on their travels related to their growing, processing, and delivering of crops.

The account of John Hook's slave Will reflects the range of market activities of these slaves. Will had the largest account in the slave ledger, and his purchases alone represented 17 percent of all the slave debts. His page begins with a nearly £2 debt transferred from the previous ledger. More than a year later, on Christmas Day 1806, Will delivered 145 pounds of tobacco to the store in payment. In August 1807 Will purchased a wool hat, and near Christmas that year he bought household ceramics, including a dozen plates. In February 1808 he stopped in for a knife; in April, a pair of cotton cards. The next day he returned with another 630 pounds of tobacco, but Hook deducted one-third of that amount for rent, presumably of a parcel of land, leaving several pounds of credit. On May 1 and 11, Will bought two hats and a "pair of stout men's shoes." In September he may have been preparing to preserve food, as he purchased three jars. The small amounts of tobacco used in payment do not suggest full-time farming; between 1800 and 1807, a full-time laborer grew on average 1,500 pounds of tobacco and Will grew less than half of that.[25] Nonetheless, the economic relationship with Hook, whatever its nature, allowed Will to grow tobacco.

Five men—three belonging to Hook and two others to a neighboring farmer named Meador—worked land in some form of arrangement with John Hook. He rented land to them, extended them credit for necessary goods, accepted agricultural products as payment, and deducted the price of the rent from their commodities. White planters occasionally entered into these kinds of arrangements with free blacks, but such economic affiliation between slaves and their owners was extraordinary in turn-of-the-century Virginia. This atypical arrangement would, of course, be recast as the norm after slaves' freedom in the form of sharecropping and the company store.

Will represents one end of the spectrum of slave activity—his farm products and store purchases demonstrate an active pursuit of his own wealth. His ability to devote spare time to cropping suggests he was a single man, and notations in Hook's inventory list him as being about 30 years old with "nots on his hams," scars on his legs.

Among the 110 slaves listed in the inventory of Hook's estate on his death in 1809, 6 males and 5 females had family groups. The name of each of the male heads of household appears at least once in the store ledger, and several are accompanied by lengthy lists of purchases made during regular visits. The sole female account belongs to the woman most prominently identified as the head of a large family. Most of these slaves were also rented out at Hook's death, and often again are listed by family in the ledger.

The extensive inventory-based documentation of these purchasers helped me reconstitute these black families and allowed me to analyze their consumption patterns as *households*—a task that can seldom be achieved when the subjects are the poor whites of the region. Yet in undertaking this reconstitution, I had to depend primarily on the view of the white, usually male, observer, which means that information I was able to uncover about the activity of individual African American women is limited.

An examination of the slave households illuminates those relations and sheds light on their expression through the world of goods. Phebe is the only named black woman who appears in Hook's ledger. In the mid-1780s Hook accepted Phebe and two other young girls as payment on a debt owed him. In 1801, 26-year-old Phebe and her three children Lucy (10), Tom (6), and Rachel (1) lived on Hook's smallest plantation. Eight years later she headed a large household of unrelated women and children all noted as "Phebe's family." Hook's death resulted in the separation of the larger female group. Lucinda was about 12 when she was listed with Phebe in 1801; she would be rented along with her two children to Benjamin Booth in 1809. Daughter Lucy and her child were rented out to a third planter, Isiah Harrison. Phebe and the now four remaining children were rented to John Hook's partner and son-in-law Bowker Preston. The low rental fee that Preston paid for Phebe and the multiple children suggests that she was providing child care. Phebe's new home was not far away from her old one.

No other woman stands so clearly apart among Hook's slaves as Phebe: at no point is she ever listed with an adult male. In May 1805 she purchased six yards of rolls—an inexpensive, relatively coarse, and likely undyed textile—at Hook's store. Six yards was a generous amount of fabric; perhaps she made a new mattress for moving her young children Tom and Rachel to separate beds, or perhaps each family member received a new apron.

Charles, identified in 1801 as a 24-year-old carpenter valued at £150, was one of the two highest valued slaves in the estate. His special status as a craftsman enabled him to indulge in thirty-eight purchases during the ledger's three years—paying with cash and household goods he had fabricated, ranging from a bedstead to a wooden bowl. Unlike most slaves, he purchased no alcohol. But his choice of textiles and clothing—including three hats, three handkerchiefs, shoes, a pair of buckskin pantaloons, and upper leathers for two pair of shoes—indicates he had a strong concern with appearance. He augmented his diet with store-bought shad, sugar, and molasses. He even loaned money. His purchases also suggest the presence of a woman—ribbon, a pair of cotton stockings, and numerous items for sewing, such as a thimble, buttons, pins, and Virginia cloth, a finer grade of linen homespun than the osnaburg usually issued by owners.

According to evidence in the inventories, he formed a household with Aley or Alice, whom the 1801 inventory takers had described as a "likely negro girl" age 14. By 1809 the pair had two children, Ned and Fanny. Being a skilled craftsman conferred status, so his small family stayed near him when he was rented to another of Hook's sons-in-law.

Another account entry in Hook's ledger also links specific men and women through consumer goods. Jacob purchased a hat for Celia on November 17, 1805, and charged it to his account. Jacob, then age 28, lived at the Maggoty Creek plantation in 1801 along with several other young unattached men. In 1809 he remained grouped with young unattached men, most of whom also shopped at Hook's store. Celia lived on the farthest-flung of Hook's plantations (in neighboring Montgomery County) and would have been 15 the year she received the hat from the older man. For everyday work Celia likely did not need such a hat; perhaps she wore her new hat to a party, such as one of the Negro balls recorded in Franklin County. One white passerby in 1794 "met with about 30 Negroes at a Ball in what they call a Negroe House." As one former slave later recalled, they held most big dances at night where they "would dance awhile then go to other room and drink coffee, corn whiskey, and apple brandy, sometimes some of us would get drunk."[26] Slaves themselves, and their white observers, document dressing well, even competitively, for such occasions (pl. 10).

Celia's situation was atypical—her mother Nancy had sued for the freedom of herself and her eight children in 1802. In court Nancy Page claimed that she was the indentured daughter of a white woman and had been unjustly enslaved by Thomas Jones in North Carolina, from whom Hook obtained her and her infant son as payment of a debt in 1787. Virginia law allowed the indenture of mulatto children up to the age of 31; Nancy Page brought her suit after Hook rented her to another planter when she was 30. The court awarded her the freedom of herself and her children in 1804; however, Hook continued to appeal the ruling. At Hook's death, she did not appear in the estate inventory of slaves, but her children did.

The hat thus becomes a poignant symbol. Celia and her younger siblings—Billey, Daniel, Rachel, and Ellick (Alexander)—are listed in the 1809 inventory without any special notation, and they may all have worked on Hook's Montgomery County plantation. Four years after receiving the hat as gift, and five years after the court sided with her mother Nancy, Celia was not free.

The story continues. The inventories list Celia's brother David first as a "bright mulattoe boy" and later as "white" and a "tollerable scholar." Hook also wrote that Billey worked in the store in Franklin County. The account book that lists the slave purchases is simply labeled "blacksmith's ledger." Yet it also contains the slave accounts and a number of pages on which handwriting was practiced. No other Hook book contained such unofficial business. David the tolerable scholar may have kept the slave books.

Like the white people's store accounts, slaves' purchases do more than divulge relationships; they also reveal purchasing preferences. The slave com-

munity bought many textiles and items of clothing at Hook's store.[27] Like
white customers in the backcountry, slaves had a need and desire to warm,
cover, and adorn their bodies. Nearly 90 percent of their accounts indicate
purchase of some of these items. Their motives for particular choices were
complex; however, shedding the discomfort of basic coarse clothing likely
figured high on most lists. Franklin County's most famous black resident,
Booker T. Washington, spent his youth at Hale's Ford, the location of Hook's
store, some forty years after the merchant's death. In his autobiography he
vividly recalled that "the most trying ordeal that I was forced to endure as a
slave boy was the wearing of a flax shirt." He compared the torture of wearing that shirt to "the feeling that one would experience if he had a dozen or
more chestnut burrs or a hundred small pinpoints, in contact with his flesh."[28]
Few have more eloquently expressed the discomfort caused by cheap textiles
made with coarse materials (in the eighteenth century osnaburg or "Negro
cloth," sold at a third the price of "finer cloth").[29]

Fabrics had other appealing features. The protean nature of clothing allowed individuals to transform identities and identify the status of others.
Both runaway advertisements and descriptions from white observers reveal
the care with which slaves cultivated their appearance. Indeed some owners
appropriated the special regard that slaves had for clothing as a means to re-
ward or punish slaves.[30] David Ross's 1813 instructions on clothing his slaves
included detailed instructions on the garb allowed to the various skilled laborers at his ironworks. Wagoners were to have coats, vests, and pantaloons
of cotton—other laboring groups were assigned special clothes by rank.
Slave Edmund "was to be particularly attended to"—he received blue cotton for a coat and pantaloons, scarlet flannel for a vest. After describing the
ironworks' two watermen as "rascals" who deserved to be sold to the "Carolina Hogg drivers," Ross made his displeasure most clear by giving them
no new clothes.[31]

The flood of western garb that constituted David Ross's hierarchy of
prestige certainly impacted traditional patterns of how slaves measured one
another. But like most contests between cultural groups where consumer
goods are exchanged, one party can appropriate the meanings of such goods
and make them work within preexisting cultural practices.[32]Archaeological
and pictorial evidence combines to show the use of cowry shells, beads and
coins on strings, and ribbons, demonstrating how slaves continued to par-
ticipate in traditional patterns of body decoration and how they adapted inexpensive jewelry to this art. Such changes may have represented an attempt
to construct class and/or racial identities through dress in ways unimagined
by slave owners. If London the slave wore his purchased necklace over his
slave cloth uniform, it did not change his standing in the eyes of his master

Caldwell or most other whites; however, among fellow slaves it could well have signaled a mocking of white fashion.[33] In all these ways and more, ribbons, hats, and textiles may have provided slaves a means of differentiating "self" from others in a world of owner-issued loose-fitting uniforms made of durable inexpensive materials.[34]

Household goods constituted a second major group of items that slaves purchased. Unlike textiles, some of these objects survive as archaeological evidence at the sites of slave households. This evidence has revealed considerable data about the ways slave households were differentiated in terms of material comfort and access to consumer goods. Although scholarly debates still rage over how slaves acquired these items, the likely explanations are that slaves acquired some goods as castoffs from white owners, that they pilfered some, and as Hook's accounts indicate, that they purchased yet others.[35]

Thomas Jefferson's rural retreat Poplar Forest lay five miles from Hook's New London store. While Jefferson was seldom in residence, slaves continuously occupied the plantation between 1790 and 1812. Artifacts excavated from the house yards of three slave quarters there include ceramics (131 vessels), fragments of cast-iron pots, tools, lead shot, writing slate fragments, furniture hardware, marbles, and padlocks. In addition, there is important evidence of independent slave production: pipes made of locally available schist and wasters from pipe production, barrel-making tools, and agricultural equipment. That evidence, in combination with local store records, enables a unique two-tiered level of analysis of slave possessions.[36]

Slaves purchased numerous household goods at Hook's store. The mirrors, knives and forks, and straight pins they bought all belonged to the growing tide of consumer goods and changing behaviors that formed the heart of the consumer revolution.[37] They also reveal the ways in which slaves adopted the larger Anglo-American references in the realm of foodways. Hook's slave Will purchased a dish, a dozen plates, an undesignated part of a pitcher, and three jars. A dozen plates had little use if one consumed the standard slave diet—meals that heavily relied upon ground corn served in a semi-liquid state. That Will used plates indicates that he had adopted the concepts of separate portions of multiple foods, an idea embedded in Anglo-American foodways. Similarly, knives and forks signify a cultural acceptance of the growing European taboos against touching food with the hands. Between April and October 1808, Meador's Tobe chose a set of teacups and saucers in addition to his thirteen purchases of hard liquor, and they cost him the equivalent of three quarts of his well-beloved whiskey. That many archaeologists' sites have unearthed teacups and saucers at slave sites further emphasizes the breadth of slave participation in the Anglo-Virginian consumer world around them.

Yet neither the record of sales nor archaeological survivals show the tea-cups, forks, pins, or ribbons in use; they remain mute about what meanings those objects may have held for their owners. Suckey's choice of a looking glass and a ribbon in 1774 provides only a glimpse of the intersection between the world of goods and the world of slaves. It does not reveal what Suckey did after she made her purchase and left the store. Perhaps she tied her ribbon in a bow for the front of her shift, or wound it around her neck or the brim of her hat, or laced it through her hair. And perhaps she then admired herself in the mirror. We have followed Suckey to the door, and now we need to consider whether Suckey's mirror had meanings for her that the English craftsman who made it, the Scottish merchant who stocked it, and the Virginia planter who owned her never imagined.

MIRRORS AND MEANINGS

Mirrors are in many ways the most magical of consumer goods. Before the nineteenth century they were most often called "looking glasses," and they were to *look*: to look into and look beyond, at one's face or into other worlds. They told the truth and predicted the future. As such, looking glasses had long played important roles in both myths and folk cultures. Prometheus created fire with a looking glass. Moses obtained the brass for a tabernacle from the many mirrors amongst the women gathered. When the Brothers Grimm recorded the folktale of Snow White in the early nineteenth century, mirrors could still listen and speak the truth.

Thus, any in-depth understanding of Suckey's choice of a looking glass must begin with magical, mythical mirrors. During ancient times the round mirrors crafted by the Egyptians spread through the ancient worlds of Greece, Asia, and China. By the Middle Ages, craftsmen had perfected multiple forms: flat, curved (to distort shapes), burning (to create fire) and "magic" (to serve in sorcerer's kits). Most were small and exotic items made of metal or crystalline or blown glass and framed and backed with precious materials. Venetian craftsmen perfected the skills necessary to produce crystalline glass and to blow glass into cylinders, which revolutionized mirror making. Larger plates allowed mirrors to become wall decorations and their expense was soon measured in their size, not precious materials.

Even after they became more common, mirrors still carried deep symbolism. When artists of the Renaissance began to master the powers of light and its depiction, mirrors became a favorite artistic trick (is it real or a reflection?) and served as iconographic devices in which to present moral issues.[38] They often used mirrors as symbolic icons for female vanity, and a painter's elite audience well understood the association: at least in Europe, vanity was a woman's weakness. While mirrors continued to convey deep moral play about self-admiration and false images, by the age of the Enlightenment, mirrors also connoted the ability to see with clarity, and hence became signs of science and rationality.[39] Artists thus also used *men* in combination with mirrors and light to symbolize a new way of thinking. Mirrors at the end of the eighteenth century in Europe represented the dualisms of vanity/clarity, false sight/true sight, and men/women.

Chinese, Japanese, Turkish, and pre-Columbian peoples also had traditions of viewing and decorating using reflective surfaces. But a special use developed: very small pieces of glass combined to produce glittering light effects that spread from the East. Moorish conquests took mirrors throughout the Mediterranean. Persians, Indians and Africans all used tiny fragments of silvered glass. That blending of cultures finds northern Africans using the powers of the reflection of light to protect people and places from the "evil eye."

So mirrors had special powers that far transcended their role as a manufactured good.[40] On the whole they exemplified the reflexivity of material culture and the way symbolic investment could transform a commodity. This dualism of the ability to view one's self (to critically examine, to preen, to decorate) and to reflect (to heighten available light and to flash or flicker when turned) provides additional keys to understanding Suckey's looking glass.

By the late eighteenth century, Virginia merchants could offer their customers inexpensive face-sized mirrors or large wall mirrors. Suckey could purchase a small one for a mere 2½ shillings, while F. Maddison could spend £3 for Hook's "largest looking glass" (pls. 11 and 12).[41] Among the well-to-do, looking glasses belonged to the realm of genteel fashion and lighting. In their houses the triad of pier mirror, window, and candle provided maximum glitter and refraction. The expense of making large sheets of glass gave these large mirrors a very real stamp of prestige; the greatest sparkle and most accurate representation came at high cost.[42] Middling householders in more urbane places joined the queue of purchasers and increasingly placed a mirror over the fireplace in the best room, allowing it to reflect back the figurines aligned on the mantel even as it captured the actions of figures in the room. The new wish for nighttime sociabilities—card games, tea parties, and dances—placed a premium on lighting and mirrors played a significant role in this because they multiplied the available light.

But Suckey stood with only one foot in that world. Furthermore, even though mirrors came with complex referents to European culture, they could also have been used in precise ways to distinguish slaves from any broader eighteenth-century Anglo-Virginian world. Such evidence is far more difficult to obtain, but material culture sometimes gives us a way to piece together shattered images.

Mirrors did have a deep resonance in West African culture. They functioned in a Bakongo ritual tradition that valued light and transparency, enabling sight into another world. In the nineteenth century and before, particular beetle wings offered such qualities and metaphorically fused the shine of the spirit with one's ability to see to another world through flight. But the arrival of manufactured goods extended and intensified the metaphor and mirrors soon became a fundamental component in West and sub-Saharan African spiritualism.[43] A Bakongo anthropomorphic figure might hold a mirror and medicine pack in his belly, in order to repel the divining witches who cause illnesses.[44]

That spiritualism crossed the Atlantic aboard the slave ships. African American slaves, like their African cousins, believed mirrors could capture, attract, or repel a spirit, and this belief played out in numerous faith practices, superstitions, and customs. Mirrors and black cats (perhaps not coincidentally retaining superstitions in American culture today) were required to make specific charms or *nkisi*. Mirrors allowed gifted individuals supernatural sight—the ability to see ghosts, the future, or things out of vision, that is to say, invisible or far away.[45] Buried outside or standing next to the front door, a mirror could flash back evil spirits that wished to cross the portal. That flash of spiritualism has been carried forward to modern times, as is apparent in some African American yard art.[46] The desire to link the living to the dead helps explain the work of Cyrus Bowen in a black cemetery in Sunbury, Georgia, and cemetery decoration. He made his wife's marker in the 1920s of clay painted yellow and roughly cut in an open hand with a mirror glittering in its palm.[47] Broken dishes, lamps, glassware, mirrors, tin foil—all have been recorded on African and African American graves. Finally, mirrors could also be quite dangerous around the dead. Many white families, in the North as well as the South, practiced the custom of covering mirrors in the presence of death, following a European superstitition.[48] The custom of covering mirrors before burial is likely of European origin, and the treatment of the grave with flash is of African origin.

The case of twentieth-century African American ritual practices that incorporate mirrors can be used to understand Suckey's looking glass purchase, even though historical evidence linking West African practices to time and space in colonial America is ephemeral. We must continue to look back from some nineteenth-century sources. The Igbo or Ebo peoples were quite commonly enslaved to Virginia in the eighteenth century, and one recently imported Igbo man lived on Hook's plantation in 1809.[49] Tom was 45 years old and listed with his wife Anne, age 35, and children (possibly three), in Hook's inventory. Scrawled by his name was the word "outlandish." When rented to Hook's son-in-law with his wife and 18-month-old daughter Silvey, he was noted as "Ebo Tom." That the white men described Tom as "Ebo" and "outlandish" is important, for seldom did Virginia planters identify slaves with a specific African place-name. Moreover, the use of the word "outlandish" suggests that Tom was foreign-born (perhaps a recent importation from Africa) or that his behavior was odd, strange, or bizarre. Tom was clearly not like many of the Afro-Virginians around him in Franklin County at the turn of the nineteenth century.

Tom's status as an Igbo encourages us to take a deeper look at specific Igbo practices, specifically the historical accounts of mirrors in the areas occupied by multiple subgroups of the Igbo people. In 1832 traders Laird and Oldfield stipulated red cloth, velvet, and coral beads along with "looking glass and snuff-boxes of Venetian manufacture" as essential items of trade.[50] Subsequently Oldfield noted in his journal that the Igbo manifested a great desire for "rum, small looking glasses, and cowries."[51] Over the years he presented at least a dozen looking glasses as gifts to dignitaries on his trade route. When visiting Obie, king of the Igbo, the long list of gifts included an armchair (made by the carpenter on board the ship) and a large looking glass. On being seated in the chair, the king called for the looking glass: "He then proceeded to examine himself in it, and burst into a loud laugh, thinking himself, no doubt, the happiest of monarchs. He remained there surveying and laughing at himself alternatively for some time."[52]

That the mirror and not the western chair caused the king's delight is evidenced in his later admiration of mirror gifts.[53] Yet this raises questions about what caused the ruler's amusement. Was viewing his image—so much clearer than that previously seen in water or other natural reflective surfaces—new and exciting? Or was he happy because he foresaw the power such an object gave him? The early trade narratives of Europeans in Africa seldom mention mirrors, but other evidence exists that indicates how Africans had integrated mirrors into ritual practices by the mid-nineteenth century, and perhaps earlier. Titled Igbo women carried mirrors in finely carved wooden frames.[54] European missionaries two decades later penetrated the interior at Onitsha, where an Igbo trading group had been active for a century. The phrase "the glass is very dazzling" is recorded in the ex-slave Samuel Crowther's translations of Douda language in 1854.[55]

When he returned there in 1857, Crowther documented a telling story. The missionaries had earlier presented a mirror to an African, a great doctor who drove out *moa* (spirits), a service for which the people accorded him much respect. One day, wanting to exhibit wonders to them, the doctor told his people that he had "been to see Beke or Oibo, his moa companions and

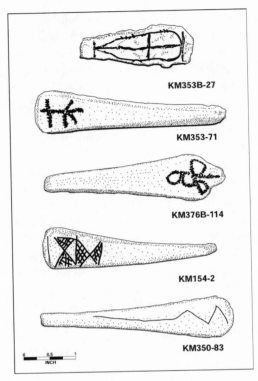

FIGURE 6.1. Sample of carved designs on pewter spoon handles from Kingsmill Quarter, York County, Virginia. Fig. 8.7 in Patricia M. Samford, *Subfloor Pits and the Archaeology of Slavery in Colonial Virginia* (Tuscaloosa: University of Alabama Press, 2007). My thanks to Samford for permission to publish her work.

they had given him a wonderful reflector." He placed it among the divinity markers and unfortunately smashed it to pieces. He needed another mirror to continue his power; however, the missionaries refused, as they decided it would only encourage ungodly superstitions.[56]

Archaeological evidence found in Virginia slave dwellings provides a remarkably strong case for the endurance of spiritual practices long after slaves' arrival from Africa. Some objects, like knife handles, have been carved and cut in ways similar to Kongo cosmograms and other forms of African expression.[57] Most striking are the nineteen pewter spoon handles found in Kingsmill Quarter, all purposely broken (several of them shaped into a point) and three-fourths of them engraved with postproduction decoration that suggests their use as extremely significant markers of Igbo rituals of ancestor veneration in personal shrines (fig. 6.1).[58] The incorporation of new objects into old ritual expression evinces both a symbolic appropriation and an artistic transfiguration, and in combination both work as one way to resist cultural oppression.[59]

Mirror glass also has a history among eighteenth-century African Americans: Suckey bartered for her mirror from John Hook in 1774; "Negro Jack" purchased one from William Allason in 1761.[60] Archaeologists have recovered mirror glass in numerous slave quarters. An investigation of the quarter at Carter's Grove near Williamsburg uncovered three pieces in a root cellar, a space that many slaves apparently used to store their personal items, including knives and forks, pins, and rum bottle glass, all items that slaves could have acquired from a cornucopia of consumerism like John Hook's and all of which may have played a role in the spiritual world of African Americans.[61]

Let us return to John Hook's store on that February day and attempt to understand Suckey's specific choice of a ribbon and a mirror. Like Benjamin Ruff and Joseph Stewart, she chose multicolored, multipurpose, and inexpensive ribbons. Like seven other customers at John Hook's store in the autumn of 1771—men and women, black and white—she bought a mirror that cost 2½ shillings. She could have chosen a dozen creamware plates for 1 shilling less.

Focusing the spotlight on Suckey alone permits consideration of her as an individual and an assessment of the ways in which she fit into those white and black worlds as well as the meanings that the mirror might have carried for her. At the turn of the nineteenth century, nearly thirty years after her purchase of the mirror and ribbon, Suckey's owner Richard Stith died, leaving his wife Lucy as executrix of his estate. Finding an "extensive family of Negroes and other estate superfluous to her," Lucy chose "to be rid of the trouble of such estate" and allowed her sons and daughters to divide the property. She kept only three slaves. One was Old Suckey, valued at only £18.[62] Lucy's decision intimates that Suckey was a house servant, perhaps one who had assisted her for years. If so, the much younger Suckey was likely a black woman in a white household when she purchased a manufactured consumer good imbued with extraordinarily complex meaning.

Such knowledge encourages reconsideration of the other slaves found in Hook's store accounts. The families that lived on Hook's plantation also lived in a world bounded by whites; their lives were perhaps profoundly different from Suckey's, yet they nonetheless allow a clearer picture of slave lives and slave cultures, although their precise living arrangements remain undefined. That the multiple Hook inventories grouped some slaves as families suggests a few family living arrangements existed amidst the larger number of mostly male slaves grouped on several plantations. Archaeological evidence elsewhere in Virginia suggests that they lived in small log structures, some of which may have had multiple root cellars that provided storage as well as space for privacy, personal use, or religious expression.

The purchases that these men and women made add a new dimension to any understanding of their hierarchy of living standards. A Scottish traveler stumbled on a settlement of a dozen log slave dwellings on a visit to Mount Vernon in 1823 and was "astonished at not finding male, female or child in any of them." Padlocks secured half of the cabins. Peeking in the holes of the walls of locked structures, he "perceived things a little cleaner, and in better order" and "was led to suppose then even in such slavery, there were grades of comfort, and enjoyment."[63] While he did not delineate what he saw, the slaves' decisions to secure these dwellings imply domestic spaces were marked by varying levels of consumer goods—goods that the householders considered both valuable and, more importantly, *not shared by all.* The traveler's experience at Mount Vernon is reinforced by archaeological excavations near the slave quarters at Poplar Forest, which yielded a significant number of locks, keys, and parts during a similar time span.[64]

The scene on our consumer stage often blurs and shifts—maddeningly so—whenever the attention focuses on slaves in action as consumers and users. Our view, like that of the Scottish visitor, is too often devoid of people; only the *result* of the slaves' actions is known. Questions still abound: did the young man Charles wear his new clothes when he courted Alice? Did Phebe share the large amount of coarse fabric with the three adult women in her household? Was Celia's hat a fine fashionable gift for a partially white woman trapped in a slave society? Slaves like Celia, Alice, or Phebe only appear as glimmers in routine documents. But it is through their purchases at John Hook's store that these slaves exercised powers of agency. The choices of particular consumer goods reveal desires spelled out in terms of material things. Does that put them into the new consumer world defined in Anglo-American culture? The wealth of new things at lower prices, a greater supply through the retail trade, a greater freedom to travel and trade, and knowledge of market economies were all critical to the ability of slaves to acquire these small comforts and conveniences. Despite the horrors of their servitude, they too participated, in the smallest of ways, in a consumer world.

As an institution, a store brought together and financially rewarded those who "belonged" together in a mutual reinforcement of structure and hierarchy. But it also operated as a business with the goal of making money by exchanging agricultural products and cash for goods. A store therefore brought together many who did not "belong" together; a slave stood before the same counter as the wife of the wealthiest planter. At Hook's, both faced a locally disliked Scottish merchant. And the objects for sale there bound men and women in America and all across the British Empire together in the experiences of shopping and consumer choice, of learning about new products and of negotiating price. For some customers, the goods represented the world of international gentility that required appropriate props for new genteel behaviors. For others, they made tasks more convenient or a hard life more bearable. And for others still, they may have, just may have, led down mystical paths, paths unseen and unknown by people who had authority over these buyers. If only we had that all-seeing mirror.

Country Gentleman in a New Country

John Hook's Beef

JOHN HOOK SUED many people during his long mercantile career and, judging from his ultimate wealth, successfully collected debts. Yet in one case he got caught in his own snare. His ultimate fame—or infamy—resulted from bringing a case to district court in New London in which he claimed an army commissary in 1781 had illegally taken two of his steers. The defendants hired Patrick Henry as their lawyer. William Wirt's biography of Henry in 1817 records a scene of both magnificent oratory and hilarity. Hook wanted payment for the property the army had appropriated. Henry mounted a simple defense; he emotionally manipulated the crowd and ridiculed John Hook. In Henry's argument, the ragtag suffering army was on trial, not the army commissioner, and Hook was no American if he could refuse to feed such heroes.

As Wirt tells it, Henry's humiliation of Hook is vivid. Henry painted a picture of "the American army, exposed almost naked to a winter's sky and marking the frozen ground over which they marched with the blood of their unshod feet." In stock courtroom drama, Henry's voice rose and fell as he appealed to the jury, until he reached the dramatic moment, at which point he thrust out his arm and pointed an accusatory finger:

> Where was the man who had an American heart in his bosom, who would not have thrown open his fields, his barns, his cellars, the doors of his house, the portals of his breast, to have received with open arms, the meanest soldier in that little band of famished patriots? Where is the man? *There* he stands—but whether the heart of an American beats in his bosom, you gentlemen are to judge.[1]

Henry continued to carry the jury by the "powers of their imagination" to the plains around York. He described the victory, the surrender, the "shouts of victory . . . and the cry of Washington and Liberty as it rung and echoed throughout the American ranks, and was reverberated from the hills and shores of the neighboring river." Henry paused. "But hark! What notes of discord are these that disturb the general joy . . . —they are the notes of *John Hook,* hoarsely brawling through the American camp, *beef, beef, beef!*"

The audience convulsed with laughter. Rather than despoil the sanctity of his office, court clerk James Steptoe raced outside and rolled "in the grass in the most violent paroxysm of laughter." Hook, also seeking relief, came out and in the Scottish brogue that Wirt so carefully records, asked: "Jemmy Steptoe, what ails ye, mon?" Steptoe could only say *"he could not help it."* Patrick Henry had worked up the audience into such an uproar, first laughter then outrage at such Tory audacity, that Hook's lawyer could not even respond. Soon, according to Wirt, the echoing cries of *"beef, beef"* were replaced with *"tar and feather,"* and only a fast horse could save John Hook.

By the time that William Wirt's account of the famous beef trial appeared in 1817, John Hook was long dead. His end was rather ignominious. His lawsuit with David Ross had dragged on and required that Hook often travel from Hale's Ford to Richmond to deal with court business. Returning home at the end of March 1809, he fell ill. He wrote a will that strangers witnessed and then passed away. His sons and sons-in-law later refused to stand as executors. A state marker erected two centuries later identifies New London as an early town and singles out Henry's involvement in the court case as the most historically interesting thing to have happened there. Perhaps the skill of Patrick Henry—Wirt reported that his contemporaries called him the "SHAKESPEARE AND GARRICK COMBINED!"—led to the melodramatic pathos that caused the new nation to heap scorn on John Hook and in some ways brought to an end the Revolutionary saga of this Scottish merchant.

John Hook's personality made him easy to dislike. His letters reveal a man who alternated between pessimism and bravado; his fear of failure necessitated vigilance against disadvantage. He spent countless hours in the saddle traveling to courthouses pressing for debts; his papers include a concise reference list of several county courts along with their meeting days. Between 1772 and 1774, Hook undertook forty-six prosecutions in Bedford County Court alone for collection of back debts. In 1774, he filed twenty-seven more. In addition to suing wealthy men like William Mead and James Callaway, he also hounded poorer men.[2] Thirty-one years later, when one long-standing Virginia clan got entangled in a suit with John Hook, they turned to Hook's former-partner-turned-nemesis, David Ross. The Preston family wanted to be "released from the grip of that most avaricious and worst of Scotchmen," and they planned to capitalize on Ross's willingness to "indulge . . . his own resentment against a man that he despises."[3]

John Hook fits the stereotype that had developed in the late 1760s of Scottish merchants: cheap, quarrelsome, and greedy. If we are to believe any of several people, every Scottish merchant harbored Tory sensibilities. In John Hook's case, his actions seem almost contrary to good sense. He obdurately refrained from declaring his loyalties to the American cause until an angry mob threatened him with physical harm. He began busily acquiring more land in preparation of his move to a plantation. He stubbornly acted as if the law of property was inviolate, even in chaotic wartime. Such actions raise questions about which of his other actions engendered antagonism as the desire for goods and economic vicissitudes combined.

Hook enjoyed a full life; he married well, raised seven children, and acquired huge amounts of land and an astonishing number of slaves. His holdings spread across so many Virginia counties and on to points westward that they are estimated to have totaled hundreds of thousands of acres. At his death the house that he had sketched out in 1782 was filled with the lavish trappings of a rich merchant and wealthy planter.

The men who took the 1809 inventory worked methodically through the house room by room. A desk and bookcase, six walnut tables, fifteen leather-bottom chairs, six Windsor chairs, a looking glass framed in walnut, and a case of liquor bottles stood in his central hall. Beds stood in the downstairs chamber as well as in the garret over the chamber and hall. The dining room held porcelain tea ware, silver serving pieces, Queen's ware dishes, and fine tablecloths. Curtains hung at the windows, carpets covered the floor, all showing a new, more comfortable world, suitably expressing wealth, and providing the appropriate environment for top-notch genteel entertaining, right down to dram glasses with which to raise a toast, once filled with the liquor from the cut-glass decanters. John Hook himself "bought into the world of goods" that had become de rigueur for appropriate living and entertaining among wealthy and connected people across the nation.

The most surprising item in the inventory is "George the third and his Queen" valued at £1, an amount that suggests they were prints rather than paintings. The position in the inventory listing makes their location ambiguous. They come immediately after the "walnut table in the hall garret" and just above the large listing of porcelain and dining room items. Their precise location may offer another explanation for why John Hook was so disliked. If Hook had been an unreformed old Loyalist, he may have used them to visually taunt his guests at dinner, or perhaps he simply kept them upstairs for more private admiration.

In the local context, Hook's success measures up to that of his competitors. Rival merchant James Callaway lived similarly well in his home near the Franklin County court. But the contents of both men's household inventories in 1809 are stark indeed by comparison with those of wealthy men living in eastern and more urbane places in Virginia. The 1815 tax imposed on luxury items reveals how few households in Bedford or Franklin counties had mahogany furniture of any kind. Newly fashionable forms such as chests of drawers or sideboards were absent, even those taxable ones made from local woods. Few local homes had mirrors hanging on walls or silver salvers sitting on tables.[4] Only a very few of very well-to-do planters had possessions that linked them to their peers across the state. The broad middle swathe still did not "buy into the world of goods" at least as defined by fine furnishings.

Hook's mercantile enterprise had changed markedly in the forty years since he had established his business with David Ross. He no longer operated a store in the burgeoning town of New London nor did he function as a Scottish merchant in the Atlantic economy. The purchases made at his second store were quite different. In 1771, the top five items sold were rum, buttons, osnaburg, hats, and handkerchiefs; in 1799, they were brandy, cider, whisky, nails, and salt; and in 1809 they were cotton cards, brandy, iron plate, leather uppers, and butter pots. The last group constitutes neither high-status goods nor small luxuries. They filled simple, basic, unrefined, rural needs. In 1771 the retail trade at John Hook's store revolved around a general mercantile line that included good-quality goods firmly linked to style centers in England. Hook's departure from the Scottish trade muted the influence of the Atlantic world on the goods he offered. In 1799 all the top items sold could have been locally made and were for household consumption. In 1809 the top items show that the local economy was now centered on the production of a new staple crop (cotton), involved in new industries (iron and hat making), and probably supplied foodstuffs to the new towns developing nearby (butter). Hook's manufactured goods came from Philadelphia, Baltimore, and Richmond. He no longer imported rum from colonies around the Atlantic rim; instead he operated a still that transformed local corn to local whiskey.

The success of competing towns also brought changes. In 1804 John Howell Briggs visited Sweet Springs, one of the newly popular mountain spas. On his way home he passed the homes of old Bedford County elite, notably: "Colo. Callaway's and Mr. Steptoe's which appear[ed] to be handsome situations, well improved." Although the old merchants and clerks of court had prospered, the town of New London had not, for "a number of handsome and comfortable houses were tenantless" and the traveler saw but few inhabitants. Briggs attributed the decay to the removal of the court but added that nearly the whole town belonged to Colonel Callaway. He optimistically noted that the town still had a boarding school for young ladies and a close-by college "for the education of youth."[5]

New London had lost its bright future, and Lynchburg, located on the river a few miles away, gained regional prominence. In 1791 the peripatetic Richard Venable reported: "Improvements are arising fast" at Lynchburg; only three years before there were but two or three small houses, "now there are numbers of small houses and about 20 very good houses." It was a boomtown—"all things look new, stumps and grubs not taken out of the main street."[6]

Twenty-five years later the local newspaper profiled the town: more than three thousand residents lived in over three hundred principal dwellings and numerous other houses "of inferior grade." Their community had a courthouse, market house, bank, fire engine, mason's hall, and toll bridge. Seven public tobacco warehouses, three flour mills, three cotton and woolen factories, a paper mill, and a carding machine graded, managed, or transformed local agricultural projects into consumer goods. Thirty-four dry good stores, twenty-two groceries, and four commission merchants serviced retail customers. Four apothecaries, four saddlers, and three cabinetmakers provided goods and services. Finally, Lynchburg boasted of ten milliners and mantua makers to vend and make clothing and accessories.[7]

The economy of the countryside in the early national era continued to show how large landowners prospered. Relative patterns of land ownership in Franklin County during this thirty-year period (using 1786, 1799, and 1815 as points of measure) demonstrate that the number of landholdings of more than five hundred acres increased, and holdings of more than two thousand acres particularly surged (table E.1).

The planter-merchants James Callaway and John Hook and the farming Wade family fared quite differently in those thirty years. James Callaway had arrived in Bedford County with his family in the 1750s. Following in his father's footsteps, young Callaway held county office and acquired large tracts of land. Like John Hook, he formed a partnership in the tobacco trade and, as was the case with Hook, the American Revolution ended that international mercantile business. Callaway became commander in chief of the Bedford County militia in 1778. He formed a partnership with his father-in-law, Jeremiah Early, and purchased an ironworks. By 1779 they renamed it Washington Iron Works in honor of the commander in chief of the Revolutionary army. By 1783 the partners owned twelve thousand acres, much of it timberland that they harvested to feed the ravenous furnace of the iron foundry and to grow food for the thirty-seven slaves who were owned by the firm and probably worked there. Callaway also individually owned over three thousand acres of land and a dozen slaves.

The Callaway family had established itself locally at about the time that John Hook arrived in the colony as a 13-year-old apprentice. When Hook

TABLE E.1. Land Ownership Patterns in Franklin County, 1786–1815

Property size	1786	1799	1815
1–99 acres	12.1%	18.1%	14.4%
100–199	34.9	33.4	33.2
200–299	21.3	19.0	17.7
300–399	10.5	9.1	10.6
400–499	8.0	7.1	7.3
500–999	8.2	8.4	10.5
1,000–1,999	4.1	3.2	4.0
2,000+	1.0	1.7	2.2

Source: Franklin County Land Tax Book, Library of Virginia.

moved still westward to Franklin County, the family was a power to be reckoned with, and their influence continued to expand. James Callaway dictated the placement of the courthouse on his land in Franklin County in 1787, much to Hook's fury, and Hook predicted that Callaway would have much business in the court because of his "being very largely in Trade in the said County and very Rich and Powerful."[8] By 1799 Callaway had tripled his personal ownership of land and halved his slave population.

The shoppers at John Hook's Hale's Ford store lived far differently from people like the Callaways. Eight out of ten households in Franklin County had no slaves, so many of them lacked the investment in capital that often led to more wealth. Most families either rented land or had farms of several hundred acres. The Wade family exemplifies this group. Several men in the Wade clan lived in Franklin County during the thirty years John Hook operated a store there. They passed the little land they owned from one generation to the next. John Utley Wade, the illegitimate son of John Utley and Angelina Wade, moved westward to Franklin County from the nearby eastern Piedmont about 1788. When he died in 1799, he left 350 acres but no slaves. His teenaged son Bradley still lived at home but already owned a horse. In 1815, Bradley, the youngest son of many children, owned land (probably he had inherited from his father) and lived in a cabin with his wife Rachel. That cabin, surrounded by other cabins inhabited by other Wades, remained in the family for another 150 years.

Abstract concepts about lineage, wealth, property, and consumer goods can now be pinned to people. John Hook arrived in Virginia with nothing; he came to work for a Scottish merchant and hoped to make a fortune in the colony and return home to live a genteel life. When he ended his partnership with David Ross, he owned fifteen hundred acres in Franklin County.

As astonishing, he then more than tripled his landholdings by 1799. He was remarkably successful in gaining property, yet he spent much of his life in litigation and likely had strained family relationships. Callaway family members figured among the earliest settlers in the region and their decision to pursue political office further augmented their wealth and power. John Utley Wade moved into the region a few decades later, arriving with personal property (a cupboard) and acquired real property (land) that he passed on to his son.

William Mead's life story offers even more drama. Arriving from Pennsylvania by the valley route, he and his wife Ann settled in Bedford County in 1754, and he became an important local leader. Officer, vestryman, patriot, he also led the mob that threatened John Hook's life and property. He and Ann had seven children; with his second wife Martha, he had six more.[9] Mead created the gentry life that Virginia elites chose to both promote and cement their authority. In the early 1770s he ordered a quite expensive clock and other fine furnishings through merchant John Hook. He and Ann trained their sons to raise horses, dance, and play music. Mead planned carefully for all his sons to have an appropriate inheritance so that they too could live like those at the top of the social hierarchy.

Following the Revolution, William Mead followed the pull of the frontier once more, relocating to a large plantation near Augusta, Georgia. He left large tracts of land in Bedford County, on which he settled two sons. In 1793, his third son Stith returned to Bedford County to look after his lands. While there, Stith fell under the sway of the sweeping religion that lawyer Venable had warned about earlier and wrote a pious autobiography that details his battles with the wickedness of his father, brothers, and old friends. The old gentry lifestyle of his father—dancing, card playing, and fine dress—deserved damnation. Brother Samuel Mead's Christian rebirth proved annoyingly short-lived, as he lapsed when he returned to Georgia. The Meads loved to dance.

Samuel Mead's sudden death in 1793 enraged Stith, and he accused his father of sending his own son to hell. "The Indulgence of Fiddling and dancing has ever been your beseting Sin," he hissed. He cast opprobrium on his father for "training his children up for the DEVIL." William's protests that he was himself a good man failed to slow Stith's venomous attack. The old man was too "glewed to the World" to fear the fires of the next, too fond of "sensual delights" to embrace the ascetic forbearance of an evangelical lifestyle, too attached to the social pleasures of "the Association of the Augusta Gentlemen and Ladies" to give up simple entertainment. In 1805 William Mead passed away at his home at Cupboard Creek in the even newer frontier of Georgia. Only months before, he had experienced conversion.[10]

In 1771, John Hook's store stood in a bustling town in which four merchants competed for business. Exotic goods from around the British Empire flowed to southwestern Virginia. The county enjoyed the palpable excitement of newness: it was a new town with new settlers and new consumer goods. Yet, by 1809 the story had changed. His store stood on a plantation and served a much different market. The contested edge of backcountry had long moved on, past Daniel Boone, past Kentucky to Tennessee and to parts of Georgia. The burning evangelism that swept across the Virginia Piedmont and backcountry had begun its transition to settled churches that did not challenge planters' lifestyle choices or their authority over wife or slave. Sunday dress and consumer display by Bedford/Franklin region church members would no longer be decried.

John Hook's tantalizing world of goods fades and blends into images of rural stores that dotted the nineteenth-century landscape of America. Those stores still offered new consumer goods and the fashions still changed, yet the goods were no longer as new and they were more widely available.

After Hook's death, his son-in-law Bowker Preston began the long task of helping settle his father-in-law's estate. On forty-five different days between January 4 and October 9, Bowker recorded sales and auctions of John Hook's store goods and household possessions. The world of goods had come full circle.

What does this study tell us about consumer behavior and the world of goods? First, a consumer good must be affordable, available, and desirable to reach the point where it might be acquired, and its acquisition involves a cognitive process of evaluating need, questioning value (what "this" must I give up to gain "that"?), measuring fitness (is this the best choice I can make in the eyes of my social peers who are critically examining my selection?), and experiencing pleasure (does it stoke a desire, cement a relationship? Is it sensory or sensual?).

Second, an array of choices affects behavior. The explosion of available consumer goods presented one kind of new choice: a fine linen shirt or a coarse one, a printed handkerchief or one left plain. But, in a larger sense, a consumer had multiple choices when positioning him- or herself in relation to the world of goods. This explains the double meaning of the phrase "buying into" the world of goods: each consumer could choose among cultural practices and systems to adopt, reject, simplify, or hybridize "taken for granted" cultural patterns.

A third principle is that consumer transactions involved a triangulation among merchant, customer, and object. The ephemera of daily action—such as the jotted notes, the scratched-out letters, the scribbled names—allows insight into businesses and transforms the documented sliver of seemingly impenetrable letters and numbers into actions and process. Deconstructing a document like an account book means looking for larger patterns by quantifying the quotidian. It then makes people from names by building biographies. Finally, it asks, "why did they choose that?" The drama continues. Finding wives and daughters and enslaved men and women draws attention to the actions of the disfranchised, highlighting relationships and behaviors. Putting them in an architectural space where all might shiver from cold or squint in darkness as they shopped under the watchful eye of a merchant behind a counter makes the process dramaturgical. By adding in the active object, analyzing commodities as artifacts, and examining their hidden meanings and powers, we have completed the triangle of commerce, desire, and meaning.

Finally, theoretical insight tells us that objects are complex bundles of meanings, both cultural and personal. Nowhere does the sheer magnitude of the power of objects become more obvious than in pressing for their meanings. They work as signifiers of status and prestige as well as promise and sexuality. Mirrors are the most potent signifiers of all. In exploring Suckey's choice of a ribbon and a mirror, we are transported to a world unseen and unknown, asked to interpret objects in the double consciousness of blacks in the Atlantic world, compelled to wonder about how the disfranchised used things to provide pleasure, ameliorate conditions, build relations, even venture into the spiritual world. Just as some backcountry white people rejected consumer culture, some Africans and African Americans embraced it and shaped it to their own use. Material culture study merely asks that we find and follow the paths.

So what do these findings tell us about us? Can we find ourselves among the people of John Hook's world? By the time the colonies became a nation, Americans had already moved from moral certitude to ambiguity about consumption. A call to the "simple life" has reverberated throughout our history, particularly through small nonconformist groups, often grounded in religious practice, but has never succeeded in curbing the flow of consumer goods. Polarities of meaning, such as luxury/corruption or hipster/rube still reverberate in our national anxieties. A long line of people whose job it is now to bring goods to our purview, guide our choices, and take our money has replaced the likes of John Hook. So too, local standards are fading as chain stores are built in Appalachia and Alaska. We seldom hide the sensual and spiritual; a ribbon no longer can function so boldly as a metonymic stand-in for sex, for instance, and mirrors contain few surprises.

But the power of objects remains. Objects still carry expressions of human caring and evidence of relationships. We only have to look as far as our

FIGURE E.I. John Hook's store, Franklin County, 2003. Photograph by Ann Smart Martin. A dozen years before, this structure was in decay. The roof was breached—the first sign of impending collapse—and weeds and vines had encroached. Owner Warren Moorman soon took steps to have it reroofed, repaired, and revitalized. This rare still-standing example of an eighteenth-century store has now earned a place on the Virginia Register of Historic Buildings.

national and religious holidays to see revelries of gift giving. Our society loves to play with the meaning of things, and in this moment of late capitalism in America we spurn silly jingles and didactic advertising campaigns. People on geographic, racial, or economic fringes can pick and choose, take what is useful, and move between and around the lines of constraint. The cutting and marking that enslaved Virginians performed to transform spoons or pipes or storage holes in the eighteenth and nineteenth centuries became a booming form of twentieth-century consumer savvy and pleasure. Successful mass-produced consumer goods, such as kits to personalize already distressed jeans, allude to that creation and power. The art world no longer views the "found object" with disdain.

The rural general store's particular architectural form is now an anomaly (fig. E.1). If saved, the building might have another use, to house a nostalgic antique shop or community business. Its legacy is immense yet contradictory.

Five-and-dime stores were one set of natural heirs, for their owners pulled household goods, notions, and trinkets from behind counters and placed them on low shelves, which gave customers a new sense of delight and pleasure. Big urban department stores were another. They used large plate-glass windows to beckon customers inside and displayed goods in glass cases that enabled longing gazes. But a merchant or a surrogate clerk still offered service and served as a point of power between person and consumer good.

The most recent but very different heir to the rural general store is Wal-Mart. Its founder, Sam Walton, saw an underserved rural population ripe for retail expansion. He had to teach such people how to buy freely and with great pleasure by objectifying value, a love of thrift, and an acceptance of desire and change as natural and worthwhile. He needed to devise more efficient supply lines and to standardize consumer choice. Goods from around the world now flow freely, and China has again emerged as a mass producer of western-style goods.[11] In the same way, more than two centuries ago, John Hook vended goods from a global economy and dreamed of an extended chain of stores from Tidewater Virginia throughout the backcountry. After a century of decline, the Scottish store model is victorious. In all these ways and more, "buying into the world of goods" is a drama that never ends.

Preface

1. William Blake, *For Children: The Gates of Paradise* (1793). Reproduced in David Bindman, *William Blake: His Art and Times* (New Haven, CT: Yale Center for British Art, 1982), 120–21.

Introduction. In Backcountry Time

1. Hook to Walter Chambre, December 28, 1773, John Hook Letterbook, Library of Virginia.

2. Mrs. Geo. Callaway, June 24, 1772, John Hook Petty Ledger, 1771–76, p. 14, Hook Papers, Rare Book, Manuscript, and Special Collections, Perkins Library, Duke University.

3. Benjamin Ruff, May 16, 1773, John Hook Mercantile Ledger, 1773–75, p. 9, Hook Papers, Duke.

4. Tarleton East, October 28, 1773, John Hook Mercantile Ledger, p. 19.

5. James Smith, July 20, 1774, John Hook Petty Ledger, p. 33.

6. John Hook's extant papers include 7,289 items and 103 account volumes stored in the Rare Book, Manuscript, and Special Collections at Duke University's Perkins Library. (Most relate to his son-in-law's business at a later period than that studied here.) Scratch copies of letterbooks and other miscellaneous items are found in the John Hook Papers, Business Records Collection, Library of Virginia. Parts of these collections are on microfilm at Colonial Williamsburg and the University of Virginia. Five letters are found in the Brock Collection at the Huntington Library. An additional eighteenth-century ledger is in family hands. Only two in-depth studies of John Hook have ever been produced. See Willard Pierson Jr., "John Hook: A Merchant of Colonial Virginia" (honors thesis, Duke University, 1962), and Warren Moorman, "John Hook: New London Merchant," *Journal of the Roanoke Valley Historical Society* 11 (1980): 40–54.

7. Yi-fu Tuan, *Space and Place: The Perspective of Experience* (Minneapolis: University of Minnesota Press, 1977). For the larger South as place, see *The Encyclopedia of Southern Culture*, ed. Charles Reagan Wilson and William Ferris (Chapel Hill: University of North Carolina Press, 1989), and for details of this specific region, see Terry G. Jordan-Bychkov, *The Upland South: The Making of an American Folk Region and Landscape* (Santa Fe, NM: Center for American Places, 2003).

8. Hook to William Donald, New London, May 29, 1768, Hook Papers, Duke.

9. See Lula Jeter Parker, *Parker's History of Bedford County, Virginia*, ed. Peter Viemeister (Bedford: Hamilton's, 1988), 7.

10. A single store in a town might have a market radius of 10 to 20 miles or between three and twelve hundred square miles. James O'Mara, *An Historical Geography of Urban System Development: Tidewater Virginia in the Eighteenth Century*, York University Geographical Monographs 13 (Downsview, Ontario: Department of Geography, Atkinson College, York University, 1983).

11. John S. Salmon and Emily J. Salmon, *Franklin County, Virginia, 1786–1986: A Bicentennial History* (Rocky Mount, VA: Franklin County Bicentennial Commission, 1993), 26. The Salmons's history of Franklin is quite simply a fine piece of modern local scholarship. John Salmon generously shared portions of his research with me in a far earlier day.

12. Warren R. Hofstra, *The Planting of New Virginia: Settlement and Landscape in the Shenandoah Valley* (Baltimore: Johns Hopkins University Press, 2004).

13. T. H. Breen, *Tobacco Culture: The Mentality of the Great Tidewater Planters on the Eve of Revolution* (Princeton, NJ: Princeton University Press, 1985).

14. Bernard Bailyn, *The Peopling of British North America: An Introduction* (New York: Knopf, 1986), 112.

15. Hook to James Lyle, New London, March 7, 1771, John Hook Letterbook, Library of Virginia.

16. The mid-Atlantic uplands contained "dual economies." Harry L. Watson, "Slavery and Development in a Dual Economy: The South and the Market Revolution," in *The Market Revolution in America: Social, Political, and Religious Expressions, 1800–1880*, ed. Melvin Stokes and Stephen Conway (Charlottesville: University Press of Virginia, 1996), 47.

17. Neil McKendrick, John Brewer, and J. H. Plumb, *The Birth of a Consumer Society: The Commercialization of Eighteenth-Century England* (Bloomington: Indiana University Press, 1982).

18. See, for example, Richard Bushman, *The Refinement of America: Persons, Houses, Cities* (New York: Knopf, 1992), and Cary Carson, "The Consumer Revolution in Colonial British America: Why Demand?" in *Of Consuming Interests*, ed. Cary Carson, Ronald Hoffman, and Peter J. Albert (Charlottesville: University Press of Virginia for the United States Capitol Historical Society, 1994), 483–697. The importance of mobility is the central proposition of Carson's article (523–24). These ideas about how the provincial elite defined themselves and their sociability have been further developed in the incisive work of David S. Shields; see *Civil Tongues and Polite Letters in British America* (Chapel Hill: Published for the Institute of Early American History and Culture, Williamsburg, Virginia, by the University of North Carolina Press, 1997).

19. Two critical volumes of essays are Larry E. Hudson Jr., ed., *Working toward Freedom: Slave Society and Domestic Economy in the American South* (Rochester, NY: University of Rochester Press, 1994), and Philip D. Morgan, *Slave Counterpoint: Black Culture in the Eighteenth-Century Chesapeake and Lowcountry* (Chapel Hill: Published for the Omohundro Institute of Early American History and Culture, Williamsburg, Virginia, by the University of North Carolina Press, 1998).

20. Benjamin Franklin to Timothy Folger, London, September 29, 1769, in

Franklin: Writings, ed. J. A. Leo Lemay (New York: Library of America, 1987), 847. "Blackamore, on Molatto Gentleman," *Pennsylvania Gazette*, August 30, 1733, in *Franklin: Writings*, 219.

21. John Hatcher, "Labour, Leisure and Economic Thought before the Nineteenth Century," *Past and Present* 160 (1998): 79.

22. William Eddis, *Letters from America*, ed. Aubrey C. Land (Cambridge, MA: Belknap Press, 1969), 51–52. Originally self-published in 1792.

23. Adam Smith, *An Inquiry into the Nature and Causes of the Wealth of Nations*, ed. Edwin Cannan (New York: Modern Library, 1937), 821. The view that man's desires are relative to his social universe is neatly summed up by Karl Marx, who wrote, "Our needs and enjoyments spring from society; we measure them, therefore, by society, and not by the objects of their satisfaction" ("Wage-Labour and Capital," in vol. 1 of *Selected Works* [London: Lawrence and Wishart, 1947], 268–69).

24. Smith, *Wealth of Nations*, 274. Bernard Mandeville, one of the earliest to point to the relationship between social rank and socially defined standards of living, noted dryly that "some people call it but decency to be served in plate, and reckon a coach-and-six among the necessary comforts of life." *Fable of the Bees; or, Private Vices, Public Benefits*, ed. Douglas Garman (1721; repr., London: Wishart, 1934), 191–92.

25. Adams, *The Works of John Adams*, 10 vols. (Boston: C. C. Little and J. Brown, 1850–56), 6:94.

26. Ann Smart Martin, "Material Things and Cultural Meanings: Notes on the Study of Early American Material Culture," *William and Mary Quarterly*, 3rd ser., 52, no. 1 (1996): 5–12.

27. John Styles, "Manufacturing, Consumption and Design in Eighteenth-Century England," in *Consumption and the World of Goods*, ed. John Brewer and Roy Porter (London: Routledge, 1993), 527–54.

28. Arjun Appadurai hence urges us to look at commodities in various "regimes of value" as they enter particular contexts that change through space and time ("Commodities and the Politics of Value," in *The Social Life of Things: Commodities in Cultural Perspective*, ed. Arjun Appadurai [Cambridge, UK: Cambridge University Press, 1986], 3–4). Appadurai introduces Georg Simmel and the idea of exchange in exciting ways that bring history and anthropology together in this edited volume.

1. The Business of Revolutions

1. I thank Anne Carter Lee, Rocky Mount, Virginia, for this extraordinary find.

2. "John Hook, Loyalist," *Virginia Magazine of History and Biography* 34, no. 2 (1926): 149–50. See also Hook to Henry Hook, Pages, August 28, 1764, John Hook Letterbook, Rare Book, Manuscript, and Special Collections, Perkins Library, Duke University.

3. Alan L. Karras, *Sojourners in the Sun: Scottish Migrants in Jamaica and the Chesapeake, 1740–1800* (Ithaca, NY: Cornell University Press, 1992).

4. Hugh Jones, *The Present State of Virginia*, ed. Richard L. Morton (Chapel Hill: University of North Carolina Press, 1956), 73.

5. Much of the following overview is discussed in more detail in Ann Smart Martin, "Buying into the World of Goods: Eighteenth-Century Consumerism from London to the Virginia Frontier" (Ph.D. diss., College of William and Mary, 1993).

6. One tradesman of this kind was Scotsman William Allason, who came to Virginia with parcels of goods for sale known as "cargoes." A brief discussion of Allason's early years as a supercargo is found in Edith E. B. Thompson, "A Scottish Merchant in Falmouth in the Eighteenth Century," *Virginia Magazine of History and Biography* 39 (1931): 108–17.

7. William Gooch to the board of trade, April 9, 1730, Public Record Office CO 5/1322, ff. 147–48.

8. For a study of the consignment trade, see Samuel Rosenblatt, "The House of John Norton and Sons: A Study of the Consignment Method of Marketing Tobacco from Virginia to England" (Ph.D. diss., Rutgers University, 1961). For more on John Norton and Sons, see Jacob Price, "Who was John Norton? A Note on the Historical Character of Some Eighteenth-Century London Virginia Firms," *William and Mary Quarterly*, 3rd ser., 19, no. 3 (1962): 400–407. The published letters of John Norton and Sons are found in Frances Norton Mason, ed., *John Norton and Sons, Merchants of London and Virginia* (Richmond: Dietz Press, 1937). See also Jacob Price, "The Last Phase of the Virginia-London Consignment Trade: James Buchanan and Co., 1758–1768," *William and Mary Quarterly*, 3rd ser., 43, no. 1 (1986): 64–98.

9. See, for instance, A Schedule of Goods Wanted from London by Hart and Marshall of Hanover Town from John Norton and Sons, in John Norton and Sons Papers, Folder 18, microfilm, John D. Rockefeller Jr. Library, Colonial Williamsburg Foundation.

10. Jacob M. Price, *Capital and Credit in British Overseas Trade: The View from the Chesapeake, 1770–1776* (Cambridge, MA: Harvard University Press, 1980), 25.

11. Roger Atkinson to Messrs. Lionel and Samuel Lye, July 5, 1769, transcribed in William Bundy Bynum, "Roger Atkinson, Merchant-Planter in Revolutionary Virginia" (master's thesis, University of Virginia, 1981), 51.

12. Robert Polk Thomson, "The Tobacco Export of the Upper James River Naval District, 1773–75," *William and Mary Quarterly*, 3rd ser., 18, no. 3 (1961): 396.

13. Ian Charles Cargill Graham, *Colonists from Scotland: Emigration to North America, 1707–1783* (Ithaca, NY: Cornell University Press, 1956), 124.

14. Another young Scot, Alexander Wilson, apprenticed in the small urban market town of Alexandria and explained his duties to his parents. See Karras, *Sojourners in the Sun*, 90.

15. Hook to Andrew Ramsay, August 28, 1766, John Hook Letterbook, Duke.

16. Hook to Duncan Hook, Warwick, August 1, 1763, Hook Papers, Duke.

17. Thomson, "The Tobacco Export of the Upper James River," 396.

18. Alexander Wilson began his apprenticeship at an annual wage of £10 with a £5 annual increase. Karras, *Sojourners in the Sun*, 90.

19. Hook to Henry Hook, Pages, March 1764, John Hook Letterbook, Duke.

20. Hook to Henry Hook, Pages, August 28, 1764, John Hook Letterbook, Duke.

21. Hook to Crawford and Gammele, Pages, December 12, 1765, John Hook Letterbook, Duke.

22. Hook to Crawford and Gammele, Pages, December 12, 1765, John Hook Letterbook, Duke.

23. Hook to Andrew Ramsay, August 28, 1766, John Hook Letterbook, Duke.

24. Hook to Andrew Ramsay, Pages, May 25, 1766, John Hook Letterbook, Duke.

25. Hook to Andrew Ramsay, August 28, 1766, John Hook Letterbook, Duke. Hook to William Donald, New London, December 9, 1766, John Hook Letterbook, Duke.

26. John Mair, *Book-keeping Methodiz'd: A Methodical Treatise of Merchant-Accompts, According to the Italian Form* (Edinburgh: Sands, Donaldson, Murray, and Cochrane, 1757), 333.

27. William Allason to ?, June 15, 1761, and William Allason to James Mitchell, Falmouth, August 19, 1760, William Allason Letterbook, 1757–70, Library of Virginia.

28. Francis Jerdone to Neil Buchanan, April 16, 1742, Francis Jerdone Account and Letterbook, 1739–44, Manuscripts Collections, Swem Library, College of William and Mary.

29. Arthur Morson to Neil Jamieson, Neil Jamieson Papers, Library of Congress (microfilm, John D. Rockefeller Jr. Library, Colonial Williamsburg Foundation). For more complaints about damage from moths and rats, see Francis Jerdone to Samuel Rickards, Israel Mauduit and Company, December 14, 1754, in "Letter Book of Francis Jerdone," *William and Mary College Quarterly Historical Magazine* 14, no. 3 (1906): 141–44.

30. Henry Fleming to Fischer and Bragg, Norfolk, July 29, 1774, Henry Fleming Letterbook, 1772–75, Cumbria County Council Archives Department (microfilm, John D. Rockefeller Jr. Library, Colonial Williamsburg Foundation).

31. James Lawson to John Semple, Glasgow, March 18, 1759, and James Lawson to James Russell, January 9, 1760, James Lawson–John Semple Accounts, Scottish Public Record Office, Currie-Dal Miscellaneous Bundle 20 (microfilm, John D. Rockefeller Jr. Library, Colonial Williamsburg Foundation). For a discussion of Semple's various entrepreneurial ventures, see David Curtis Scaggs, "John Semple and the Development of the Potomac Valley, 1750–1773," *Virginia Magazine of History and Biography* 92, no. 3 (July 1984): 282–308.

32. George Beeby to Jones and Bragg, July 13, 1759, William Bragg Papers, Duke; James Lawson to John Semple, August 31, 1759, James Lawson–John Semple Accounts.

33. For instance, he found that an agent usually provided working materials such as iron to poor workers, mostly women and children, who returned finished products in a week. That agent then shipped the goods off to a principal in London or Birmingham. Joshua Johnson to "the firm," April 17, 1772, in *Joshua Johnson's Letterbook 1771–1774: Letters from a Merchant in London to His Partners in Maryland,* ed. Jacob M. Price (London: London Record Society, 1979), 33.

34. William Allason also gives partial information on suppliers with occasional

subheadings under invoice totals in his invoice books. A few shop notes are also scattered throughout his loose papers. Both his books and papers are at the Library of Virginia. Shop notes are also occasionally found in the Hook Papers, Duke.

35. James Lawson to John Baddeley at Shelton near Newcastle-under-Lyne, Glasgow, January 2, 1759, James Lawson–John Semple Accounts. John Baddeley Sales Book, 1753–61, vol. 101, Aqualate Papers, Staffordshire Record Office. Baddeley's production is discussed in John Mallot, "John Baddeley of Shelton: An Early Staffordshire Maker of Pottery and Porcelain," *English Ceramic Circle Transactions* 6, pt. 2 (1967): 124–66 and *English Ceramic Circle Transactions* 6, pt. 3 (1967): 181–247.

36. All of these items are found in letterbook and daybooks, particularly Bundle 20, Box 2, No. 1/10, Daybook of Maryland Concern, 1757–June 1760, Scottish Record Office (microfilm, John D. Rockefeller Jr. Library, Colonial Williamsburg Foundation).

37. A parcel of broadcloth that was a good "pennyworth" was sent along to William Allason (Walker and Company, Glasgow, to William Allason, September 26, 1759, William Allason Letterbook [microfilm, John D. Rockefeller Jr. Library, Colonial Williamsburg Foundation]). This notion of advance is nicely summed up in Price, *Capital and Credit,* appendix A, 149–51. Henry Fleming also discusses it in a letter to Fisher and Bragg, undated 1772, Henry Fleming Letterbook, 1772–75. Lengthy testimony about long and short prices granted based on credit, drawbacks, and bounties are found in the court case of Freeland v. Heron, Lenox, U.S. Circuit Court, Richmond, Virginia, Record Book no. 13, May–December 1818, Library of Virginia. Long prices are "internal" prices on taxed or subsidized items, prices given when the firm goes to the trouble and expense to get the bounty or drawback from customs. Short prices leave any drawbacks or bounties to the shipper. James and Archibald Freeland's partnership agreement with Nathaniel Heron and Company of London showed that goods were to be charged only with the "usual commission" and shipping charges and that the Freeland partnership was entitled to all bounties, drawbacks, and abatements received by the London house. The agreement also stipulated that 15 percent of the cost of the sterling goods was to be charged in lieu of importation fees, to which was added the current exchange. Much of the case revolved around what was considered "usual."

38. For dropping advance, see Francis Jerdone to Messr. Samuel Rickards, Israel Mauduit and Company, December 14, 1764, Francis Jerdone Account and Letterbook; John Robinson to James Turner, October 4, 1768, and John Robinson to John Likely, October 6, 1771, reprinted in T. M. Devine, ed., *A Scottish Firm in Virginia, 1767–1777: W. Cuninghame and Co.* (Edinburgh: Clark Constable for the Scottish History Society, 1982), 9–45. For showing invoices to planters, see James Robinson to William Henderson, October 10, 1769, in Devine, *Scottish Firm,* 17.

39. Henry Fleming to Fisher and Bragg, Norfolk, June 19, 1772, Henry Fleming Letterbook, 1772–75.

40. All these were noted in correspondence between James Lawson and John Semple. Cited in Jean B. Lee, *The Price of Nationhood: The American Revolution in Charles County* (New York: W. W. Norton, 1994), 39.

41. Walker and Company to William Allason, Sept. 26, 1759, William Allason Letterbook, 1757–70. Allason chose Falmouth as a likely town in 1759. Neil Jamieson also chose Falmouth for his new store. Because he felt that new customers were easier to get than wooing old ones away from an established merchant, Jamieson chose a town in a less populated new area. Robert Thomson, "The Merchant in Virginia, 1700–1775" (Ph.D. diss., University of Wisconsin, 1955), 4.

42. Bedford County tobacco may have been especially prized for its quality; William Donald told his son that it brought a higher price than any other shipped from his stores. Deposition of Andrew Donald, April 12, 1806. Richard Crump testified in November of that year that Andrew Donald came to Virginia to collect debts for his father (Callaway v. Dobson, U.S. Circuit Court, Library of Virginia). These depositions all refer to pre-Revolutionary Virginia.

43. Peter Bergstrom, "Markets and Merchants: Economic Diversification in Colonial Virginia, 1700–1775" (Ph.D. diss., University of New Hampshire, 1980), table 5.4, p. 145. Thomson, "The Tobacco Export of the Upper James River," 394.

44. James Robinson to Thomas Gordon, August 23, 1770, William Cuninghame and Company Letterbook, reprinted in Devine, *Scottish Firm*, 34–35. Gordon was opening a store in Halifax County for the Cuninghame chain.

45. James Robinson to John Turner, Falmouth, October 8, 1771, in Devine, *Scottish Firm*, 44–48.

46. This sense that country stores were most numerous "wherever the middling classes are a considerable proportion of the population" because the wealthy either raised everything they needed or shopped in town is articulated clearly in a description of Louisiana on the eve of the Civil War. Lewis Atherton, *The Southern Country Store, 1800–1860* (Baton Rouge: Louisiana State University Press, 1949), 20.

47. John Tabb to William Patterson Smith, April 15, 1806. William Patterson Smith Papers, Rare Book, Manuscript, and Special Collections, Perkins Library, Duke University.

48. James Robinson to John Turner, October 6, 1771, in Devine, *Scottish Firm*, 47.

49. James Robinson to William Cuninghame, October 8, 1771, in Devine, *Scottish Firm*, 49.

50. Robert Rives, Charlotte Court House, to Richard Blow, March 9, 1785, and Robert Rives, Charlotte Court House, to Richard Blow, April 9, 1785, 7, fols. 9 and 10, Blow Family Papers and Scrapbook, 1770–1815, Manuscripts Collections, Swem Library, College of William and Mary.

51. Hook to William Donald, New London, December 9, 1766, John Hook Letterbook, Duke.

52. Callaway's store was already in business when Thomas Walker passed through in 1750; Ruth Hairston Early, *Campbell Chronicles and Family Sketches: Embracing the History of Campbell County, Virginia, 1782–1926* (Lynchburg, VA: J. P. Bell, 1927), 3.

53. Hook to William Donald and Company, Bedford Court House, December 2, 1767, and May 29, 1768, John Hook Letterbook, Duke.

54. Hook to William Donald, New London, May 29, 1768, John Hook Letterbook, Duke.

55. James Callaway v. Matthew and Joshua Dobson, administrators of Jn. Dobson, deceased, U.S. Circuit Court, Richmond, Virginia, 1811, unrestricted, Oversize File 2, Box 221, 1810–12, Library of Virginia. My thanks to John Salmon for alerting me to this important, and previously undiscussed, reference. Dobson, Daltera, and Walker were a Liverpool firm that seems to have functioned as a consignment house, supplying goods in lots to a large number of independent Virginia merchants. Callaway and Trents were but one of their many concerns. The result was that they were the largest English firm exporting tobacco from the Upper James River between 1773 and 1775. Thomson, "The Tobacco Export of the Upper James River," 397–98.

56. Hook to Ross, January 17, 1772, John Hook Letterbook, Duke.

57. Hook to William Donald Jr., New London, June 14, 1769, John Hook Letterbook, Duke.

58. Hook to James Nowell Jr., New London, March 15, 1771, John Hook Letterbook, Duke.

59. For example, see Hook to Archibald Gowan, Bedford Court House, January 10, 1771, John Hook Letterbook, Duke.

60. Hook to N.D., December 6, 1770, Hook Papers, Duke.

61. Hook to James Lyle, New London, March 7, 1771, John Hook Letterbook, Duke.

62. Hook to James Lyle, New London, March 7, 1771, John Hook Letterbook, Duke.

63. Hook to James Lyle, New London, March 7, 1771, John Hook Letterbook, Duke.

64. Hook to James Lyle, New London, May 30, 1771, John Hook Letterbook, Duke.

65. Hook to Ross, December 31, 1771, John Hook Letterbook, Duke.

66. Hook to James Lyle, New London, April 21, 1771, John Hook Letterbook, Duke.

67. Hook to James Lyle, New London, June 14, 1771, John Hook Letterbook, Duke.

68. *Virginia Gazette*, Purdie and Dixon, August 19, 1771, 3.

69. Price, *Capital and Credit*, 39.

70. Jackson Turner Main, "The One Hundred," *William and Mary Quarterly*, 3rd ser., 11, no. 3 (1954): 354–84.

71. For a brief description of the Farish Print Shop, see Ralph Emmett Fall, *Hidden Village, Port Royal, Virginia, 1744–1981* (Port Royal: R. E. Fall, 1982). The Farish Shop has one fewer dormer window for lighting the upstairs storage area, and the office and storage area are of slightly different dimensions. The chimney is also placed differently. Overall, however, the forty- by twenty-foot size, the organization of the space, and the fenestration of the first floor are remarkably similar; Hook even mistakenly wrote the dimensions "40 x 20" on his plan, although the dimensions of his room added up to forty-two by twenty feet. The structure may have been used

as a tavern in the late eighteenth century. Port Royal, like New London, was also a small mercantile town, home to five or six Scottish merchants and about twenty or thirty houses in 1775, although it lay on navigable water. Robert Honyman, *Colonial Panorama, 1775: Dr. Robert Honyman's Journal for March and April,* ed. Phillip Padelford (Freeport, NY: Books for Libraries Press, 1971), 1.

72. Alexander Stewart, Robert Donald's factor at Rocky Ridge, merely explained that they intended closing this store and opening another where there was less competition. Alexander Stewart to John Smith, February 23, 1772, Pocket Plantation Papers, Small Special Collections Library, Harrison Institute, University of Virginia.

73. Ross to Hook, Richmond, February 6, 1772, Hook Papers, Duke.

74. Ross to Hook, March 11, 1773, John Hook Letterbook, Library of Virginia. This may be Hook's personal scratch letterbook.

75. Hook to Ross, New London, March 2, 1772, Hook Papers, Duke.

76. Alexander Stewart to John Smith, Rocky Ridge, October 20, 1772, Pocket Plantation Papers. Stewart may ultimately have joined William Cuninghame and Company. Smith's important account was taken by Alexander Banks, the firm's factor in Manchester who wrote, "nothing in my power shall be wanting to continue you as a customer." Alexander Banks to John Smith, Manchester, November 7, 1772, Pocket Plantation Papers.

77. Ross to Hook, Richmond, May 23, 1772, Hook Papers, Duke.

78. Ross to John White Holt, Petersburg, August 17, 1772, Hook Papers, Duke.

79. Richard B. Sheridan, "The British Credit Crisis of 1772 and the American Colonies," *Journal of Economic History* 20, no. 2 (1960): 161–86.

80. Ross to Hook, Suffolk, August 25, 1772, Hook Papers, Duke.

81. Ross to Hook, Suffolk, August 25, 1772, Hook Papers, Duke.

82. Ross to Hook, Suffolk, August 25, 1772, Hook Papers, Duke.

83. Ross to Hook, Petersburg, October 12, 1772, Hook Papers, Duke.

84. Ross to Hook, Petersburg, September 16, 1772, Hook Papers, Duke.

85. Agreement to Fix Advances on Most Common Items Sold, October 5, 1772, New London.

86. Agreement of Bedford County Merchants, October 6, 1772, New London.

87. *Virginia Gazette,* Purdie and Dixon, October 17, 1771.

88. *Virginia Gazette,* Purdie and Dixon, November 25, 1773, 2.

89. *Virginia Gazette,* Purdie and Dixon, November 25, 1773, 2.

90. *Virginia Gazette,* Purdie and Dixon, November 25, 1773, 2.

91. Hook to E. Brisbane, New London, March 15, 1773, John Hook Letterbook, Library of Virginia.

92. *Virginia Gazette,* Purdie and Dixon, November 23, 1773.

93. Quoted in Drew McCoy, *The Elusive Republic: Political Economy in Jeffersonian America* (Chapel Hill: Published for the Institute of Early American History and Culture, Williamsburg, Virginia, by the University of North Carolina Press, 1980), 59.

94. "The Examination of Doctor Benjamin Franklin, before an August As-

sembly, relating to the Repeal of the STAMP-ACT, &c," February 13, 1766, in *The Papers of Benjamin Franklin*, 36 vols., ed. Leonard W. Labaree et al. (New Haven, CT: Yale University Press, 1959), 13:143.

95. Hook to E. Brisbane, New London, March 15, 1773, John Hook Letterbook, Library of Virginia.

96. G. C. Callahan, "Some of the Meads," *William and Mary College Quarterly Historical Papers* 10, no. 3 (1902): 193–96.

97. Memorandum of Goods for Mead, September 9, 1772, Hook Papers, Duke.

98. Barbara Crawford and Royster Lyle Jr., *Rockbridge County Artists and Artisans* (Charlottesville: University Press of Virginia, 1995), 130.

99. Personal communication, George Dalgleish, acting head of Museum of Scotland International, April 2002.

100. David S. Landes, *Revolution in Time: Clocks and the Making of the Modern World* (Cambridge, MA: Belknap Press, 1983).

101. Martin Bruegel, "'Time That Can be Relied Upon': The Evolution of Time Consciousness in the mid-Hudson River Valley, 1790–1869," *Journal of Social History* 28, no. 3 (Spring 1995): 547–64.

102. Joseph T. Rainer, "'Commercial Scythians' in the Great Valley of Virginia: Yankee Peddlers' Trade Connections to Antebellum Virginia," in *After the Backcountry: Rural Life in the Great Valley of Virginia, 1800–1900*, ed. Kenneth E. Koons and Warren R. Hofstra (Knoxville: University of Tennessee Press, 2000), 62.

103. Suzanne Coffman, "Timepiece Ownership and Use in Fairfax County, Virginia, 1752–1825: Evidence of the Consumer Revolution in Everyday American Life" (master's thesis, George Washington University, 1984).

104. Benno Forman, "German Influences in Pennsylvania Furniture," in *Arts of the Pennsylvania Germans*, ed. Scott T. Swank and Catherine E. Hutchins (New York: W.W. Norton for the Winterthur Museum, 1983), 148.

105. Details of William Mead's life are captured in Christine Leigh Heyrman, *Southern Cross: The Beginnings of the Bible Belt* (New York: Knopf, 1997), 118–20. Primary documentation is from Callahan, "Some of the Meads."

2. Getting the Goods

1. Carole Shammas uses the powerful concept of "sovereign consumption" to highlight the degree of freedom to consume that must be aligned within any supply system: indeed, "hierarchically structured consumer demand" was inevitable (*The Pre-Industrial Consumer in England and America* [Oxford, UK: Clarendon Press, 1990], 203).

2. Orders for 1770, Henry Fitzhugh Accounts, Rare Book, Manuscript, and Special Collections, Perkins Library, Duke University.

3. John Mercer to George Mercer, letter begun December 22, 1767, and ended January 28, 1768, when the river thawed enough for it to be posted, *George Mercer Papers Relating to the Ohio Company of Virginia*, ed. Lois Mulkearn (Pittsburgh: University of Pittsburgh Press, 1954), 211–20.

4. Richard Morriss, Hanover County, Green Springs, to James Maury, Liver-

pool, February 11, 1788, Morriss Family Papers, no. 38–79, Small Special Collections Library, Harrison Institute, University of Virginia.

5. Peter Lyon to John Norton, September 25, 1771, John Norton and Sons Papers, John D. Rockefeller Jr. Library, Colonial Williamsburg Foundation.

6. William Lee to the Honorable George W. Fairfax, Esq., January 19, 1770, William Lee Letterbook, 1769–71, Robert E. Lee Memorial Foundation, Stratford Hall (microfilm, John D. Rockefeller Jr. Library, Colonial Williamsburg Foundation).

7. Many examples can be found in the letters of Virginia planters to their partners in England. Rebecca Chamberlayne was indebted to Mrs. Norton for the selection of her petticoat (Chamberlayne to John Norton and Sons, July 28, 1770, John Norton and Sons Papers). Mrs. Downman was anxious that Mrs. Athawes or her daughters choose for her "a half-yard Spanish purple poplin shot with yellow" as well as cotton (Raleigh Downman to Edward and Samuel Athawes, March 31, 1776, Downman Letterbook, Library of Congress [microfilm, John D. Rockefeller Jr. Library, Colonial Williamsburg Foundation]). Mrs. Campbell helped in the choice of an elaborate brocade gown for Henry Fitzhugh's daughter (Fitzhugh to Jno. Stewart and Campbell, January 28, 1771, Fitzhugh Letterbook, Rare Book, Manuscript, and Special Collections, Perkins Library, Duke University). For promise that Mrs. Lee will supervise purchases, see William Lee to George W. Fairfax, January 19, 1770, William Lee Letterbook, 1769–71.

8. William Preston's Memorandum for Williamsburg, July 1771, Box 3, 688, William Preston Papers, Virginia Historical Society. For the spread of creamware, see Ann Smart Martin, "'Fashionable Sugar Dishes, Latest Fashion Ware': The Creamware Revolution in the Eighteenth-Century Chesapeake," in *Historical Archaeology of the Chesapeake,* ed. Paul Shackel and Barbara J. Little (Washington: Smithsonian Institution Press, 1994), 169–87.

9. David Richard to John Smith, July 20, 1769, Pocket Plantation Papers, Small Special Collections Library, Harrison Institute, University of Virginia (microfilmed in "Records of Antebellum Southern Plantations: From the Revolution to the Civil War," series E: part 1, Reels 11–13).

10. John Hook Memorandum Book, March 1773, pp. 37–38, Hook Papers, Duke.

11. For peddling in rural New England, see David Jaffee, "Peddlers of Progress and the Transformation of the Rural North, 1760–1860," *Journal of American History* 78, no. 2 (1991): 511–35.

12. Richard Beeman, ed., "Trade and Travel in Post-Revolutionary Virginia: A Diary of an Itinerant Peddler," *Virginia Magazine of History and Biography* 84 (1976): 177.

13. Beeman, ed., "Trade and Travel in Post-Revolutionary Virginia," 177, 179. For peddlers and the secondhand trade in England, see Beverly Lemire, *Fashion's Favourite: The Cotton Trade and the Consumer in Britain, 1660–1800* (New York: Oxford University Press, 1991), 115–60.

14. "Price Lists and Diary of Col. Fleming," *Virginia Historical Magazine* 5 (1897–98): 263–64. See also the Account Book of Sir Peyton Skipwith for payment

of £1.4.0 for a hat from "the peddlar" on September 14, 1795. Skipwith Papers, Account Book 2, 1775–81 (scattered notes to 1795), Manuscripts Collections, Swem Library, College of William and Mary.

15. John S. Salmon and Emily J. Salmon, *Franklin County, Virginia, 1786–1986: A Bicentennial History* (Rocky Mount, VA: Franklin County Bicentennial Commission, 1993), 114.

16. Account of Sale of the Estate of Edward Goldman, January 3, 1775, returned November 29, 1787, Bedford County Will Book 1, 1763–87, Library of Virginia.

17. Col. Francis Taylor Diary, 1786–99, Library of Virginia (microfilm, John D. Rockefeller Jr. Library, Colonial Williamsburg Foundation). It is not clear whose sale it was, but the large lots suggest it may have been a merchant's. Merchants sponsored other auctions or vendues, especially if a particular market was glutted with goods. Little is known of this source, but Matthew Read and Hugh Johnson's ledger in nearby Staunton in Botetourt County is filled with customer charges for goods bought at vendue in the late 1760s. Matthew Read and Hugh Johnson Ledger, 1761–70, Manuscripts Collections, Swem Library, College of William and Mary.

18. Matthew Read and Hugh Johnson Ledger, 1761–70.

19. Will, March 11, 1787, and Inventory, June 6, 1789, of Jacob Hickman, Franklin County Will Book 1, 1786–1812, Library of Virginia.

20. Will of Jeremiah Early, September 1779, Bedford County Will Book 1.

21. Will of Robert Ewing, March 2, 1786, Bedford County Will Book 1.

22. Will of Guy Smith, September 24, 1781, Bedford County Will Book 1.

23. Another woman was left his land, provided she pay his son William Adams the sum of £50. Will of John Adams, Bedford County Will Book 2, August 3, 1796, Library of Virginia.

24. Will of Peter Funk, July 7, 1796, Campbell County Will Book 1, 1782–1800, Library of Virginia.

25. Salmon and Salmon, *Franklin County*, 113.

26. The suit was over payment for a desk and planking (February 2, 1763, Bedford County Order Book 3, 1763–77, Library of Virginia).

27. The desk is in the collection of Salem Historical Society. It and its label are reproduced in John D. Long and Mary Crockett Hill, *A Town by the Name of Salem: The Past in Pictures* (Salem, VA: Salem Museum and Historical Society, 2002), 23. Thanks to Warren Moorman for taking me to see this object.

28. Frank Horton documented the desk in 1976 during field study for the Museum of Early Southern Decorative Arts, Winston-Salem, North Carolina. Its owner's great-grandmother had purchased it in what was then Patrick County. A Samuel Linear and a Joseph Scales were both titheables in Henry County in 1779. Loose papers, Henry County, Library of Virginia.

29. Salmon and Salmon, *Franklin County*, 33.

30. Account of the Estate of William Jones, March 3, 1785, October 6, 1785, April 1, 1790, Campbell County Will Book 1.

31. For instance, see Joan M. Jensen, "Cloth, Butter and Boarders: Women's Household Production for the Market," in *Domestic Ideology and Domestic Work*, vol.

4 of *History of Women in the United States: Historical Articles on Women's Lives and Activities*, ed. Nancy Cott (New York: K.G. Saur, 1992), 264–90. Two important studies that do take on the role of women as consumers, albeit in England, are Lorna Weatherill, "A Possession of One's Own: Women and Consumer Behavior in England, 1660–1740," *Journal of British Studies* 25, no. 2 (1986): 131–56, and Amanda Vickery, "Women and the World of Goods: A Lancashire Consumer and Her Possessions, 1751–1781," in *Consumption and the World of Goods*, ed. John Brewer and Roy Porter (London: Routledge, 1993), 274–301.

32. Jan de Vries, "Between Purchasing Power and the World of Goods: Understanding the Household Economy in Early Modern Europe," in *Consumption and the World of Goods*, 118. He suggests a more complex model of a cooperative unit— "a realm of altruism" that guided relationships within the household to a greater maximum utility. Put more simply, de Vries calls us to unlock that black box in order to get a sense of choices made within households about market participation.

33. "Narrative of the Travels of a Scotsman from Glasgow," manuscript, 1821–24, vol. 1, p. 43, New York Historical Society.

34. Jack P. Greene, "Independence, Improvement, and Authority: Toward a Framework for Understanding the Histories of the Southern Backcountry during the Era of the American Revolution," in *An Uncivil War: The Southern Backcountry during the American Revolution*, ed. Ronald Hoffman, Thad W. Tate, Peter J. Albert (Charlottesville: University Press of Virginia for the United States Capitol Historical Society), 443–44, 523.

35. Ross to Robert Richardson, January 1813, David Ross Letterbook, Library of Virginia.

36. For discussion of the multiple ways that food moved through a local economy, see Lorena S. Walsh, Ann Smart Martin, and Joanne Bowen, "Provisioning Early American Towns: The Chesapeake; A Multidisciplinary Case Study," final report to the National Endowment for the Humanities, Grant RO-22643-93, Colonial Williamsburg Foundation.

37. Edward Miles Riley, ed., *The Journal of John Harrower, An Indentured Servant in the Colony of Virginia, 1773–1776* (New York: Holt, Rinehart, and Winston, 1963), 138.

38. My thanks to Linda Sturtz for allowing me to read and comment on her manuscript copy of *Within Her Power: Propertied Women in Colonial America* (New York: Routledge, 2002), which details this wonderful chapbook scene.

39. Daniel Drake, *Pioneer Life in Kentucky, 1785–1800*, ed. Emmet Field Horine (New York: Henry Schuman, 1948), 115. Most of these activities remain unseen to the historian, unless caught in the glaring light of some form of accounting practice. Recent studies by Laurel Ulrich and Joanne Bowen Gaynor have demonstrated how such transactions were not always ad hoc but rather involved precise reciprocity of services, commodities, and cash. Laurel Thatcher Ulrich, *A Midwife's Tale: The Life of Martha Ballard, Based on Her Diary, 1785–1812* (New York: Knopf, 1990), and Joanne Bowen, "A Study of Seasonality and Subsistence: Eighteenth-Century Suffield, Connecticut" (Ph.D. diss., Brown University, 1990).

40. Advertisement found in Maude Carter Clemons Collection, Box 2, Small Special Collections Library, Harrison Institute, University of Virginia.

41. Jane Frances Walker Page and Jane Byrd Nelson Walker Commonplace Book, manuscript, Virginia Historical Society. Amy Karen Rider has written an outstanding analysis of the manuscript in "The Castle Hill Commonplace Book and the Plantation Mistress's World, 1802–1845" (honors thesis, Princeton University, 1997).

42. Lucy Bailey, August 1772–July 1773, John Hook Mercantile Ledger, 1773–75, p. 10, Hook Papers, Duke; Sarah Tisdale, August 13 and December 9, 1772, John Hook Daybook, Falling River, 1772–73, Hook Papers, Duke; Ruth Mosse, July 24, 1772, and August 27, 1772, John Hook Petty Ledger, 1771–76, Hook Papers, Duke. Laurel Thatcher Ulrich uses specific diary evidence to brilliantly illuminate how women and men had discrete responsibilities and obligations as well as how numerous neighborhood systems of exchange bypassed more institutional economic avenues. She cites a merchant's letter suggesting that women had certain "perquisites" that were clearly their own to barter or sell. That the merchant proposed stocking items to induce them to center their exchanges through his store shows that consumer items for women were no less important in Maine than Virginia. Laurel Thatcher Ulrich, "Martha Ballard and Her Girls: Women's Work in Eighteenth-Century Maine," in *Work and Labor in Early America*, ed. Stephen Innes (Chapel Hill: University of North Carolina Press, 1988), 84–86.

43. Hook to Ross, New London, November 7, 1771, John Hook Letterbook, Library of Virginia.

44. Hook to Ross, New London, November 7, 1771, John Hook Letterbook, Library of Virginia.

45. The letter is undated and torn. Hook to Ross, December 30, 1771, John Hook Letterbook, Library of Virginia.

46. Hook to Ross, New London, April 20, 1773, John Hook Letterbook, Library of Virginia.

47. Hook to Ross, New London, June 10, 1773, John Hook Letterbook, Library of Virginia.

48. Ross to Hook, Petersburg, June 23, 1773, John Hook Letterbook, Library of Virginia.

49. Hook to Walter Chambre, December 28, 1773, John Hook Letterbook, Library of Virginia.

50. Hook to Walter Chambre, New London, December 23, 1773, John Hook Letterbook, Library of Virginia.

51. John Bezís-Selfa, *Forging America: Ironworks, Adventurers, and the Industrious Revolution* (Ithaca, NY: Cornell University Press, 2004), 14.

52. Salmon and Salmon, *Franklin County*, 108–10.

53. John S. Salmon, *The Washington Iron Works of Franklin County, Virginia, 1773–1850* (Richmond: Virginia State Library, 1986), 15, describes iron making both eloquently and simply.

54. Salmon, *Washington Iron Works*, 15–17.

55. For a good conjectural drawing of the Marlboro furnace, 1772–96, see Bar-

bara Crawford and Royster Lyle Jr., *Rockbridge County Artists and Artisans* (Charlottesville: University Press of Virginia, 1995), 155. Their chapter on ironwork is also quite useful (151–65).

56. Salmon and Salmon, *Franklin County,* 109.

57. Salmon, *Washington Iron Works,* 50–52.

58. For a visual catalog of the kind of ironwares made and used in colonial America, see the trade card of Joseph Webb, Boston iron merchant, which Paul Revere engraved (housed in collection of American Antiquarian Society), illustrated in Henry J. Kauffman, *Early American Ironware, Cast and Wrought* (Rutland, VT: Charles E. Tuttle, 1966), 30.

59. I turned to many scholars for advice. It was their mutual astonishment that drove me on. Thanks to John Davis, curator of metals, Colonial Williamsburg Foundation, and Donald L. Fennimore, curator, Winterthur Museum, for their expertise and curiosity. One of the benefits of being at a world-class university is that I can walk to the next building to ask premiere metalworking scholars and artists for their insights. My thanks to professors Fred Fenster and Lisa Gralnick and graduate student Andrew Thurlow in the metals section of the art department at the University of Wisconsin–Madison for explaining and debating casting and finishing processes via close study of Franklin County plates.

60. Martin, "Fashionable Sugar Dishes, Latest Fashion Wares,'" 169–87.

61. These plates are documented in the fieldwork research files at the Museum of Early Southern Decorative Arts in Winston-Salem, North Carolina. A final example has been found from either Smyth or Washington County, Virginia, and just published in Betsy K. White, *Great Road Style: The Decorative Arts Legacy of Southwest Virginia and Northeast Tennessee* (Charlottesville: University of Virginia Press, 2006), fig. 174, p. 184.

62. Crawford and Lyle, *Rockbridge County Artists and Artisans,* 163.

63. Edward S. Cooke Jr., "Making Furniture in the Salisbury Iron Region: The Case of Bates How," *Yale Journal of Criticism* 11, no. 1 (1998): 85–93. I am grateful for Cooke's perceptive analysis.

3. Accounting for Life

1. Answer of John F. Price to the Interrogatories of John Hook, sworn June 15, 1808, Ross v. Hook, U.S. Circuit Court, Richmond, Virginia, Hook Papers, Library of Virginia.

2. Answer of John F. Price to the Interrogatories of John Hook, sworn June 15, 1808, Ross v. Hook, U.S. Circuit Court, Richmond, Virginia, Hook Papers.

3. Questions of John F. Price by John Hook, June 15, 1808, Answer of John F. Price to the Interrogatories of John Hook, sworn June 15, 1808, Deposition of George Turnball and Skelton Taylor, acting commissioners, September 5, 1801, and other testimony, Ross v. Hook, U.S. Circuit Court, Richmond, Virginia, Hook Papers.

4. Answer of John F. Price to the Interrogatories of John Hook, sworn June 15, 1808, Ross v. Hook, U.S. Circuit Court, Richmond, Virginia, Hook Papers.

5. John Mair, *Book-keeping Methodiz'd: A Methodical Treatise of Merchant-*

Accompts, According to the Italian Form (Edinburgh: Sands, Donaldson, Murray, and Cochrane, 1757), 4.

6. Remarks on the Cash and Tobacco Accounts Taken from John Hook's Books up the Date of the Compromise at Capital in Richmond 1808, Box 58, XIII, 8, p. 27, Hook Papers, Library of Virginia.

7. John Hook Daybook, 1771–72, John Hook Ledger, 1773–74, John Hook Petty Ledger, 1773–75, John Hook Mercantile Ledger, 1773–75, all found in the Hook Papers, Rare Book, Manuscript, and Special Collections, Perkins Library, Duke University.

8. The term "frontcountry" is used by Warren Hofstra to describe a landscape of dispersed farms and market towns in *The Planting of New Virginia: Settlement and Landscape in the Shenandoah Valley* (Baltimore: Johns Hopkins University Press, 2004), 329.

9. Richard B. Sheridan, "The British Credit Crisis of 1772 and the American Colonies," *Journal of Economic History* 20, no. 2 (1960): 161–86.

10. For example, Charles Farmer found that 48 percent of total annual sales were made between November and January at James Murdoch's store in nearby Halifax County. December volume was the greatest for any month and was six times that of August. Similar patterns were found in the sales of other Southside merchants ("Country Stores and Frontier Exchange Systems in Southside Virginia during the Eighteenth Century" [Ph.D. diss., University of Maryland, 1984]). A more recent study of frontier stores for a later period is Elizabeth Perkins, "The Consumer Frontier: Household Consumption in Early Kentucky," *Journal of American History* 78, no. 2 (1991): 486–510.

11. Analysis based on a 1775 memorandum book listing customers, locations, and debts (Box 55, Hook Papers, Duke).

12. Hook and Ross also ran a smaller and more rural store located on the Staunton River to the south and east of New London. This accommodated both traffic from the wagon road west from Petersburg and increasing river traffic (Falling River). Hook had hired John White Holt to be storekeeper there, a position he held until he returned to Scotland with the general wartime exodus.

More of a trading post, the Falling River store is less well documented than its larger, more urban cohort in New London. Nevertheless, a fragment of a daybook exists for May 2–24, 1773, recording ninety-one different customers. The most common items sold were the same as those sold at the New London store: inexpensive fabrics (osnaburg and rolls) and alcohol (rum and brandy).

13. Alexander Steward to John Smith, January 17, 1769, Pocket Plantation Papers, Small Special Collections Library, Harrison Institute, University of Virginia.

14. Lorena S. Walsh, Ann Smart Martin, and Joanne Bowen, "Provisioning Early American Towns: The Chesapeake; A Multidisciplinary Case Study," final report to the National Endowment for the Humanities, Grant RO-22643-93, Colonial Williamsburg Foundation.

15. *Virginia Gazette,* in Paton Yoder, "Tavern Regulation in Virginia," *Virginia Magazine of History and Biography* 87 (1979): 275.

16. Cited in Mary R. M. Goodwin, *The Colonial Trade,* Colonial Williamsburg Foundation Research Report Series (1966), 33–35.

17. A sample of customers at William Allason's store at the fall line at Falmouth between 1769 and 1772 also demonstrated that textiles, notions, and sewing items made up just under half of all purchases. This fits the pattern in other studies of stores throughout Virginia in the eighteenth century. The Allason study was based on a sample of thirty-three customers making 1,238 purchases between 1769 and 1772. William Allason Papers, Ledger 1, Library of Virginia (microfilm, John D. Rockefeller Jr. Library, Colonial Williamsburg Foundation). Other studies can be found in Farmer, "Country Stores and Exchange Systems," and Harold B. Gill, "The Retail Trade in Colonial Virginia" (unpublished manuscript, January 1984, John D. Rockefeller Jr. Library, Colonial Williamsburg Foundation).

18. Disappearance of clothing onto the backs of others is one factor in the underrepresentation of clothing in probate inventories. That problem aside, it is the immense *replacement* cost of these items that is not captured in inventories. For further detail on the Bedford probate study, see Ann Smart Martin, "'Fine Feathers Make Fine Birds': Clothing and Consumerism in the Eighteenth-Century Virginia Store Trade" (paper presented at the Clothing and Consumerism in Early Modern England and America Conference, Victoria and Albert Museum, London, June 26–27, 1992).

19. The authority on women's clothing and textiles in Virginia is Linda Baumgarten, curator of textiles at Colonial Williamsburg. See Baumgarten, *What Clothes Reveal: The Language of Clothing in Colonial and Federal America* (New Haven, CT: Colonial Williamsburg Foundation with Yale University Press, 2002). Laurel Thatcher Ulrich examines cultural roles of women's textile production in *The Age of Homespun: Objects and Stories in the Creation of an American Myth* (New York: Alfred A. Knopf, 2001).

20. Invoice of Goods Shipped by Walter Chambre on the Milham for Norfolk and James River, Virginia by Order of Eilbeck, Ross, and Company, Hook Papers, Duke University.

21. Invoice of Goods Shipped by Walter Chambre on the Milham for Norfolk and James River, Virginia by Order of Eilbeck, Ross, and Company, Hook Papers.

22. The suit probably set him back £11 in Virginia currency. Edward Dixon, a merchant in Caroline County in eastern Virginia, also imported two suits in 1769, although he kept one for himself. These varied only slightly from the ones stocked by John Hook. Dixon Ledger B, 1768–71, Library of Virginia. Cited in Gill, "Retail Trade in Colonial Virginia."

23. Invoice of Goods to Be Bought by Captain James Ward for Account of Charles Yates and Daniel Payne, August 23, 1780, microfilm, John D. Rockefeller Jr. Library, Colonial Williamsburg Foundation. Jones and Bragg to George Beeby, Petersburg, Virginia, April 15, 1769, William Bragg Papers, Rare Book, Manuscript, and Special Collections, Perkins Library, Duke University.

24. For example, see Jones and Bragg to Mr. George Beeby, Petersburg, Virginia, April 15, 1769. William Bragg Papers, Special Collections, Duke University.

25. Hook to Ross, New London, April 20, 1773, John Hook Letterbook, Library of Virginia.

26. Another merchant crowed that nothing contributed so well toward the cheap purchase of tobacco as a ready supply of good osnaburg, cottons, and other coarse cloth. Cited in Calvin B. Coulter Jr., "The Import Trade of Colonial Virginia," *William and Mary Quarterly*, 3rd ser., 2, no. 3 (1945): 303.

27. Linda Baumgarten, "'Clothes for the People': Slave Clothing in Early Virginia," *Journal of Early Southern Decorative Arts* 14, no. 2 (1988): 28–70.

28. Survey of *Virginia Gazette* advertisements for runaway servants from 1760–70, Colonial Williamsburg Foundation. My thanks to Linda Baumgarten for sharing her files.

29. Devereux Jarratt, *The Life of the Reverend Devereux Jarratt, Rector of Bath Parish, Dinwiddie County, Virginia Written by Himself. In a Series of Letters to the Reverend John Coleman* (1806; repr., NY: Arno Press, 1969), 27.

30. Paul Clemens estimated that a family of four producing two thousand pounds of tobacco spent some 40 percent on clothing or £1 per person (*The Atlantic Economy and Colonial Maryland's Eastern Shore: From Tobacco to Grain* [Ithaca, NY: Cornell University Press, 1980]). This must have been for the most basic kinds of clothing as several planters estimated that £1 sterling was the cost of clothing a slave. My thanks to Lorena Walsh for that information from her *"Motives of Honour, Pleasure, and Profitt": Plantation Management in the Colonial Chesapeake, 1607–1763* (Chapel Hill: University of North Carolina Press, forthcoming).

31. For slave value, see table 4.2. Hook's prices are from his mercantile and petty ledgers. Other prices are from: Account of Barbering, Richard Morriss with Joseph Brand, 1771–72, Morriss Family Papers, Virginia Historical Society. On attending the play in Williamsburg, see Thomas Jefferson Memorandum Book, 1767–70, Thomas Jefferson Papers, Series 4, Library of Congress (microfilm, John D. Rockefeller Jr. Library, Colonial Williamsburg Foundation); on attending the fireworks display in Annapolis, William Ennals Memorandum Book, 1771–74, Library of Congress.

32. Herbert J. Stoeckel, "Down the Years to Babylon in the Making of Blank Books," *Bookbinding and Book Production* 25 (1937): 22–24.

33. C. Clement Samford and John M. Hemphill II, *Bookbinding in Colonial Virginia* (Charlottesville: University Press of Virginia for Colonial Williamsburg, 1966), 7, 47.

34. My thanks to Janie C. Morris, research services librarian, Rare Book, Manuscript, and Special Collections, Perkins Library, Duke University, for examining the details of size and condition in these accounts. Shreds on the spine of the 1771–72 ledger suggest that portion of the covers was of leather.

35. My thanks to Jeanne Solensky, librarian, Joseph Downs Collection of Manuscripts and Printed Ephemera, and Catherine Cooney, senior librarian, Printed Book and Periodical Collection, both at the Winterthur Library, and Gail Greve, special collections librarian and associate curator of Rare Books and Manuscripts, John D. Rockefeller Jr. Library, Colonial Williamsburg Foundation, for personal discussion and information from their collections databases.

36. Personal communication, John Krill, senior paper conservator, Winterthur Museum, Garden, and Library, February 4, 2004.

37. William Birch advertisement, c. 1790–1814, no. 75 x 228.1, Joseph Downs Collection of Manuscripts and Printed Ephemera, Winterthur Library.

38. Ronald L. Hurst and Jonathan Prown, *Southern Furniture, 1680–1830: The Colonial Williamsburg Collection* (Williamsburg, VA: Colonial Williamsburg Foundation with Harry N. Abrams, 1997), 452–57.

39. Charles Lamb, "The South Sea House," in *Elia; Essays which Have Appeared Under that Signature in the London Magazine* (London: Taylor and Hessey, 1823), 4.

40. Lamb, "The South Sea House," 3.

4. Living the Backcountry

1. William Eddis, *Letters from America*, ed. Aubrey C. Land (Cambridge, MA: Belknap Press, 1969), 67. Originally self-published in 1792.

2. Eddis, *Letters from America*, 51–52.

3. Henry H. Glassie, *Material Culture* (Bloomington: Indiana University Press, 1999), 47.

4. Evarts B. Greene and Virginia D. Harrington, *American Population before the Federal Census of 1790* (New York: Columbia University Press, 1932).

5. John S. Salmon and Emily J. Salmon, *Franklin County, Virginia, 1786–1986: A Bicentennial History* (Rocky Mount, VA: Franklin County Bicentennial Commission, 1993), 69–72.

6. Allan Kulikoff, *Tobacco and Slaves: The Development of Southern Cultures in the Chesapeake, 1680–1800* (Chapel Hill: University of North Carolina Press, 1986), 153 and table 16; for more details on regional patterns of slave ownership, see Philip D. Morgan and Michael L. Nicholls, "Slaves in Piedmont Virginia, 1720-1790," *William and Mary Quarterly*, 3rd ser., 46, no. 2 (1989): 211–51. A nicely updated and nuanced study of the Southside is Clifton Ellis, "Dissenting Faith and Domestic Landscape in Eighteenth-Century Virginia," in *Exploring Everyday Landscapes, Perspectives in Vernacular Architecture* 7, ed. Annmarie Adams and Sally McMurry (Knoxville: University of Tennessee Press, 1997), 23–40.

7. Dell Upton, "Ethnicity, Authenticity, and Invented Traditions," *Historical Archaeology* 30 (1996): 1–7.

8. Edward Chappell, "Acculturation in the Shenandoah Valley," in *Common Places: Readings in American Vernacular Architecture*, ed. Dell Upton and John Michael Vlach (Athens: University of Georgia Press, 1985), 27–57. Cynthia G. Falk, "Symbols of Assimilation or Status?: The Meanings of Eighteenth-Century Houses in Coventry Township, Chester County, Pennsylvania," *Winterthur Portfolio* 33, nos. 2–3 (1998): 107–34.

9. For example, Heinz W. Pyszczyk has carefully studied the buying patterns of various ethnic minorities in the late eighteenth- and early nineteenth-century fur trade of western Canada. He found that consumption similarities existed among various ethnic groups and even persisted in forts across the West ("Consumption

and Ethnicity: An Example from the Fur Trade in Western Canada," *Journal of Anthropological Archaeology* 8, no. 3 (1989): 213–49.

10. Salmon and Salmon, *Franklin County*, 187–88.

11. For evidence of the settlement of Quakers, see Douglas Summers Brown, *A History of Lynchburg's Pioneer Quakers and their Meeting House, 1754–1936* (Lynchburg, VA: J. P. Bell, 1936); Marlene Lewis, "The South River Monthly Meeting of Friends, 1757–1800: A Socio-religious Study" (master's thesis, Utah State University, 1976).

12. Mrs. Fletcher O. Thomas, "A Brief Sketch of the Presbyterian Churches in Bedford County, Virginia," probably 1938, Bedford County File, Library of Virginia. The Baptists in Bedford County are listed in Morgan Edwards, *Materials Towards a History of the Baptists*, 2 vols., ed. Eve B. Weeks and Mary B. Warren (Danielsville, GA: Heritage Papers, 1984), 2:51.

13. Michael Connors, "The Eighteenth-century Cuban Sacristy Chest of Drawers," *Magazine Antiques* 165, no. 2 (2004): 66–73.

14. Jonathan Prown, "The Backcountry," in Ronald L. Hurst and Jonathan Prown, *Southern Furniture, 1680–1830: The Colonial Williamsburg Collection* (Williamsburg, VA: Colonial Williamsburg Foundation with Harry N. Abrams, 1997), 35–46.

15. Benno Forman put forth many of the guiding principles for Pennsylvania German furniture in "German Influences in Pennsylvania Furniture," in *Arts of the Pennsylvania Germans*, ed. Scott T. Swank and Catherine E. Hutchins (New York: W.W. Norton for the Winterthur Museum, 1983), 102–70. For western Maryland and Virginia, see Sumpter Priddy III and Joan K. Quinn, "Crossroads of Culture: Eighteenth-Century Furniture from Western Maryland," in *American Furniture*, ed. Luke Beckerdite (Hanover: University Press of New Hampshire for the Chipstone Foundation, 1997), 127–69, and Wallace Gusler, "The Furniture of Winchester, Virginia," in *American Furniture*, 228–65. For North Carolina, see Michael H. Lewis, "American Vernacular Furniture and the North Carolina Backcountry," *Journal of Early Southern Decorative Arts* 20, no. 1 (1994): 1–38, and Johanna Miller Lewis, *Artisans in the North Carolina Backcountry* (Lexington: University Press of Kentucky, 1995).

16. The evidence here is from the private collection of J. Francis and Laquita Amos of Franklin County. Additional information is from Roderick Moore, director of the Blue Ridge Institute of Ferrum College, Ferrum, Virginia, and utilizes photographs and information from his archives and pieces from his personal collection.

17. The tulip motif on Pennsylvania architectural hardware can be seen in Herbert, Peter, and Nancy Schiffer, *Antique Iron: Survey of American and English Forms, Fifteenth through Nineteenth Centuries* (Exton, PA: Schiffer, 1979).

18. Joel Cephas Flora, *A Genealogy and History of Descendants of Jacob Flora, Senior, of Franklin County, Virginia* (Dayton, OH, and Myerstown, PA: Church Center Press, 1951). John W. Boitnott, *Naff and Related Families: Swiss Ancestors of Naffs & Neffs in the U.S. A.* (Harrisonburg, VA: Boitnott, 1979), 24–25.

19. Dell Upton, "Form and User: Style, Mode, Fashion, and the Artifact," in *Living in the Material World: Canadian and American Approaches to Material Culture,*

ed. Gerald L. Pocius (St. John's, Newfoundland: Institute of Social and Economic Research, Memorial University of Newfoundland, 1991), 156–69.

20. The Presbyterian church measured forty by twenty feet. Edwards, *Materials Towards a History of the Baptists*, 51.

21. House plan found in Hook Papers, Rare Book, Manuscript, and Special Collections, Perkins Library, Duke University. Photostat in Hook Papers, Library of Virginia. For more on the development of the passage, see Dell Upton, "Vernacular Domestic Architecture in Eighteenth-Century Virginia," *Winterthur Portfolio* 17, nos. 2–3 (1982): 95–119.

22. Hook to Ross, New London, December 16, 1771, Hook Papers, Duke. Ross had chastised his new partner that his chosen method of payment for the building of the house and store—"to have work valued when finished" rather than settling on a fixed price in advance—was the most expensive (Ross to Hook, Goochland Courthouse, October 21, 1771, Brock Papers, Huntington Library). Hook replied that he was most uneasy with building the store and house for "the manner of ingaging workmen is what I'm unskill'd in" and that he wished for "an able advisor to instruct me." He had already agreed to provide the workmen with money to buy all provisions, but they were to bring their charges, and if there were disagreements, they would be referred to "Men of Good Character, reputed for their Skill in Building" (Hook to Ross, New London, October 26, 1771, John Hook Letterbook, Library of Virginia).

23. *Virginia Gazette*, Petersburg, May 19, 1788.

24. Plan of a house to be built for William Cabell of Nelson County, Virginia, in 1784. Illustrated in Mark R. Wenger, "The Central Passage in Virginia: Evolution of an Eighteenth-Century Living Space," in *Perspectives in Vernacular Architecture* 2, ed. Camille Wells (Columbia: University of Missouri Press, 1986), 141. My thanks to Wenger for his insights into this plan and the similarity to the Cabell plan.

25. Plans of Building for the Forrest Plantation, August 1782, Hook Papers, Duke.

26. Undated scrap on microfilm 135-13-1, Hook Papers, Duke.

27. Complaint of John Hook, New London, January 18, 1777, Hook Papers, Duke.

28. Camille Wells, "The Planter's Prospect: Houses, Outbuildings, and Rural Landscapes in Eighteenth-Century Virginia," *Winterthur Portfolio* 28, no. 1 (1993), table 5, p. 7. John Hook's house was later enlarged to become the Hook property that still exists today.

29. Gabrielle M. Lanier and Bernard L. Herman, *Everyday Architecture of the Mid-Atlantic: Looking at Buildings and Landscapes* (Baltimore: Johns Hopkins University Press, 1997), 73–83.

30. Edward A. Chappell, "Acculturation in the Shenandoah Valley: Rhenish Houses of the Massanutten Settlement," *Proceedings of the American Philosophical Society* 124, no. 1 (1980): 27–57.

31. Fieldwork study of extant late eighteenth- and nineteenth-century log cabins from Texas to Wisconsin has suggested that two rooms, often the same size, be-

came the norm. For example, see Warren E. Roberts, "German American Log Buildings of Dubois County, Indiana," *Winterthur Portfolio* 21, no. 4 (1986): 265–74, and William H. Tishler, "Fachwerk Construction in the German Settlements of Wisconsin," *Winterthur Portfolio* 21, no. 4 (1986): 275–92.

32. Will of Jacob Hickman, March 11, 1789, Franklin County Will Book 1, 1786–1812, Library of Virginia.

33. Richard Beeman, *The Evolution of the Southern Backcountry: A Case Study of Lunenburg County, Virginia, 1746–1832* (Philadelphia: University of Pennsylvania Press, 1984), 160–85. Beeman attributes this to attitudes about deference.

34. These lists do not include slaves, as they were already counted under the personal property tax. My thanks to Anne Carter Lee for the manuscript copy of these tax lists and other primary materials from Franklin and Henry counties ("A List of Whit [sic] People & Buildings in the Bounds of Capt. Rubles Company," Henry County Courthouse, Martinsville, Virginia). A brief analysis was compiled by R. Gravely and provided to me by Lee. This report is also cited and discussed in Salmon and Salmon, *Franklin County*, 75–76. Tax lists from Halifax County to the south reveal similar findings; see Mick Nichols, "Building the Virginia Southside: A Note on Architecture and Society in the Eighteenth Century," unpublished paper on file, John D. Rockefeller Jr. Library, Colonial Williamsburg Foundation.

The manuscript is not uniform, and thus the evidence needs to be carefully examined. While each district enumerator varied in the detail he reported, most lists include the number of houses, cabins, and types of outbuildings and the number of white inhabitants in each household. Further confusion over taxation is also revealed by the inclusion of slaves by name on some lists, although slaves were already listed and taxed under personal property tax provisions. This new tax was imposed to establish each state's burden of "common defence and general welfare" based on land and its improvement under the Articles of Confederation. William Hening, *The Statutes at Large*, 13 vols. (1819–23; repr., Charlottesville: Published for the Jamestown Foundation of the Commonwealth of Virginia by University Press of Virginia, 1969), 11:415–16.

35. "To be added to Captain Salmon's list," Henry County Tax Lists, 1785.

36. After continued county splitting, the farthest eastern part of Bedford County, virtually at the New London line, became Campbell County. Bernard L. Herman, "An Introduction to the Folk Building Traditions of Campbell County," in *Lest it Be Forgotten: A Scrapbook of Campbell County, Virginia* (Campbell County, VA: Altavista, 1976), 56–73.

37. Herman, "An Introduction to the Folk Building Traditions of Campbell County," 58.

38. Salmon and Salmon, *Franklin County*, 35.

39. Pedro Sloan, "The Way of Life in Turner's Creek Valley Sixty Years Ago," typescript, 1941, General File, Franklin County Library.

40. Israel Christian v. William Bates, 1773, Bedford County Court Determined Causes, Library of Virginia.

41. John Hook Memorandum Book, May 1772, p. 13, Hook Papers, Duke.

Madison also needed a few appropriate implements to live in a way that might be considered proper in such a house: a dressing glass, one-half dozen tea- and a half-dozen coffee cups and saucers, a copper coffee pot, a bell-metal skillet, and twenty-five pounds of brown sugar.

42. This echoes the building behavior of the Anglican gentry in Virginia's Halifax County, who believed they had "little to gain from building a central passage or by furnishing a room with the accoutrements of fine dining" if such action did not impress local Baptist neighbors. See Ellis, "Dissenting Faith and Domestic Landscape in Eighteenth-Century Virginia," 35. For overall building hierarchy, see Wells, "The Planter's Prospect," table 5. According to Bernard L. Herman, probably at least 85 percent of all houses in southern Delaware in the late eighteenth and early nineteenth centuries were one-story frame or log structures measuring less than twenty by twenty-five feet. The most common size was eighteen by twenty feet. Bernard L. Herman, *The Stolen House* (Charlottesville: University Press of Virginia, 1992), 183.

43. He also found two dry goods stores, one grocery, and two taverns. Richard Beeman, ed., "Trade and Travel in Post-Revolutionary Virginia: A Diary of an Itinerant Peddler," *Virginia Magazine of History and Biography* 84 (1976): 181.

44. *Andrew Bailey, Jr. Chronicles: Life in Virginia During the 17–1800's*, ed. Eunilee Leath Bailey and Frank T. Bailey Jr. (Pfafftown, NC: privately published, 1989), 14–15.

45. Thomas Anburey, *Travels through the Interior Parts of America*, 2 vols. (Boston: Houghton Mifflin, 1923), 2:187.

46. Daniel Drake, *Pioneer Life in Kentucky, 1785–1800*, ed. Emmet Field Horine (New York: Henry Schuman, 1948), 115.

47. Francis Calley Gray, *Thomas Jefferson in 1814, Being an Account of a Visit to Monticello, Virginia* (Boston: Club of Odd Volumes, 1924), 36.

48. Glassie, *Material Culture*, 270.

49. Will of Edward Bright, July 2, 1784, and Inventory Returned May 23, 1785, Bedford County Will Book 1, 1763–87, Library of Virginia.

50. Bedford County Will Book 1. Lois Green Carr and Lorena S. Walsh, "Changing Lifestyles and Consumer Behavior in the Colonial Chesapeake," in *Of Consuming Interests*, ed. Cary Carson, Ronald Hoffman, and Peter J. Albert (Charlottesville: University Press of Virginia for the United States Capitol Historical Society, 1994), 59–166.

51. The high incidence of knives and forks in Bedford County may be measured in another way. Just over half of the Bedford probates did not contain knives and forks in the approximate decade before the American Revolution. Yet Barbara Carson's study of probate inventories in Washington, D.C., from half a century later found that about 40 percent of the decedents still did not own knives and forks. Barbara Carson, *Ambitious Appetites: Dining, Behavior, and Patterns of Consumption in Federal Washington* (Washington, D.C.: American Institute of Architects Press, 1990), 31.

52. Quoted in Ellen Eslinger, "The Great Revival in Bourbon County, Kentucky," (Ph.D. diss., University of Chicago, 1988), ch. 5, p. 23.

53. Quoted in S. Allen Chambers Jr., "Revelations from the Records: The Documentary Research at Poplar Forest," *Lynch's Ferry: A Journal of Local History* (Spring/Summer 1991): 7–12.

54. Richard Venable Diary, January 22, 1791–November 30, 1792, Virginia Historical Society.

55. Richard Venable Diary, January 22, 1791–November 30, 1792.

56. Richard Venable Diary, January 22, 1791–November 30, 1792.

57. Christine Leigh Heyrman brilliantly lays out the multiple ways that such challenges were felt in her book *Southern Cross: The Beginnings of the Bible Belt* (New York: Knopf, 1997). The quote is from "Letter to a Young Friend (Miss Elizabeth A. Morton) who had lately made a Public Profession of Religion," written by Conrad Speece, published in *Virginia Argus*, March 8 and 21, 1811; see "The Writings of Conrad Speece," manuscript volume, Brock Collection, Huntington Museum.

58. Elliott J. Gorn, "'Gouge and Bite, Pull Hair and Scratch': The Social Significance of Fighting in the Southern Backcountry," *American Historical Review* 90, no. 1 (1985): 18–43. Compare this to T. H. Breen, "Horses and Gentlemen: The Cultural Significance of Gambling among the Gentry of Virginia," *William and Mary Quarterly*, 3rd ser., 34, no. 2 (1977): 239–57.

59. Gorn, "Gouge and Bite."

60. Anburey, *Travels through the Interior Parts of America*, 2:202–3.

61. Anburey, *Travels through the Interior Parts of America*, 2:202–3.

62. Salmon and Salmon, *Franklin County*, 214.

63. Richard Beeman, ed., "Trade and Travel in Post-Revolutionary Virginia," 174–88. The unknown peddler was visiting Bedford County's courthouse in Liberty after Campbell County had been carved out of Bedford County. The remembrances of childhood are found in William Eldridge Hatcher, *The Life of J. B. Jeter* (Baltimore: H. M. Wharton, 1887).

64. Thomas Jones v. Thomas Prunty, ACC 23707, May 1789, Franklin County Suit Papers, Library of Virginia. Quoted in Salmon and Salmon, *Franklin County*, 221–22.

65. Drawing on the theories of Victor Turner, Joseph Gusfield describes a similar middle ground or liminality in modern culture where hierarchy and manners are temporarily suspended in the highly structured act of drinking ("Passage to Play: Rituals of Drinking Time in American Society," in *Constructive Drinking: Perspectives on Drink from Anthropology*, ed. Mary Douglas [Cambridge, UK: Cambridge University Press, 1987], 73–91).

66. The failure to wipe the bowl may have caused the offense. Philip Vickers Fithian listed some hypothetical causes for a brawl he witnessed in 1774, including that one of the brawlers offered the other "dram without wiping the mouth of the bottle." The point is that the smallest failure to observe drinking rituals could result in violence. Fithian, *Journal and Letters of Philip Vickers Fithian: A Plantation Tutor of the Old Dominion, 1773–1774*, ed. Hunter Dickinson Farish, 2nd ed. (Charlottesville: University Press of Virginia, 1968), 183.

67. Edward Willson v. John England, Franklin County Suit Papers, August 1789. Quoted in Salmon and Salmon, *Franklin County*, 221–22.

68. Indenture between George Callaway and Adam Brown, 1770, Suit, Brown v. Callaway, March 1772. See also Forquoran v. Buford, 1772. All of these documents are to be found in Bedford County Court Determined Causes.

69. James Finley v. Thomas Pate, November 29, 1766?, John Hale v. George and Robert Baber, August 1766, Bedford County Court Determined Causes.

70. A. G. Roeber, "Authority, Law, and Custom: The Rituals of Court Day in Tidewater, Virginia, 1720 to 1750," *William and Mary Quarterly*, 3rd ser., 37 (1980): 29–52.

71. J. Franklin Jameson, ed. "The Diary of Edward Hooker," *American Historical Association Reports*, vol. 1 (1896): 842–929.

72. Franklin Jameson, ed. "The Diary of Edward Hooker," 895.

73. Richard Venable Diary, July 22, 1791.

74. Interview, Margaret Ferguson Gonzalez, August 10, 2004.

75. Igor Kopytoff, "The Cultural Biography of Things: Commoditization as Process," in *The Social Life of Things: Commodities in Cultural Perspective*, ed. Arjun Appadurai (Cambridge, UK: Cambridge University Press, 1986), 64–73.

76. Michael Ann Williams, *Homeplace: The Social Use and Meaning of the Folk Dwelling in Southwestern North Carolina* (Athens: University of Georgia Press, 1991). While it is nearly impossible to quantify such data, at least two-thirds of the people interviewed had lived in one-room spaces as children. George McDaniel also interviewed modern occupants of single-room houses such as log structures in St. Mary's County, Maryland; see his *Hearth and Home, Preserving a People's Culture* (Philadelphia: Temple University Press, 1981), 149–86.

77. Forman, "German Influences in Pennsylvania Furniture."

78. Bradford L. Rauschenberg, "A Study of Baroque and Gothic Style Gravestones in Davidson County, North Carolina," *Journal of Early Southern Decorative Arts* 3, no. 2 (1977): 24–51. Kay Moss, *Decorative Motifs: From the Southern Backcountry, 1750–1825* (Gastonia, NC: Schiele Museum of Natural History, 2001), 25. My thanks to Sally Gant for this reference.

79. Sloan, "The Way of Life in Turner's Creek Valley."

5. Setting the Stage, Playing the Part

Epigraph: Hook to William Donald, New London, December 9, 1766, John Hook Letterbook, Library of Virginia.

1. Property Sale Advertisement of Theodorick Bland in Prince George County, *Virginia Gazette*, July 23, 1767.

2. Inventory of the Estate of John Bates, Merchant, Goods in Poplar Spring Storehouse, June 10, 1720, York County Order and Will Book 15, 1716–20, John D. Rockefeller Jr. Library, Colonial Williamsburg Foundation. Johnathan Newell's store inventory from 1672 included coarse men's castor hats "eaten with the Ratts around the Brims," a dozen women's castors, some "damnified," and "4 dozen and 4 Ratt eaten Cabbidge Nets," February 29, 1671/72, York County Deeds, Orders, and Wills 6, 1677–84, John D. Rockefeller Jr. Library, Colonial Williamsburg Foundation.

3. James Robinson to John Turner, April 22, 1769, in Devine, *A Scottish Firm in Virginia, 1767–1777: W. Cuninghame and Co.* (Edinburgh: Clark Constable for the Scottish History Society, 1982), 12.

4. Henry Fleming to Fischer and Bragg, July 29, 1774, Fleming Letterbook,

1772–75, Cumbria County Council Archives Department (microfilm, John D. Rockefeller Jr. Library, Colonial Williamsburg Foundation). In this instance, Fleming decries the quality of ladies' gloves sent in a recent order.

5. Inventory of Richard Walker, March 7, 1728, Middlesex County Will Book B, 1714–34, pp. 335–43, John D. Rockefeller Jr. Library, Colonial Williamsburg Foundation. Walker's total estate (including personal goods) was valued at more than £1,300.

6. Inventory of John Hook's Property Relieved by the Supersedens Issued from the High Court of Chancery, Sworn 16 January 1802, Ross v. Hook, U.S. Circuit Court, Richmond, Virginia. Hook Papers, Rare Book, Manuscript, and Special Collections, Perkins Library, Duke University.

7. Inventory of William Parrott, January 8, 1798, Richmond City Hustings Court Deed Book 2, 1792–96, pp. 391–95, and Mutual Assurance Society, vol. 13, no. 297, Reel 2. Both documents can be found at the Library of Virginia.

8. An earlier version of this analysis can be found in Martin, "Buying into the World of Goods: Eighteenth-Century Consumerism from London to the Virginia Frontier" (Ph.D. diss., College of William and Mary, 1993), 198–210. The database for this expanded study comes from multiple sources and was created with help from many (see the essay on sources).

9. *Charleston Courier,* January 14, 1803. The ultimate solution to the merchant's dilemma—the competing pressures to control and display his goods—was thus found in a relatively small material culture innovation. Small glass cases might be used on a counter to protect valuables like jewelry. But the expense of glass was prohibitive. With changing technology, however, glass could be made in larger sheets and at a smaller price. The same process that enabled larger shop windows could also address the continual problems of theft, dirt, and order. By the later nineteenth century, glass counters were advertised as a means to promote viewing (and consumer desire), prevent shoplifting (seemingly rampant when goods were left unguarded on counters), and keep goods clean (from dust and too much handling). The most important theme throughout advertisements for these store fittings was that "goods can be displayed without risk from the nimble fingers of the shoplifter." These three issues were the heart of the eighteenth-century merchant's dilemma, with the largest concerns being to prevent access to the goods and control the behavior of poorer sorts. Elaine Abelson ultimately argues it is the consumption palace that released consumer desire, sometimes in ways that could not be controlled by the individual; see *When Ladies Go A-Thieving: Middle-Class Shoplifters in the Victorian Department Store* (New York: Oxford University Press, 1990).

10. Judith R. Hiltner, ed., *The Newspaper Verse of Philip Freneau: An Edition and Bibliographical Survey* (Troy, NY: Whitson, 1986), 487. Thanks to Vanessa Patrick for this reference.

11. Give "all good usage and drink in abundance," James Robinson advised young merchant John Turner in an October 4, 1768, letter (Devine, *Scottish Firm,* 11).

12. "Inventory of Household and Other Furniture on hand belonging to the Concern of Hooe and Harrison at Alexandria, December 31, 1779," Hooe, Stone,

and Company Invoice Book, 1770–84, New York Public Library (microfilm, John D. Rockefeller Jr. Library, Colonial Williamsburg Foundation). For sleeping in the store, see *Virginia Gazette,* September 16, 1737. Mr. Lidderdale's storekeeper and another man were sleeping in the store in Prince George County, as Lidderdale was away, when three "rogues" came to the store and demanded entry on the pretense of leaving a letter; they "rush'd in, bound the Two Men, and stole about 70 pounds in Cash, a Watch, A pair of Pistols, several Shirts, etc."

13. *Virginia Gazette,* September 20, 1754.

14. Estimates of square footage of Virginia dwellings come from newspapers and tax lists. For advertised properties, see Camille Wells, "The Planter's Prospect: Houses, Outbuildings, and Rural Landscapes in Eighteenth-Century Virginia," *Winterthur Portfolio* 28, no. 1 (1993): 6. Rare tax information on house size from Virginia is described in Pamela L. Higgins, "Lands, Houses, and Slaves: The 1798 Federal Direct Tax in Spotsylvania County, Virginia," *Journal of Fredericksburg History* 1 (1996): 59, 65.

15. Sargent Bush Jr., ed., "The Journal of Madam Knight," in *Journeys in New Worlds: Early American Women's Narratives,* ed. William L. Andrews (Madison: University of Wisconsin Press, 1990), 105–6. Although Knight's disdain here is clear—and no doubt colors her perception—the rest of her journal is a precise recording of real events, and there is no reason to suspect that she did not witness such a scene. The generous Sarge Bush provided this reference.

16. Jack P. Greene, ed., *The Diary of Colonel Landon Carter of Sabine Hall, 1752–1778,* 2 vols. (Charlottesville: University Press of Virginia, 1965), 2:950.

17. Crow v. Bell, October 1765, Augusta County Court Judgements, Deposition of Elizabeth Hog, October 18, 1765. Lyman Chalkley, *Chronicles of the Scotch-Irish Settlement in Virginia: Extracted from the Original Court Records of Augusta County, 1745–1800,* 3 vols. (1912; repr., Baltimore: Genealogical Publishing Company, 1965), 1:491–92. My thanks to Gail Terry and Turk McClesky for this reference and for the biographical information.

18. Elizabeth Kowaleski-Wallace, *Consuming Subjects: Women, Shopping, and Business in the Eighteenth Century* (New York: Columbia University Press, 1997).

19. Daniel Defoe, *The Complete English Tradesman* (1727; repr., New York: Augustus M. Kelly, 1969), 178–79.

20. Rhys Isaac, *The Transformation of Virginia, 1740–1790* (Chapel Hill: University of North Carolina Press, 1982), 57: "women—even widows who controlled property—did not, it seems, go into stores to make purchases"; the world outside of the home was a male landscape, and at stores the "men gathered, drank, swore, and even boxed."

21. Carole Shammas, *The Pre-Industrial Consumer in England and America* (Oxford, UK: Clarendon Press, 1990), 269. Allan Kulikoff, *Tobacco and Slaves: The Development of Southern Cultures in the Chesapeake, 1680–1800* (Chapel Hill: University of North Carolina Press, 1986), 225.

22. Reporting this problem, Hook requested Ross to find him a "young Man that can write well *& experiences, if to be had to keep my Books" (December 30, 1771, Hook Papers, Duke).

23. This visitation figure was arrived at by adding up the number of differing names per day. Cash purchases were added at the simple rate of one visitation per day that cash activity was recorded, although the number is quite likely much higher. Finally, all those who were listed as third parties, such as spouses or other family members, were added to the total.

24. Ross to Hook, Goochland Courthouse, October 21, 1771, Box 257, Brock Collection, Huntington Library.

25. Hook to Ross, Bedford Courthouse, October 26, 1771, Hook Papers, Duke.

26. Hook to Ross, New London, November 7, 1771, Hook Papers, Duke.

27. Thomas Stevens Account, Dr. Peter Donald Account Book, 1771, loose papers, Bedford County Courthouse, Liberty, Virginia.

28. Henry Brown's large family included six daughters. The special visitor was Elizabeth, Aley, Hannah, Ann, Mary, or Sarah (Bedford County Will Book 2, January 9, 1796, Library of Virginia).

29. Will of John Read, June 3, 1767, Returned May 24, 1773, Bedford County Will Book 1, 1763–87, p.181, Library of Virginia. The will lists some of John Read's land, including tracts located on either side of Falling River and off the south branch. The family was already no doubt wealthy; by 1782 William was taxed for twenty-two slaves, thirteen cattle, and six horses.

30. Edward A. Chappell and Julie Richter, "Wealth and Houses in Post-Revolutionary Virginia," in *Exploring Everyday Landscapes, Perspectives in Vernacular Architecture* 7, ed. Annmarie Adams and Sally McMurry (Knoxville: University of Tennessee Press, 1997), 3–22.

31. William K. Bottorff and Roy C. Flanagan, eds., "The Diary of Frances Baylor Hill of Hillsborough, King and Queen County, Virginia (1797)," *Early American Literature Newsletter* 2, no. 3 (1967): 33.

32. Bottorff and Flanagan, eds., "The Diary of Frances Baylor Hill," 23, 40.

33. Young women also charged to their father's accounts at William Allason's store in Falmouth, Virginia. Mary Ann Knight visited the store five times in 1770, often with her brothers, but maintained her own account. Her purchases were small niceties like a teapot, a snuffbox, black ribbon, or a pair of leather gloves. Her biggest purchase was for eight yards of fine calico at 7 shillings a yard, and her debts in two years were over £8. She paid for most of her calico in cash and her father made another payment in the fall of the following year. We know little about the Knights but that they owned their own house—probably placing them in comfortable ranks—but nowhere does Mary Ann appear in the official records of Stafford County. William Allason Papers, Ledger 1, October 1769–72, Library of Virginia. Ann Smart Martin, "Textiles and Clothing at Eighteenth-Century Virginia Stores" (paper presented at the Third Textile History Conference, North Andover, Massachusetts, September 21–23, 1990).

34. In 1831, Alexis de Tocqueville noted that in America, "paternal discipline is very relaxed and the conjugal tie very strict." *Democracy in America,* 2 vols. (New York: Knopf, 1945), 2:213.

35. Older teens and unmarried women in their young twenties had greater mobility than did those still in school (16 or younger) (Cathy Hellier, "The Adolescence

of Gentry Girls in Late Eighteenth-Century Virginia" [paper presented at the Southern Association of Women's Historians Conference, 1994]). My thanks to Hellier for her help with this larger idea of visiting and other documentary references to girls visiting stores.

36. John Thompson's will was returned on February 2, 1778 (Bedford County Will Book 1, p. 291). He lists three daughters as heirs of his estate after the death of his wife. While Elizabeth is listed, there is no Esther.

37. Lucinda Lee Orr, *Journal of a Young Lady of Virginia: Lucinda Lee, 1787* (Richmond: Whittet and Shepperson for the Robert E. Lee Association, 1976), 35–36.

38. Diary of Eliza Lavalette Barksdale, 1836–37, manuscripts 5:1, Virginia Historical Society.

39. The ultimate gendering of consumption and technology is the theme of Steven Lubar, "Men, Women, Production, Consumption," in *His and Hers: Gender, Consumption, and Technology,* ed. Roger Horowitz and Arwen Mohun (Charlottesville: University Press of Virginia, 1998), 7–38.

40. Richard Venable remembered the Election Day in Patrick County at which proffered sweet cakes were the license for caresses from the mountain lasses. The linkage of sweet cakes and "gifts" is hence a thick construction (Diary, April 25, 1791, Virginia Historical Society).

41. I am again indebted to Carole Shammas (*Pre-Industrial Consumer,* 203) for this concept.

42. One such story of disappointed consumers revolves around a son sent to the fair by his mother and sisters, each of whom supplied him with money to bring home a particular fairing. To their thorough disgust, each of his purchases was flawed; for example, the sought-after green ribbon was, under inspection, blue. Author of the *Mystic Cottager of Chamouny, The Observant Pedestrian; or, Traits of the Heart; in a Solitary Tour from Caernarvon to London: In Two Volumes, by the Author of the Mystic Cottager* (London: 1795), 2:27–32.

43. Diana O'Hara, *Courtship and Constraint: Rethinking the Making of Marriage in Tudor England* (Manchester, UK: Manchester University Press, 2000), 67–68. O'Hara explains that "complimentary gifts, cakes, and sweets and presents given and brought from [a fair], were described as fairings in contemporary parlance, but even they were subject to various interpretations" (67).

44. "Invoice of Goods to be Sent with all the dispatch Posible to Cathn. Rathell in Williamsburg Virginia," January 31, 1771. Mary A. Stephenson, "Milliners of Williamsburg in the Eighteenth Century," Report, Colonial Williamsburg Foundation (September 1951), 8. For an image displaying a multitude of ribbons used on the clothing of wealthy Londoners and their servants, see John Collet's print *High Life below Stairs* (London, 1763). Ribbons bedeck the hats of the mistress, adorn the neck of a young woman and the queue of her suitor, and the caps and aprons of the servants.

45. For example, see the portrait of Maryland resident Henry Whitely by James Peale, in the collection of the Winterthur Museum, dated 1807 (1976.108). The initials on the verso are "HCW" for Henry and his bride, Catherine Whitely. The miniature, set as a locket, is in its original case where it could have been kept. It

might also have been kept in a pocket or drawer. Although the silk ribbon that is attached to it was likely added later, it alludes to how the miniature could also have been hung either on a longer ribbon or a cord from one's neck or else on a wall. The high degree of embellishment on the reverse, an added expense, would be only as public as the wearer chose to make it. My thanks to Anne Verplanck for this example.

46. Samuel Hale Account, Boston, June 25, 1771, no. 56 x 3.1, Joseph Downs Collection of Manuscripts and Printed Ephemera, Winterthur Library.

47. Letter from Abigail Smith Adams to Lucy Cranch Greenleaf, April 2, 1786, in *Letters of Mrs. Adams, the Wife of John Adams*, 2 vols., 2nd ed. (Boston: Little Brown, 1840), 2:129–30.

48. Ann Cooper Whitall, 1716–1797, "Diary of Ann Cooper Whitall," October 1761, in Hannah Whitall Smith, *John M. Whitall: The Story of His Life* (Philadelphia: privately published, 1879), 8.

49. Mair, *Book-keeping Methodiz'd: A Methodical Treatise of Merchant-Accompts, According to the Italian Form* (Edinburgh: Sands, Donaldson, Murray, and Cochrane, 1757), 349–50.

50. *The Charms of Chearfulness; or, Merry Songster's Companion* (London: Printed for W. Lane, 1783).

51. Alice Morse Earle, "Old-Time Marriage Customs in New England," *Journal of American Folklore* 6, no. 21 (1893): 97–98.

6. Suckey's Looking Glass

1. The literature on the internal economy of slavery is rapidly growing and will only partially be cited here. A critical volume of essays is Larry E. Hudson Jr., ed., *Working toward Freedom: Slave Society and Domestic Economy in the American South* (Rochester, NY: University of Rochester Press, 1994). See also Roderick A. McDonald, *The Economy and Material Culture of Slaves: Goods and Chattels on the Sugar Plantations of Jamaica and Louisiana* (Baton Rouge: Louisiana State University Press, 1993); Betty Wood, *Women's Work, Men's Work: The Informal Slave Economies of Lowcountry Georgia* (Athens: University of Georgia Press, 1995); and Harry L. Watson, "Slavery and Development in a Dual Economy: The South and the Market Revolution," in *The Market Revolution in America: Social, Political, and Religious Expressions, 1800–80*, ed. Melvyn Stokes and Stephen Conway (Charlottesville: University Press of Virginia, 1996), 43–74.

2. Ira Berlin and Philip D. Morgan, "Introduction," in *The Slaves' Economy: Independent Production by Slaves in the Americas*, ed. Ira Berlin and Philip D. Morgan (Portland, OR: Frank Cass, 1991), 1–9.

3. Larry E. Hudson Jr., "'All That Cash': Work and Status in the Slave Quarters," 77–94, in *Working toward Freedom*.

4. Henry John Drewal, "Introduction: Yoruba Art and Life as Journeys," in *The Yoruba Artist: New Theoretical Perspectives on African Arts*, ed. Rowland Abiodun, Henry J. Drewal, and John Pemberton III (Washington, DC: Smithsonian Press, 1994), 195.

5. See, for example, Robert Olwell, "'Loose, Idle and Disorderly': Slave Women

in the Eighteenth-Century Charleston Marketplace," in *More than Chattel: Black Women and Slavery in the Americas,* ed. David Barry Gaspar and Darlene Clark Hine (Bloomington: Indiana University Press, 1996), 97–110.

6. Norfolk Borough Records, August 1, 1764, June 29, 1773, and December 20, 1783, reprinted in Brent Tartar, ed., *The Order Book and Related Papers of the Common Hall of the Borough of Norfolk, Virginia, 1736–1798* (Richmond: Virginia State Library, 1979), 142, 175, 217.

7. See, for example, Petersburg Common Council Minutes, July 16, 1785, Richmond Common Hall, January 2, 1793.

8. Henry Bradshaw Fearon, *Sketches of America* (New York: Benjamin Blom, 1969), 287.

9. Anne Cary Randolph Slave Crop Accounts, reprinted in Gerard W. Gawalt, "Jefferson's Slaves: Crop Accounts at Monticello, 1805–1808," *Journal of the Afro-American Historical and Genealogical Society* 13, nos. 1–2 (1994): 19–38.

10. Barbara Heath, "Engendering Choice: Slavery and Consumerism in Central Virginia," in *Engendering African American Archaeology,* ed. Jillian E. Galle and Amy L. Young (Knoxville: University of Tennessee Press, 2004), 23–26.

11. Jane Frances Walker Page Commonplace Book, Virginia Historical Society. Amy Rider provides a sophisticated analysis of this book in "The Castle Hill Commonplace Book and the Plantation Mistress's World, 1802–45" (honors thesis, Princeton University, 1997), 61.

12. Orra Langhorne, *Southern Sketches from Virginia, 1881–1901,* ed. Charles E. Loynes (Charlottesville: University Press of Virginia, 1964), 117.

13. April 16, 1810. Act published in the *Alexandria Daily Gazette, Commercial and Political.* My thanks to Michael Nichols for this material.

14. John Davis, *Travels of Four Years and a Half in the United States of America* (London: 1803), 388. Cited in Pat Gibbs, "Hominy, Ashcakes, and Other 'Belly Timber': Slave Diet in the Early Chesapeake to 1825," forthcoming, Colonial Williamsburg Foundation.

15. A compact summary of a vast literature on the increasing use of household goods discovered in archaeological digs and through primary sources is found in Lorena S. Walsh, "Fettered Consumers: Slaves and the Anglo-American 'Consumer Revolution'" (paper presented at the annual meeting of the Economic History Association, September 1992), and in Dylan C. Penningroth, *The Claims of Kinfolk: African American Property and Community in the Nineteenth-Century South* (Chapel Hill: University of North Carolina Press, 2003). It seems that during the antebellum period, slaves owning property may have become more and more common. At the end of the Civil War, the new government in the South had to acknowledge and adjudicate whose property was taken by Union soldiers. Former slaves brought friends, family members, and former owners, all testifying to slaves' ability to accumulate a fair amount of petty capital.

16. Washington as quoted in Mechel Sobel, *The World They Made Together: Black and White Values in Eighteenth-Century Virginia* (Princeton: Princeton University Press, 1987), 51.

17. Louise Pecquet du Bellet, *Some Prominent Virginia Families,* 4 vols. (Lynchburg, VA: J. P. Bell, 1907), 2:779–80. Merchants were proscribed from receiving goods from or selling goods to slaves without written permission by the "Act Concerning Servants and Slaves," October 1705 (William Hening, *Statutes at Large,* 13 vols. [1819–23; repr., Charlottesville: Published for the Jamestown Foundation of the Commonwealth of Virginia by University Press of Virginia, 1969], 3:451). Merchants could not vend alcohol that was expected to be drunk on site. A pint met that legal standard ("An Act for Regulating Ordinaries, and Restraint from Tippling Houses," Hening, *Statutes at Large,* 6:74).

18. *Andrew Bailey, Jr. Chronicles: Life in Virginia During the 17–1800's,* ed. Eunilee Leath Bailey and Frank T. Bailey Jr. (Pfafftown, NC: privately published, 1989), 15.

19. Anne Frame Account Book, Charles Town, Berkeley County, Virginia (now West Virginia), manuscript, Virginia Historical Society.

20. John T. Schlotterbeck, "Internal Economy of Slavery in Rural Piedmont Virginia," in *The Slaves' Economy: Independent Production by Slaves in the Americas,* ed. Ira Berlin and Philip D. Morgan (Portland, OR: Frank Cass, 1991), 176.

21. William Johnston's account book can be found in the Francis Jerdone Account and Letter Book, 1736–37, 1738–44, Manuscripts Collections, Swem Library, College of William and Mary.

22. John Glassford and Company Records for Virginia, Colchester Store Ledger B, 1760–61, and Ledger H, 1767, Library of Congress (microfilm, John D. Rockefeller Jr. Library, Colonial Williamsburg Foundation).

23. See, for example, Dylan C. Penningroth, "Remaking Kinship and Community," in *The Claims of Kinfolk: African American Property and Community in the Nineteenth-Century South* (Chapel Hill: University of North Carolina Press, 2003), 162–86.

24. The location of Hunt's plantation is unknown but perhaps is the site referred to in litigation as the home of several slaves in Montgomery County.

25. Lorena Walsh, "Slave Life, Slave Society and Tobacco Production in the Tidewater Chesapeake, 1620–1820," in *Cultivation and Culture: Labor and the Shaping of Slave Life in the Americas,* ed. Ira Berlin and Philip D. Morgan (Charlottesville: University Press of Virginia, 1993), 175.

26. John S. Salmon and Emily J. Salmon, *Franklin County, Virginia, 1786–1986: A Bicentennial History* (Rocky Mount, VA: Franklin County Bicentennial Commission, 1993), 246–47.

27. Hook Ledgers, 1786–1814, 13 F, Box 62, Hook Papers, Rare Book, Manuscript, and Special Collections, Perkins Library, Duke University.

28. Booker T. Washington, *Up From Slavery* (New York: Airmont Books, 1967), 20.

29. Richard Henry Lee Memorandum Book, 1776–94, Folder 2, pp. 68–69, Brock Collection 52, Huntington Library. Price information in Folder 6, p. 244, Brock Collection 52, Huntington Library. My thanks to Julie Richter for this reference. The coarser nature of slave clothing was acknowledged in Richard Henry

Lee's payment to a weaver for "Negro cloth" and "finer cloth" for counterpanes and "Children's cloth."

30. Shane White and Graham White, "'Too Good for Any of His Colour': Slave Clothing in the Eighteenth and Nineteenth Centuries" (paper presented at the Southern Historical Association Meeting, Orlando, Florida, 1993).

31. Ross to William J. Dunn, Richmond, January 1813, David Ross Letterbook, manuscript, Virginia Historical Society.

32. Phyllis M. Martin's powerful study of clothing and jewelry in French Equatorial Africa demonstrates how the introduction and later flood of western textiles and garb impacted traditional patterns of prestige in ways that puzzled Europeans ("Contesting Clothes in Colonial Brazzaville," *Journal of African History* 35 [1994]: 405).

33. Purchase by G. Caldwell's Slave, London, June 26, 1774, Mercantile Ledger, 1773–75, Hook Papers, Duke. Jonathan Prude, "To Look Upon the 'Lower Sort': Runaway Ads and the Appearance of Unfree Laborers in America, 1750–1800," *Journal of American History* 78 (1991): 155.

34. Linda Baumgarten, "'Clothes for the People': Slave Clothing in Early Virginia," *Journal of Early Southern Decorative Arts* 14, no. 2 (1988): 27–70.

35. For examples, see Theresa A. Singleton, "The Archaeology of Slave Life," in *Before Freedom Came: African-American Life in the Antebellum South*, ed. Edward D. C. Campbell Jr. (Richmond: Museum of the Confederacy, 1991), 155–75.

36. Barbara J. Heath, "Archaeological and Documentary Evidence of Slaves as Consumers" (paper presented at the Society for Historical Archaeology Annual Meeting, January 1997).

37. Joan Thirsk has demonstrated that it was the increasing production of just these small consumer goods in seventeenth-century England that may have laid the groundwork for the new consumerism of the eighteenth century (*Economic Policy and Projects: The Development of a Consumer Society in Early Modern England* [Oxford, UK: Oxford University Press, 1978]).

38. Jonathan Miller, *On Reflection* (New Haven, CT: Yale University Press for the National Gallery, London, 1998).

39. Serge Roche, Germain Courage, and Pierre Devinoy, *Mirrors* (New York: Rizzoli, 1985).

40. For numerous examples, see Stith Thompson, *The Motif Index of Folk Literature* (Bloomington: Indiana University Press, 1956), especially D1323.

41. The note says "if desired." John Hook Memorandum Book, January 1773, Hook Papers, Duke.

42. See, for instance, Elizabeth Donaghy Garrett, "Looking Glasses in America: 1700–1850," in *American Tables and Looking Glasses in the Mabel Brady Garvan and other Collections at Yale University*, ed. David L. Barquist (New Haven, CT: Yale University Art Gallery, 1992), 26–36. The problem of accurate representations can be seen in an advertisement by John Elliott of Philadelphia, who offered to "new quicksilver or re-frame old looking glasses" and "undertake to cure any English

Looking glasses, that shew the face either too long or too broad, or any other way distorted" (*Pennsylvania Gazette*, November 24, 1763).

43. Robert Farris Thompson and Joseph Cornet, *The Four Moments of the Sun: Kongo Art in Two Worlds* (Washington, DC: National Gallery of Art, 1981), 198–99. For the items of trade, see Graham Connah, *African Civilizations* (New York: Cambridge University Press, 1990), 147. Thanks to Gray Gundaker for this reference and her generous and able introduction to the ideas and currents of African and African American folklore and material culture scholarship.

44. *Art and Healing of the Bakongo Commented by Themselves: Minkisi from the Laman Collection,* trans. and ed. Wyatt MacGaffey (Stockholm: Folkens Museum, 1991), 14.

45. One informant suggested that to acquire supernatural powers, one bury a mirror at a crossroad and then dig it up in three days (Harry Middleton Hyatt, *Hoodoo, Conjuration, Witchcraft, Rootwork: Beliefs Accepted by Many Negroes and White Persons, These Being Orally Recorded Among Blacks and Whites,* 5 vols. [Hannibal, MO: Western, 1970], 1:193–94). Another informant said to go into the graveyard with a mirror and a new pair of scissors. At exactly midnight, if one called out the name of the deceased and dropped the scissors, the reflection of the dead man would appear and one would be able to see the reflection of the dead and ask him for what one wanted. The scissors meanwhile would cut away one's fear (Newbell Miles Puckett, *Folk Beliefs of the Southern Negro* [Chapel Hill: University of North Carolina Press, 1926], 140).

Mirrors were also strongly linked with black cats. With some variation, the custom required catching a black cat and boiling it. When the flesh was off the bones, each bone was put in the mouth. When the "lucky bone" was in one's mouth, one's image would disappear. What is most compelling—though too tentative to be more than speculative—is that similar beliefs about lucky bones (from unlucky cats) are recorded among both black and white North Carolinians. However, only the black versions include a mirror. See Puckett, *Folk Beliefs,* 256–57, and Hyatt, *Hoodoo, Conjuration,* 86–90.

46. Robert Farris Thompson, "The Song That Named the Land: The Visionary Presence of African-American Art," in *Black Art: Ancestral Legacy* (Dallas, TX: Dallas Museum of Art, 1989), 104–7; Gray Gundaker, "Tradition and Innovation in African-American Yards," *African Arts* 26, no. 2 (1993): 58–96.

47. *Drums and Shadows: Survival Studies Among the Georgia Coastal Negroes,* Georgia Writers Project, Works Project Administration, Athens (1940; repr., Athens: University of Georgia Press, 1986), 117. John Michael Vlach, *By the Work of Their Hands: Studies in Afro-American Folklife* (Charlottesville: University Press of Virginia, 1991), 47.

48. William D. Hand, ed. *Frank C. Brown Collection of North Carolina Folklore: Popular Beliefs and Superstitions from North Carolina,* 7 vols. (Durham, NC: Duke University Press, 1964), 7:80. Puckett found that this was a custom picked up by Southern blacks from whites. He suggests that because of interaction between slaves and owners, practices up to the interment are often European in form but that grave

decoration and avoidance of spirits are more African in origin (*Folk Beliefs of the Southern Negro,* 80).

49. Allan Kulikoff documents that the majority of new slaves were from that region in the first half of the century in *Tobacco and Slaves: The Development of Southern Cultures in the Chesapeake, 1680–1800* (Chapel Hill: University of North Carolina Press, 1986), 322.

50. MacGregor Laird and R. A. K. Oldfield, *Narrative of an Expedition into the Interior of Africa by the River Niger,* 2 vols. (London: Richard Bentley, 1837), 1:167.

51. Laird and Oldfield, *Narrative,* 2:181.

52. Laird and Oldfield, *Narrative,* 1:385.

53. Laird and Oldfield, *Narrative,* 1:389.

54. Herbert M. Cole and Chike C. Aniakor, *Igbo Arts: Community and Cosmos* (Los Angeles: University of California, Museum of Cultural History, 1984), 54.

55. Samuel Crowther, *Journal of an Expedition of the Niger and Tshadda Rivers Undertaken by Macgregor Laird in Connection with the British Government in 1854* (London: Frank Cass, 1970), 224.

56. Samuel Crowther and John Christopher Taylor, *The Gospel on the Banks of the Niger: Journals and Notices of the Native Missionaries Accompanying the Niger Expedition of 1857–59* (London: Dawsons of Pall Mall, 1968), 261.

57. Patricia Samford, "The Archaeology of African-American Slavery and Material Culture," *William and Mary Quarterly,* 3d ser., 53, no. 1 (1996): 87–114.

58. While *ofo* are traditionally made of natural materials such as the twigs of the tallow tree, the *ofo* recovered from archaeological sites along the Forcados River were made of cast bronze (Eli Bentor, "Life as an Artistic Process: Igbo Ikenga and Ofo," *African Arts* 21, no. 2 [1988]: 67). Cole and Aniakor simply state that "*ofo* is doubtless the most important medicinal object in Igbo life." Its phallic shape represents "maleness and paternity and are held by senior sons to represent the collective power of the ancestors and the truths given by *Chukwu*" (17). Samford's argument for the spoons is found in "'Strong is the Bond of Kinship': West African–Style Ancestor Shrines and Subfloor Pits on African-American Quarters" (paper presented at the World Archaeological Conference, South Africa, 1998), and in her book *Subfloor Pits and the Archaeology of Slavery in Colonial Virginia* (Tuscaloosa: University of Alabama Press, 2007). I am grateful for our many discussions and permission to cite her work.

59. While beyond the bounds of this paper, scholarship of traditional and modern African art helps us think about the way custom and traditional practice are also about choice and change—in essence about what we choose to remember and value about the past and incorporate into the present—and enables a clearer view of the ways new objects could be incorporated into old rituals. John Mason cites the example of how the massive export of European Catholic dolls was incorporated into Yoruba religious expression and recontextualized in altars and commemorative figures ("Yoruba-American Art: New Rivers to Explore," in *The Yoruba Artist: New Theoretical Perspectives on African Arts,* 241–50).

60. William Allason Papers, Ledger B, October 1761–September 1762, Library of Virginia.

61. The mirror glass at Carter's Grove comes from a mid-eighteenth-century context. Patricia Samford has uncovered mirror glass at a number of Virginia archaeology sites, including that of Polly Valentine, an enslaved woman of the Tucker household in Williamsburg, Virginia (1840–65). Other sites include quarters at Kingsmill, York County, Virginia (eighteenth century) and Portici at Manassas Battlefield in Virginia (early nineteenth century).

62. Will of Richard Stith, Gentleman, April 12, 1803, pp. 123–26, Campbell County Will Book. Inventory and Appraisement, June 13, 1803, p. 131, Campbell County Will Book.

63. "Narrative of the Travels of a Scotsman from Glasgow, 1821–1824," manuscript, New York Historical Society.

64. Heath, "Engendering Choice," 11. Heath cites multiple other slave quarter excavations with locks and keys in their assemblages.

Epilogue. Country Gentleman in a New Country

1. William Wirt, *Sketches of the Life and Character of Patrick Henry* (1816; repr., Ithaca, NY: Mack, Andrus, 1845), 260–62.

2. Willard Pierson, "John Hook: A Merchant of Colonial Virginia" (honors thesis, Duke University, 1962), 74; Marshall Wingfield, *An Old Virginia Court: Being a Transcript of the Records of the First Court of Franklin County, Virginia, 1786–1789* (Memphis: West Tennessee Historical Society, 1948).

3. James P. Preston to Maj. General John Preston, Smithfield, December 27, 1807, Preston Family Papers, Virginia Historical Society.

4. See, for example, Ann Smart Martin, "The Urban/Rural Dichotomy of Status Consumption: Tidewater, Virginia, 1815" (master's thesis, College of William and Mary, 1986).

5. John Howell Briggs, "Journal of a Trip to the Sweet Springs," September 11, 1804, manuscript, Virginia Historical Society.

6. Richard N. Venable, "Diary of Richard N. Venable 1791–92," *Tyler's Quarterly Historical and Genealogical Magazine* 2 (1920): 136.

7. *Lynchburg Press* (Lynchburg, VA), August 8, 1816, 3–2.

8. John S. Salmon, *The Washington Iron Works of Franklin County, Virginia, 1773–1850* (Richmond: Virginia State Library, 1986), 33.

9. G. C. Callahan, "Some of the Meads," *William and Mary College Quarterly Historical Papers* 10, no. 3 (1902): 195.

10. For his father's attachment to the ways of the world, see Stith Mead to William Mead, September 1, 1794, pp. 101–2, Stith Mead Letterbook, Virginia Historical Society. The larger dramatic story of Stith Mead's life is found in Christine Leigh Heyrman, *Southern Cross: The Beginnings of the Bible Belt* (New York: Knopf, 1997), 117–23.

11. Sam Walton with John Huey, *Sam Walton: Made in America, My Story* (New York: Doubleday, 1992).

This book uses the ledgers of mercantile business activity to establish base-lines of everyday consumption patterns. Such account books are some of the most neglected historical documents. Utilizing the information they easily tender—names, dates, and prices—requires the scholar's fortitude and patience. The storekeeper's language skills and writing talent not surprisingly bore on how he spelled customers' names, and so there can be a confusing inconsistency on this front. Particular commodity names like textiles changed quickly ("alamode" or "Persian"); some objects had names derived from a producer's vocabulary ("twiffler"); some items for sale ("twigs") simply had names that are now obsolete. Monetary systems occasionally seemed ad hoc but as often were based on complicated currency exchange.

To develop an accounting system, storekeepers in the eighteenth century might have studied Daniel Defoe's *The Complete English Tradesman* or John Mair's *Book-keeping Mecthodiz'd: A Methodological Treatise of Merchant-Accompts, According to the Italian Form* and consulted detailed tables of exchange. Mostly they relied on what they had learned during their years as junior clerks or from the letters of their partners and suppliers. In combination, such sources help scholars piece together the life of a merchant and the lifeblood of a store.

This book draws on research gleaned from my two decades of studying merchants, the commodities they sold, and the larger material culture of early America. During that time I examined hundreds of merchant records in archives from Britain to California, but the bulk reside in the mid-Atlantic states of Virginia, Maryland, and North Carolina. Four kinds of papers were integral: accounts (records of sale and payment), invoices (lists of commodities imported), correspondence, and miscellaneous business notes. John Hook is in some ways the most accommodating of merchants. His papers are voluminous and various: they include account books, invoices, letters, memorandum books, architectural plans, and notes that are stored in archives at Duke University and the Library of Virginia. Most are at Duke, but other materials can be found at various libraries. Five letters spread westward and now reside at the Huntington in San Marino, California.

The merchants' accounts and papers cited here (grouped by repository) include: William Allason Papers (Library of Virginia), Anne Frame Account Book, 1798–1812 (Virginia Historical Society), Neil Jamieson papers and John Glassford accounts (Library of Congress), Francis Jerdone Account and Letter Book, 1739–44, Blow Family Papers and Scrapbook, 1770–1815, and Matthew Read and Hugh Johnson Ledger, 1761–70 (College of William and Mary), Maude Carter Clemons Collection (University of Virginia), John Norton and Sons Papers (Colonial Williamsburg Foundation), William Bragg Papers and William Patterson Smith Papers (Duke University), Samuel Hale Account, 1771 (Winterthur Library), and Henry Fleming Letterbook, 1772–75 (Cumbria County Council Archives Department; microfilm, Colonial Williamsburg Foundation).

Invoices give the most detailed evidence of what was purchased by the merchant to sell to his customers. The business records of James Lawson and John Semple actually named the exact shop or producer in England or Scotland in their accounts (Scottish Public Record Office, Currie-Dal Miscellaneous Bundle 20; microfilm, Colonial Williamsburg Foundation), and Hooe, Stone, and Company Invoice Book, 1770–84, gave useful long runs of invoices (New York Public Library; microfilm, Colonial Williamsburg Foundation). Court battles snagged the records of many merchants, including those of Dobson, Daltera, and Walker that were sequestered by the U.S. District Court and those of James Lawson and John Semple that were stored at the Scottish Public Record Office.

Particularly significant letters were exchanged by employees of the Cunninghame firm and published by T. M. Devine in *A Scottish Firm in Virginia, 1767–1777: W. Cunninghame and Company* (Edinburgh: Clark Constable for the Scottish History Society, 1982). Similarly useful was Joshua Johnson's *Letterbook,* edited and published in 1979 by the London Record Society. Memoirs of Virginia storekeeper Andrew Bailey (Library of Virginia) provided important evidence about the successes and failures of backcountry merchants.

The accounts would remain muted without an understanding of the allure or necessity of consumer goods and the process by which they were acquired. The writings of elite planters are helpful in shedding light on both the appeal of goods and how consumers came by them. Particularly useful were the writings of Henry Fitzhugh (Duke University), Richard Henry Lee (Huntington Library), William Lee (Robert E. Lee Memorial Foundation, Stratford Hall; microfilm, Colonial Williamsburg Foundation), and Col. Francis Taylor, 1786–99 (Library of Virginia). The published writings of Phillip Fithian and Landon Carter contain key insights. The memorandum book of William Ennals, 1771–74, and several accounts of Thomas Jefferson (both in the Library of Congress) showed the relative costs of certain expenditures. Jane Frances Walker Page's Commonplace Book (Library of Virginia) keenly demonstrates the important role of women in the blending of local and market economies.

The writings of regional elites (from the Southside and backcountry) helped set a particular local pattern in the recording of consumption. Richard Venable's diary was only partially published in 1908, but the rest of the manuscript can be seen at the Virginia Historical Society. The Preston papers (Virginia Historical Society), the Pocket Plantation papers (University of Virginia), and Skipwith Papers (College of William and Mary) each tell of goods and human relationships. In her diary of 1836–37 (Virginia Historical Society), Eliza Barksdale recorded the minutia of small rural purchases, boredoms, and pleasures. William Eldridge Hatcher's work, *The Life of J. B. Jeter* (Baltimore: H. M. Wharton, 1887), highlights behaviors high and low. William Eddis's letters back to England are published as *Letters from America* (1792; repr. 1969). The writings of Conrad Speece (Huntington Library) give a strong sense of the evangelical catharsis that this area experienced at the end of the eighteenth century. John Hook's partner, David Ross, engaged in a vast range of business activities in the backcountry—everything from running iron works to maintaining a beef herd for market (Virginia Historical Society).

Producers of goods left far fewer records than the men and women who sold them. British archives included the Staffordshire potter John Baddeley's Sales Book, 1753–61, (Aqualate Papers, vol. 101, Staffordshire Record Office).

Telling a local story through profiles of the wealth, religion, or family structure of customers requires intensive study of the public documents of Bedford, Franklin, Campbell, Henry, and Patrick counties. Those include county court records (will, inventory, determined causes, loose papers, order and deed books) and general files in special collections (University of Virginia, Virginia Historical Society) and archives (Library of Virginia). Loose papers at the Bedford County Courthouse included the highly informative account book of Dr. Peter Donald. A state agency (the Virginia Division of Historic Landmarks) holds the annotated typescript "The Way of Life in Turner's Creek Valley Sixty Years Ago," by Pedro Sloan.

Studying eighteenth-century buildings was a pleasure (more detailed versions of this analysis are in Martin, "Buying into the World of Goods" (Ph.D. diss., College of William and Mary, 1993), and Martin, "Commercial Space as Consumption Arena: Retail Stores in Early Virginia," in *People, Power, Places, Perspectives in Vernacular Architecture* 8, ed. Sally McMurry and Annmarie Adams (Knoxville: University of Tennessee Press, 2000), 201–18. The database for the architectural work comes from multiple sources and was created with the help of many. (1) Architectural plans of rural stores from the Agricultural Buildings Project, Colonial Williamsburg, early 1980s, partially summed up in Edward A. Chappell, "Architectural Recording and the Open-Air Museum: A View from the Field," in *Perspectives in Vernacular Architecture* 2, ed. Camille Wells (Columbia: University of Missouri Press, 1986), 35–36. (2) Information about colonial Williamsburg's four important stores that still stand today in Colonial Williamsburg, detailed in Donna Hole, "Williamsburg's Four Original Stores: An Architectural Analysis," Colonial Williamsburg Research Report Series 188, 1980. (3) An examination by the author of eight additional stores in Fredericksburg, Petersburg, Falmouth, and the counties of Franklin, Prince George, and King George. (4) Information about Virginia stores derived from the nearly two hundred store advertisements that Camille Wells culled from the *Virginia Gazette* for her study of the paper. From that database and with additional evidence from newspapers, court cases, insurance records, and merchant records, I have documented at least the size of more than twenty additional stores. The combination of documentary and field evidence uncovered about Virginia stores spans the period from about 1740 to 1830.

Finally, one of the most neglected local sources is modern backcountry people. They drive the roads and walk the fields that most scholars can only imagine from eighteenth-century maps. They open derelict doors to show old scratch carvings or dusty books to demonstrate spidery handwriting, the inscriptions of people who lived two centuries ago. They store their everyday clothes or blankets in the chests and cupboards that form my "material culture evidence."

This primary research is framed by innovative notions and explanations about the backcountry, consumerism, material culture, object study, and economies of various stripes—tobacco, household, or petty. Each discipline has undergone exciting change over the past two decades, and its scholars are the heroes found throughout this book.

Secondary Sources

Particularly useful in sorting out the major themes and issues in the Southern backcountry is Warren R. Hofstra's eloquent *The Planting of New Virginia: Settlement and Landscape in the Shenandoah Valley* (Baltimore: Johns Hopkins University Press, 2004). Those same themes in a later time are examined in *After the Backcountry: Rural Life in the Great Valley of Virginia, 1800–1900*, ed. Kenneth E. Koons and Warren R. Hofstra (Knoxville: University of Tennessee Press, 2000). Earlier useful summaries include Albert H. Tillson Jr., "The Southern Backcountry: A Survey of Current Research," *Virginia Magazine of History and Biography* 98 (July 1990): 387–421, and Jack P. Greene, "Independence, Improvement, and Authority: Toward a Framework for Understanding the Histories of the Southern Backcountry during the Era of the American Revolution," in *An Uncivil War: The Southern Back-country during the American Revolution,* ed. Ronald Hoffman, Thad W. Tate, and Peter J. Albert (Charlottesville: University Press of Virginia for the United States Capitol Historical Society, 1985), 3–36.

The larger British backcountry as a shifting zone related to an imperial state was laid out in Bernard Bailyn, *The Peopling of British North America: An Introduction* (New York: Knopf, 1986), and more recently in Eric Hin-deraker and Peter C. Mancall, *At the Edge of Empire: The Backcountry in British North America* (Baltimore: Johns Hopkins University Press, 2003). The important work of Richard White shaped many later historical studies of the edges of European settlement. See *The Middle Ground: Indians, Em-pires, and Republics in the Great Lakes Region, 1650–1815* (Cambridge, UK: Cambridge University Press, 1991). From the vantage point of transcultura-tion, the backcountry is an unstable composition, and British consumer goods are part of a larger system of domination, resistance, and mixture. Homi K. Bhabha's recentering of the colonial experiment from core and periphery to colonial hybridity has influenced many. Jill H. Casid has helped me, not least through her book *Sowing Empire: Landscape and Colonization* (Minneapolis: University of Minnesota Press, 2005). A fine example of hybridity found in a single "entangled object" is Timothy J. Shannon, "Queequeg's Tomahawk: A Cultural Biography, 1750–1900," *Ethnohistory* 52, no. 3 (2005): 589–633.

Two major works that draw on stores as important evidence in his-torical geography are Robert D. Mitchell, *Commercialism and Frontier: Per-spectives on the Early Shenandoah Valley* (Charlottesville: University Press of Virginia, 1977), and Charles Farmer, "Country Stores and Frontier Ex-change Systems in Southside Virginia during the Eighteenth Century" (Ph.D. diss., University of Maryland, 1984). Farmer's work is particularly important as it delineates the intricate hierarchy that linked the Southside to higher-order retail places in eastern Virginia and Pennsylvania. Most re-cent are Daniel B. Thorp, "Doing Business in the Backcountry: Retail Trade in Colonial Rowan County, North Carolina," *William and Mary Quarterly* 3rd ser., 48, no. 3 (1991): 387–408, and Elizabeth A. Perkins, "The Consumer Frontier: Household Consumption in Early Kentucky," *Journal of American History* 78 (1991): 486–510.

The literature on the tobacco trade is voluminous. No one has written more about it than Jacob Price. Some of his important titles include *Capital and Credit in British Overseas Trade: The View from the Chesapeake, 1700–1776* (Cambridge, MA: Harvard University Press, 1980); "What Did Merchants Do? Reflections on British Overseas Trade, 1660–1790," *Journal of Economic History* 49, no. 2 (1989): 267–84; "The Rise of Glasgow in the Chesapeake Tobacco Trade, 1707–1775," *William and Mary Quarterly,* 3rd ser., 11, no. 2

(1954): 179–99; "Buchanan and Simson, 1759–1763: A Different Kind of Glasgow Firm Trading to the Chesapeake," *William and Mary Quarterly*, 3rd ser., 40, no.1 (1983): 3–41; and "Joshua Johnson in London, 1771–1775: Credit and Commercial Organization in the British Chesapeake Trade," in *Statesmen, Scholars, and Merchants: Essays in Eighteenth-Century History presented to Dame Lucy Sutherland*, ed. Anne Whiteman, J. S. Bromley, and P. G. M. Dickson (Oxford, UK: Clarendon Press, 1973), 153–80. See also Lois Green Carr, "'The Metropolis of Maryland': A Comment on Land Development along the Tobacco Coast," *Maryland Historical Magazine* 49 (1974): 124–45.

The most important work on the retail side of the tobacco trade is Calvin B. Coulter, "The Import Trade of Colonial Virginia," *William and Mary Quarterly*, 3rd ser., 2, no. 3 (1945): 296–314. See also his dissertation, "The Virginia Merchant" (Ph.D. diss., Princeton University, 1952). Two unpublished works that are particularly useful for their focus on the side of goods for sale in the retail trade are Harold B. Gill, "The Retail Business in Colonial Virginia" (unpublished manuscript, Colonial Williamsburg Foundation), and Mary R. W. Goodwin, "The Colonial Store" (unpublished Colonial Williamsburg Research Study, 1966).

The retail trade at large is ably handled by Carole Shammas in *The Pre-Industrial Consumer in England and America* (Oxford, UK: Clarendon Press, 1990), a work I have admired throughout this project. On the British side alone, see Hoh-cheung Mui and Lorna H. Mui, *Shops and Shopkeeping in Eighteenth-Century England* (Kingston, Ontario: McGill-Queen's University Press, 1989), and Nancy C. Cox, *The Complete Tradesman: A Study of Retailing, 1550–1820* (Aldershot, UK: Ashgate, 2000). Claire Walsh has written extensively on the English shop, with a special interest in shop design. One recent example is "Social Meaning and Social Space in the Shopping Galleries of Early-Modern London," in *A Nation of Shopkeepers: Five Centuries of British Shopkeeping*, ed. John Benson and Laura Ugolini (London: I. B. Tauris, 2003), 52–79. Finally, Elizabeth Kowaleski-Wallace takes the literary view in *Consuming Subjects: Women, Shopping, and Business in the Eighteenth Century* (New York: Columbia University Press, 1997).

The number of studies of consumer behavior and economic systems has exploded since the opening salvo by Neil McKendrick, John Brewer, and J. H. Plumb, *The Birth of a Consumer Society: The Commercialization of Eighteenth-Century England* (Bloomington: Indiana University Press, 1982). The works most important in this area to my study are Richard Bushman, *The Refinement of America: Persons, Houses, Cities* (New York: Knopf, 1992), and Cary Carson, "The Consumer Revolution in Colonial British America: Why Demand?" in *Of Consuming Interests*, ed. Cary Carson, Ronald Hoffman, and Peter J. Albert (Charlottesville: University Press of Virginia for the United States Capitol Historical Society), 483–697. These ideas about how the provincial elite defined themselves and their sociability have been further developed in the incisive work of David S. Shields, *Civil Tongues and Polite Letters in British America* (Chapel Hill: Published for the Institute of Early American History and Culture, Williamsburg, Virginia, by the University of North Carolina Press, 1997). The massive project headed by John Brewer with the Center for Seventeenth and Eighteenth Century Studies and the Clark Library at UCLA resulted in three worthy volumes. The first volume, *Consumption and the World of Goods,* ed. John Brewer and Roy Porter (London: Routledge, 1993), is the most useful for this particular project. Carson, Hoffman, and Albert's *Of Consuming Interests,* which grew out of a 1986 conference in Washington, DC, has also proved valuable. A good political analysis is T. H. Breen, *The Marketplace of Revolution: How Consumer Politics Shaped American Independence* (New York: Oxford University Press, 2004).

For the political economy of consumption, I relied on many sources but began with John E. Crowley, *This Sheba, Self: The Conceptualization of Economic Life in Eighteenth-Century America* (Baltimore: Johns Hopkins University Press, 1974), and John Sekora, *Luxury: The Concept in Western Thought, Eden to Smollett* (Baltimore: Johns Hopkins University Press, 1977). For broader political economy, see Joyce Appleby, "Consumption in Early Modern Social Thought," in *Consumption and the World of Goods,* 162–76. For an overview of the earlier period, see Cathy Matson's introduction to a special issue on the Atlantic economy, "The Atlantic Economy in an Era of Revolutions: An Introduction," *William and Mary Quarterly* 3rd ser., 62, no. 3 (2005): 357–64. For a skillfully drawn local perspective, see Paul G. E. Clemens, *Atlantic Economy and Colonial Maryland's Eastern Shore* (Ithaca: Cornell University Press, 1980). For an account of a particular place from the perspective of political economy, see Cathy D. Matson, *Merchants and Empire: Trading in Colonial New York* (Baltimore: Johns Hopkins University Press, 1998).

Information about markets, trade, and household participation are widely scattered through the literature of economic and social history. I vividly remember my argument in graduate school that these rural Virginia consumers fit neither a market nor a social-driven model of economic activity. My stubborn interest in the bridging of staple and household economies was also motivated by the evidence of petty economies and consumer choices that I found within the account books of one of the classic staple economies. I gained confidence from John J. McCusker and Russell R. Menard's *The Economy of British America, 1607–1789* (Chapel Hill: University of North

Carolina Press, 1985) and Allan Kulikoff, "The Transition to Capitalism in
Early America," *William and Mary Quarterly*, 3rd ser., 46, no. 1 (1989): 120–
44. Equally important was the call to evaluate individual and group economic interests within a single household by Jan de Vries in "Between Purchasing Power and the World of Goods: Understanding the Household
Economy of Early Modern Europe," in *Consumption and the World of Goods*,
85–132. Finally, while I have read widely, little has given me more pleasure
than Laurel Thatcher Ulrich's careful weaving of the personal webs of an
economic life in *A Midwife's Tale* (New York: Alfred A. Knopf, 1990).

In the same way, recent scholarship is dramatically reshaping our understanding of the ways in which slaves in the New World participated in the
market culture not for slave owners but for themselves. The literature on the
internal economy of slavery is rapidly growing and will only partially be
cited here. It includes Larry E. Hudson Jr., ed., *Working toward Freedom:
Slave Society and Domestic Economy in the American South* (Rochester, NY:
University of Rochester Press, 1994); Roderick A. McDonald, *The Economy
and Material Culture of Slaves: Goods and Chattels on the Sugar Plantations of
Jamaica and Louisiana* (Baton Rouge: Louisiana State University Press, 1993);
Betty Wood, *Women's Work, Men's Work: The Informal Slave Economies of
Lowcountry Georgia* (Athens: University of Georgia Press, 1995); Philip D.
Morgan, *Slave Counterpoint: Black Culture in the Eighteenth-Century Chesa-
peake and Lowcountry* (Chapel Hill: Published for the Omohundro Institute
of Early American History and Culture, Williamsburg, Virginia, by the
University of North Carolina Press, 1998); and Dylan C. Penningroth, *The
Claims of Kinfolk: African American Property and Community in the Nineteenth-
Century South* (Chapel Hill: University of North Carolina Press, 2003).
Archaeological excavation of the living quarters of enslaved peoples has si-
multaneously transformed our understanding of those economies. For a par-
ticular Virginia view, see Patricia Samford, *Subfloor Pits and the Archaeology of
Slavery in Colonial Virginia* (Tuscaloosa: University of Alabama Press, 2007).

A synthesis of the field of material culture is found in Victor Buchli's introduction to *Material Culture: Critical Concepts in the Social Sciences* (London: Routledge, 2004), Christopher Tilley, *Handbook of Material Culture*
(London: Sage Publications, 2006), and the introduction to *American Material Culture: The Shape of the Field*, ed. Ann Smart Martin and J. Ritchie
Garrison (Knoxville: University of Tennessee Press, 1997). Important methods and ideas about object study that have been formative to my own study
of the field include Henry Glassie, *Material Culture* (Bloomington: Indiana
University Press, 1999); Jules Prown, "The Truth of Material Culture: History or Fiction?" in *History from Things: Essays on Material Culture*, ed.
Steven Lubar and W. David Kingery (Washington, DC: Smithsonian

Institution Press, 1993), 1–19; Barbara Carson, *Ambitious Appetites: Dining, Behavior, and Patterns of Consumption in Federal Washington* (Washington, DC: American Institute of Architects Press, 1990), 75–103; George L. Miller, "Classification and Economic Scaling of 19th Century Ceramics," *Historical Archaeology* 14 (1980):1–40; Dell Upton, "Form and User: Style, Mode, Fashion, and the Artifact," in *Living in a Material World: Canadian and American Approaches to Material Culture*, ed. Gerald L. Pocius (St. John's, Newfoundland: Institute of Social and Economic Research, Memorial University of Newfoundland, 1991), 156–72; and Bernard Herman, *The Stolen House* (Charlottesville: University Press of Virginia, 1992). Theoretical insights also come from Daniel Miller, *Material Culture and Mass Consumption* (Oxford, UK: Basil Blackwell, 1987), and Arjun Appadurai, *The Social Life of Things* (Cambridge, UK: Cambridge University Press, 1988).

For my own reshaping of object analysis, see Ann Smart Martin, "Magical, Mythical, Practical and Sublime: The Meanings and Uses of Ceramics in America," in *Ceramics in America* (Milwaukee, WI: Chipstone Foundation, 2001), 28–46, and "Material Things and Cultural Meanings: Notes on the Study of Early American Material Culture," *William and Mary Quarterly*, 3rd ser., 52, no. 1 (1996): 5–12.

INDEX

Page numbers followed by f refer to figures; those followed by t refer to tables.